The Feminist Companion to the Bible

3

Editor
Athalya Brenner

Sheffield Academic Press

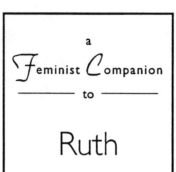

a
$\mathcal{F}$eminist $\mathcal{C}$ompanion

——— to ———

Ruth

edited by Athalya Brenner

Copyright © 1993 Sheffield Academic Press

Sheffield Academic Press Ltd
343 Fulwood Road
Sheffield S10 3BP
England

Typeset by Sheffield Academic Press
and
Printed on acid-free paper in Great Britain
by The Cromwell Press
Melksham, Wiltshire

British Library Cataloguing in Publication Data

Feminist Companion to Ruth.—(Feminist
Companion to the Bible; Vol. 3)
I. Brenner, Athalya II. Series
222

ISBN 1-85075-421-7

Contents

ACKNOWLEDGMENTS

The publishers are grateful to the following for permission to reproduce copyright material: Indiana University Press for excerpts from *Lethal Love: Feminist Literary Readings of Biblical Love Stories* by Mieke Bal; Brill for 'Naomi and Ruth' by Athalya Brenner, from *Vetus Testamentum* 33.4; the Central Conference of American Rabbis for *There is a Son born to Naomi* by Leonard Baskin, from *The Five Scrolls*; the Museum of Fine Arts, Boston, for *Harvesters Resting (Ruth and Boaz)* by Jean François Millet; Knopf for 'Ruth' by Cynthia Ozick, from *Metaphor and Memory*.

ABBREVIATIONS

AB	Anchor Bible
AnBib	Analecta biblica
BASOR	*Bulletin of the American Schools of Oriental Research*
BDB	F. Brown, S.R. Driver and C.A. Briggs, *Hebrew and English Lexicon of the Old Testament*
BKAT	Biblischer Kommentar: Altes Testament
CBQ	*Catholic Biblical Quarterly*
CSCO	Corpus scriptorum christianorum orientalium
FOTL	The Forms of the Old Testament Literature
HKAT	Handkommentar zum Alten Testament
IB	*Interpreter's Bible*
ICC	International Critical Commentary
IDB	G.A. Buttrick (ed.), *Interpreter's Dictionary of the Bible*
JPSV	Jewish Publication Society Version
JSOT	*Journal for the Study of the Old Testament*
JSOTSup	*Journal for the Study of the Old Testament*, Supplement Series
KAT	Kommentar zum Alten Testament
KB	L. Koehler and W. Baumgartner (eds.), *Lexicon in Veteris Testamenti libros*
KJV	King James Version
NAB	New American Bible
NEB	New English Bible
NRSV	New Revised Standard Version
OTL	Old Testament Library
REB	Revised English Bible
RSV	Revised Standard Version
VT	*Vetus Testamentum*
ZAW	*Zeitschrift für die alttestamentliche Wissenschaft*

INTRODUCTION

Athalya Brenner

I

The Ruth scroll is, first and foremost, a 'good yarn', superbly written[1] 'with consummate artistry'.[2] Goitein substantiates this value judgment by arguing that:

1. The plot is attractive, deflecting from tension to idyllic serenity and back again to tension, until all difficulties are resolved and a satisfactory ending is achieved.
2. The structure is appealing and easy to follow: the plot which succeeds the exposition (1.1-6) is tightly organized[3] and easy to take in.
3. The socio-cultural background (customs and norms) is familiar yet freshly illuminated.
4. The central characters—Naomi, Ruth and, to a somewhat lesser extent, Boaz—are clearly drawn and easy to identify with; the secondary characters—Orpah (ch. 1) and the apparent 'redeemer' (ch. 4)—support the main figures by serving as their symmetrical, antonymous, albeit not negative, images.
5. The message is clearly yet subtly presented: love and levirate marriage, actively sought by women, preserve the social order and invigorate it.
6. The language and style are magnificent.[4]

---

1. S.D. Goitein, *'Iyyunim ba-miqra* (Hebrew; 'Studies in the Bible'; Tel Aviv: Yavneh, 1957), p. 49.
2. P. Trible, *God and the Rhetoric of Sexuality* (Philadelphia: Fortress Press, 1978), p. 166.
3. See also Trible, *Rhetoric of Sexuality*.
4. Goitein, *'Iyyunim ba-miqra*, pp. 49-58.

Finally, Goitein writes, the scroll was possibly authored by a woman, old and wise, for the author focuses on Naomi and her interests rather than on Ruth. This is likely because (1) the story is basically a women's story, (2) the plot opens (1.6) and concludes (4.17) with Naomi, the elder person, rather than with Ruth, the younger person, (3) Naomi's advice initiates the complications necessary for advancing the plot (chs. 2–3), and (4) the scroll ends with blessings to Naomi rather than to Ruth— customarily, the ending of a biblical story is definitive for the purpose of the whole tale.[1]

Four of Goitein's points—the characters, the social background, the message of the scroll, and the issue of female authorship—are the chief preoccupations of the feminist writers who have contributed to this volume. Questions of plot, structure and language are also explored, but to a lesser extent and as auxiliary to the former issues. The reader will notice that certain overlaps, hence repetition, obtain between some contributions. In the interest of internal individual cohesion, these have not been edited out.

II

Phyllis Trible entitles her discourse on the book of Ruth 'A Human Comedy'. She starts her discussion by writing,

> A man's world tells a woman's story...the book of Ruth presents the aged Naomi and the youthful Ruth as they struggle for survival in a patriarchal environment.[2]

The fact that the Ruth scroll is 'a woman's story' makes it particularly attractive for feminist interpreters.

It seems that Trible's views on the main figures, the message, the social background, and the style basically correspond to those of Goitein but are more sharply focused:

> As a whole, the human comedy suggests a theological interpretation of feminism: women working out their salvation with fear and trembling, for it is God who works in them. Naomi

1. Goitein, *'Iyyunim ba-miqra*, p. 252: note.
2. Trible, *Rhetoric of Sexuality*, p. 166.

works as a bridge between tradition and innovation. Ruth and the females of Bethlehem work as paradigms for radicality. All together they are women in culture, women against culture, and women transforming culture. What they reflect, they challenge. And that challenge is a legacy of faith to this day for all who have ears to hear the stories of women in a man's world.[1]

In spite of disagreement about details, Trible's illuminating discussion is already regarded as a classic and has exercised great influence on subsequent interpretations, as the numerous references to it in this volume demonstrate. One aspect of her analysis, however, has recently been seriously challenged. Few readers can or do ignore the patriarchal nature of the scroll's social background:

> After all, it is a man's world, and concerns of women may well be subsumed, perhaps even subverted, by this patriarchal climate.[2]

Nor can readers ignore the largely independent action and subversive conduct of the female characters. But, although Trible allows in passing for the contingency of a female author ('She or he', pp. 168, 186; 'he or she', pp. 179, 181), she neither pursues this issue nor probes its implications for the female characters' successful 'radicality'. Trible convincingly insists on the positive values and life-giving properties exemplified by the women and their conduct. But, unlike Goitein, she does not connect this unique presentation of biblical women with the issue of authorship. She seems to imply that the scroll is the product of male literariness inasmuch as it mirrors a patriarchal order.

III

Narrational economy, which results in narrative gaps, is one of the distinctive features of biblical fiction. The filling in of these gaps is a central issue in biblical interpretation. The process is neither automatic nor self-evident: it requires close attentiveness to textual delicacies, both in the realm of reported plot

1. Trible, *Rhetoric of Sexuality*, p. 196.
2. Trible, *Rhetoric of Sexuality*, p. 196.

occurrences and in the realm of language. In other words, filling
the gaps is not simply a matter of interpretative discretion. It
constitutes a necessity for understanding the story and its plot;
the gaps often indicate narrational junctions that are significant
for the development of the tale and its central characters, yet
are not overtly reported.[1] The first three readings in this collection (Part One) are attempts to fill in some gaps, commencing
from different perspectives that nonetheless share one basic
premise: all of them are biased, gendered readings (see
Rashkow). Thus a plurality of interpretation emanates from a
common (albeit not always conscious) base of literary theory
and womanly readership.

For instance, Elizabeth Cady Stanton's 'Ruth' (first published
in 1898) deals with the following gaps (among others), utilizing
imagination as well as traditional Jewish and Christian exegesis: Ruth's missing genealogy; the textual silence concerning the
events of the women's journey to Bethlehem; emotional and
other motives for the women's behaviour throughout the story;
their daily life; Boaz's status, age, and motivation. She supplies
an explanation for the absence of such interesting details as the
marriage festivities, but (perhaps coyly?) refrains from discussing the potentially embarrassing scene at the threshing floor
until the very end of her piece. Three of her exegetical biases are
especially worth noting. One is the didactic attempt to reread
the scroll as an empowering schema for contemporary Christian
life (see Trible). Linked with this is the tendency to attribute
vigour and industry to Naomi and Ruth, implicitly alleging that
an unmarried state may perhaps not be as catastrophic as it
seems. Finally, the two central women are praised unreservedly
as exemplary figures. This pioneering feminist commentary is
thus sketchy and politicized and, precisely because of that,
historically instructive.

Ilona Rashkow writes about power and discourse. She begins
by noting that 56 out of the 86 verses of the scroll are directly
reported speech acts. Indeed, the extent to which the dialogic
narrative mode is employed in Ruth is unique in the Hebrew

---

1.   M. Perry and M. Sternberg, "Ha-melek be-mabbat ironi' ('The
King in Ironic Perspective'), *Ha-Sifrut* 1 (1968), pp. 263-92 (in Hebrew).

Bible (see also Sasson[1] and Joüon[2]). Since dialogues are the chief
vehicle for advancing the plot, Rashkow examines them in order
'to affirm the reality and significance of the female experience
reflected and place it on a par with the male [experience]'
through linguistic analysis and discourse analysis. She shows
how Naomi's and Ruth's speech acts are indexical for defining
and understanding the main figures and the story. Within the
narrative, these speech acts promote the women's case
inasmuch as they reflect their strength. Speech, perhaps even
more than but certainly not less than action, turns the women's
strength into the power to succeed in altering their circumstances. Later in this volume Carol Meyers explores the implications of the largely dialogic structure of the scroll for its
provenance as a female text.

My piece 'Naomi and Ruth' was triggered off by and written
as a response to Jack Sasson's approach in his commentary. I
loved his insights, erudition, and deep understanding of the language. Sasson chose to apply Propp's method of morphological
folktale analysis in order to elucidate the structure of the scroll.
His analysis of apparent plot and character inconsistencies,
however, left me wondering: it did not work for me because, by
and large, it did not account for difficulties such as the attribution of the newborn son to Naomi, and Ruth's disappearance at
the tale's end. Therefore, I was not sure that Ruth could be
profitably interpreted with the aid of that methodology. After
reviewing Sasson's analysis and some other attempts at
resolving interpretative problems, I tried to explain aspects of
narrative structure, plot and characterization by suggesting a
reconstruction of the (historical) processes of transmission and
literary composition. Numerous dissonances can be illuminated
by assuming two sources, a Naomi story and a Ruth story,
which were eventually combined into the Masoretic Text's

---

1. J.M. Sasson, *Ruth: A New Translation with a Philological
Commentary and a Formalist-Folklorist Interpretation* (The Biblical
Seminar, 10; Sheffield: JSOT Press, 2nd edn, 1989 [1979]).

2. P. Joüon, *Ruth: commentaire philologique et exégétique* (Rome:
Pontifical Biblical Institute, 1953; Subsidia Biblica, 9; Rome: Biblical
Insitute Press, 2nd edn, 1986).

Ruth. Needless to say, such a reading—albeit, in my view, plausible—sidesteps the issues present in the text itself in favour of its history.

IV

The Ruth scroll is a woman's story. As such it lends itself not only to (gendered) gynocentered readings but also to gynocritics—a critical discourse which posits women's writing as its primary object of investigation.[1] Feminist interest in gynocentric and female-authored texts—rather than in, or alongside, the exposure and evaluation of androcentric and male-authored texts—has been gaining ground since the early 1980s.

In biblical criticism, the first gynocritical step involves the definition of a text as a female text. Admittedly, the theoretical difficulties of so doing are many. Three essays in this collection are attempts to address these difficulties from diverse perspectives (Part Two).

Adrien Bledstein proceeds from the premise that since traces of female authorship are extant in the Bible itself, Ruth can be read as if it were written by a woman, a critical decision which affects the actual process of reading (see also Meyers). The thematics of the scroll—female companionship and social renewal—are interpreted as indices for female authorship, especially because they stand in stark contrast to the themes of anarchy and disintegration which characterize the narrative depiction of the same period in the book of Judges. An analogy with the J author of the Torah is drawn, and a suggestion made to identify both the author of Ruth and J as Tamar, daughter of David.

Fokkelien van Dijk-Hemmes minimizes the importance of gynocentrism for the scroll's authorship. She suggests that, instead of concentrating on *authorship*, we look for traces of women's *culture* in the story. She postulates three main criteria

1. The term 'gynocritics' was coined by Elaine Showalter (in E. Showalter [ed.], *The New Feminist Criticsm: Essays on Women, Literature and Theory* [London: Virago, 1986], p. 248).

for uncovering such traces: the absence of marked androcentrism; a (re)definition of reality from female perspectives; and a narrative differentiation of the views attributed to female as against male figures. Finally, she adds considerations of style and oral transmission (see Goitein[1] and Brenner[2]) to conclude that the scroll may be 'a collective creation of women's culture; a story shaped by the cooperation between wise women-narrators and their actively engaged (predominantly F [female/feminine]) audience'. The phrase 'a woman's story', applied to the scroll, thus acquires a fresh signification.

On the way to Bethlehem Naomi urges her daughters-in-law to return to their 'mother's house' (1.8). Trible views this phrase 'mother's house' as 'unexpected in a patriarchal culture' and yet 'singularly appropriate here'. According to her, the phrase conveys a binary opposition of mother-in-law and mother; it 'emphasizes the radical separation of these females from all males'; and 'it juxtaposes present reality with past and future'.[3]

The phrase *bēt 'ēm*, 'mother's house', appears three more times in the Hebrew Bible: once in Genesis (24.8) and twice in the Song of Songs (3.4, 8.2). Carol Meyers explores its significance for the scroll's authorship or, rather, dominant gendered provenance. She defines it as a socio-cultural counterpart to the Israelite basic patriarchal unit, the *bēt 'āb*, 'father's house'. She lists the common features which the *bēt 'ēm* occurrences (and the implicit 'woman's house' in Proverbs) share: all appear within women's stories; an element of female 'wisdom' is evident; women determine their own destiny and also affect others'; the setting is domestic and a marriage arrangement is involved. Thus Meyers extends the scope of her interpretation of this specific aspect of the scroll beyond the textual boundaries to the realm of sociological knowledge and literary provenance: 'When Naomi exhorts her daughters-in-law to return home to their mother's household, she allows us to hear the language of female experience. Ruth 1.8 surely constitutes a powerful evidence for the presence of a female text.'

1. *'Iyyunim ba-miqra.*
2. In this volume.
3. Trible, *Rhetoric of Sexuality*, p. 169.

My 'Naomi and Ruth: Further Reflections' is in part a response to myself in 'Naomi and Ruth' and in part a response to gynocritical moves suggested by Goitein, Bledstein, van Dijk-Hemmes and Meyers. The points I wish to highlight are: the concept of a female *voice* or *textual authority* (rather than *authorship*) which operates in the scroll, and its relatedness to women's narrative centrality and women's culture; Obed's maternity; women's retained subjectivity at the tale's end; the focalization of female desire as a dichotomy of sexuality (Ruth) and motherhood (Naomi), which is differentiated yet ultimately coalesces; the concept of orality; and the relatedness of gendered reading to gendering a text.

V

Androcentrism operates on the interpretative as well as the textual level; Meyers traces numerous examples of this practice in the ancient translations and commentaries. Leila Bronner and Jane Richardson Jensen illustrate this point by discussing two ancient, widely disparate, sources (Part Three).

Bronner discusses Ruth in rabbinic literature. Her approach is thematic. She describes the chief midrashic themes: *ḥesed*, Ruth's 'conversion', the proper names, female obedience and modesty, Ruth's looks, the marriage, and the birth. Her conclusions are that Ruth wins the Jewish sages' approval through an exegetical process of being cast—in the biblical narrative and even more so in rabbinic interpretation—into a stereotypic ideal of submissive, obedient femininity which can scarcely be cherished by contemporary feminists.

Richardson Jensen writes on Ruth in the poetic hymns of Ephrem the Syrian, a celibate deacon in the Syriac church of the fourth century CE. She shows how Ephrem, who admits Ruth's role as an ancestress of David and therefore of Jesus, does not try to obliterate her actions. His solution to the problem of Ruth's sexuality is to acknowledge, even to exaggerate, it but then to cancel it out by spiritualizing its motivation and intent. Ruth's initiative is thus neither denied nor censured, while Boaz's role is viewed as auxiliary.

VI

As Mieke Bal says, theological exegesis and literary criticism are 'metatexts'. So are works of art which are inspired by biblical passages, be they works of poetry, prose, or visual art. It follows that academic scholarship should not be privileged over art, in the sense that both constitute equally valid (or invalid) acts of interpretation. Part Four of this volume consists in three presentations which exemplify Bal's approach.

The first is Bal's own essay. Departing from Victor Hugo's poem 'Booz endormi', Bal considers issues like Boaz's focalization, as it is re-presented in Hugo's poem and presented in the biblical text (3.10); the characters' proper names; the characters' subjectivity and speech acts; subjects and the law; speech and the unconscious; analogy, history and chronology. She concludes by showing that, taken together, a series of three fabulae—Lot's daughters (Gen. 19.30-38), Tamar and Judah (Genesis 38), and Ruth—form an instance of the antichronological *mise en abyme* (embedded story) of Israelite history, in which women initiate continuity against men and their ideology. Finally, Bal evaluates her own reading in an Afterword.

Zefira Gitay uses paintings as a stepping stone for exploring the female figures of the scroll, especially the narrative role of the women of Bethlehem (end of ch. 1; and contra Trible) and the 'neighbours' (ch. 4). The binary oppositions of Naomi–Ruth and local–foreign are shown to be expressed in the biblical text as well as in artistic renderings of it. Throughout her analysis, Gitay insists on the power of women which informs the narrative as well as its underlying social milieu.

Cynthia Ozick, a well-known poet and author, demonstrates once more the irrelevance of an 'academic-scholarly-objective' versus 'literary-artistic-personal' dichotomy. She starts by gazing at two pictures—her grandfather's and Ruth's. An extensive analysis of Orpah's and Ruth's behaviour in the exposition (ch. 1) results in a definition of a normality–singularity opposition between them, which is mirrored by the opposition of Boaz–the apparent *go'el* (ch. 4; see Goitein). As the tale 'unfolds', the connection between the two pictures becomes perceptible. Ruth's recognition of the God of Israel inaugurates history (Jewish and Christian; see also Bal), thus leading to Ozick's grandfather and beyond.

Part I
GENDERED READING PERSPECTIVES

THE BOOK OF RUTH*

Elizabeth Cady Stanton

Commentators differ as to the exact period when this book was written and as to the judge who ruled Israel at that time. It must have been, however, in the beginning of the days when the judges ruled, as Boaz, who married Ruth, was the son of Rahab, who protected the spies in Joshua's reign. Some say that it was in the reign of Deborah. Tradition says that the messiah was descended from two Gentile maidens, Rahab and Ruth, and that Ruth was the daughter of Eglon, king of Moab;[1] but this is denied, as Boaz, whom Ruth married, judged Israel two hundred years after Eglon's death. However widely the authorities differ as to Ruth's genealogical tree, they all agree that she was a remarkably sincere, refined, discreet maiden, a loving daughter and an honored wife.

Elimelech, the husband of Naomi, is severely criticised by biblical writers for leaving his people and his country when in distress and seeking his fortune among the heathen Moabites, thus leading his sons into the temptation of taking strange wives. They say that the speedy deaths of the father and the sons were a proof of God's disapprobation. Naomi manifested such remarkable goodness and wisdom as a widow that one wonders that she did not use her influence to keep her husband in his native land to share the trials of his neighbors.

The tender friendship between Ruth and Naomi, so unusual with a mother-in-law, has been celebrated in poetry, in prose

---

* This article first appeared in *The Woman's Bible* (New York: European Publishing House, 1898), II.

1. Cf. Bronner in this volume [ed.]

and in art the world round. The scene between Naomi and her daughters in parting was most affectionate. As soon as Naomi decided to return to her own country, her daughters assisted her in making the necessary preparations. Ruth secretly made her own, having decided to go with Naomi to the land of Judea.

When the appointed day arrived, mounted on three gray jackasses they departed. A few miles out Naomi proposed to rest by the roadside and to say farewell, and, after thanking them for all the love and kindness they had shown her, advised them to go no farther, but return to their home in that land of plenty. She told them frankly that she had no home luxuries to offer, life with her would for them be poverty and privation in a strange land, and she was not willing that they should sacrifice all the pleasures of their young lives for her. Sad and lonely with the loss of their husbands, parting with Naomi seemed to intensify their grief. United in a common sorrow, the three women stood gazing in silence into each other's faces, until Naomi, with her usual self-control and common sense, again pointed out to them all the hardships involved in the change which they proposed.

Her words made a deep impression on Orpah. She hesitated, and at last decided to abide by Naomi's advice; but not so with Ruth. Naomi had a peculiar magnetic attraction for her, a charm stronger than kindred, country or ease. Her expressions of steadfast friendship in making her decision were so tender and sincere that they have become household words. She said, 'Entreat me not to leave thee; for whither thou goest I will go, and where thou lodgest I will lodge; thy people shall be my people, and thy God my God; where thou diest will I die, and there will I be buried. The Lord do so to me, and more also, if aught but death part thee and me.' (These words are on a bronze tablet on the stone over the grave of Robert Louis Stevenson at Samoa.)

Having bade farewell to Orpah, they journeyed together and made a home for themselves in Bethlehem. Naomi owned a small house, lot and spring of water on the outskirts of the town. After a few days of rest, Ruth said to Naomi, I must not sit here with folded hands, nor spend my time in visiting neighbors, nor in search of amusement, but I must go forth to work, to provide food and clothes, and leave thee to rest. As it was the season for the wheat and barley harvests, Ruth heard that laborers were needed in the fields. It was evident that Ruth believed in the dignity of labor and of self-support. She thought, no doubt, that everyone with a sound mind in a sound body and two hands should earn her own livelihood. She threw her whole soul into her work and proved a blessing to her mother. So Naomi consented that she might go and glean in the fields with other maidens engaged in that work.

When Naomi was settled in Bethlehem she remembered that she had a rich kinsman, Boaz, whose name means strength, a man of great wealth as well as wisdom. Ruth was employed in the field of Boaz; and in due time he took note of the fair maiden from Moab. In harvest time he needed many extra hands, and he came often among the reapers to see how the work went forward. He heard such good accounts of Ruth's industry, dignity and discretion that he ordered his men to make her work as easy as possible, to leave plenty for her to glean and to carry home in the evening. This she often sold on the way, and bought something which Naomi needed.

Naomi and Ruth enjoyed their evenings together. Naomi did not spend the day in idleness either. She had her spinning-wheel and loom to make their garments; she worked also in her garden, raising vegetables, herbs and chickens; and they talked over their day's labor as they enjoyed their simple supper of herb tea, bread and watercresses. Their menu was oft times more tempting, thanks to Ruth's generous purchases on her way home. Being busy, practical women, their talk during the evening was chiefly on 'ways and means'; they seldom rose to the higher themes of pedagogics and psychology, subjects so familiar in the clubs of American women.

It was a custom among the Israelites, in order to preserve their own line, that the nearest kinsman should marry the young widow on whom their hopes depended. So when Naomi remembered that Boaz was her kinsman, and that as age made marriage with her undesirable, Ruth would be the proper person to fill her place. With great tact on their part Naomi's wishes were accomplished.

Boaz was the son of Salmon and Rahab, and according to the

Chaldee was not only a mighty man in wealth but also in wisdom, a most rare and excellent conjunction. Boaz was of the family of Elimelech, of which Ruth, by marriage, was a part also. Moreover, as she had adopted the country of Naomi and was a proselyte to her faith, her marriage with Boaz was in accordance with Jewish custom. Naomi was told by the spirit of prophecy, says the Chaldee, that from her line should descend six of the most righteous men of the age, namely, David, Daniel, his three compeers and the king messiah.

Commentators say that Boaz was probably himself one of the elders, or the aldermen, of the city, and that he went up to the gates as one having authority, and not as a common person. They say that Ruth was neither rich nor beautiful, but a poor stranger, 'whose hard work in the fields' had withered her 'lilies and roses'. But Boaz had heard her virtue and dignity extolled by all who knew her. The Chaldee says, 'house and riches are the inheritance from fathers; but a prudent wife is more valuable than rubies and is a special gift from heaven'. Boaz prized Ruth for her virtues, for her great moral qualities of head and heart. He did not say, like Samson, when his parents objected to his choice, 'her face pleaseth me'.

In narrating the story of Ruth and Naomi to children they invariably ask questions of interest, to which the sacred fabulist gives no answer. They always ask if Ruth and Naomi had no pets when living alone, before Obed made his appearance. If the modern historian may be allowed to wander occasionally outside of the received text, it may be said undoubtedly that they had pets; as there is nothing said of cats and dogs and parrots, but frequent mention of doves, kids and lambs, we may infer that in these gentle innocents they found their pets. No doubt Providence softened their solitude by providing them with something on which to expend their mother love.

Boaz was one of the district judges, and he held his court in the town hall over the gates of Bethlehem. The kinsman who was summoned to appear there and to settle the case readily agreed to the proposal of Boaz to fill his place, as he was already married. He was willing to take the land; but as the widow and the land went together, according to the Jewish law

of inheritance, Boaz was in a position to fill the legal requirements; and as he loved Ruth, he was happy to do so. Ruth was
summoned to appear before the grave and reverend seigniors;
the civil pledges were made and the legal documents duly
signed. The reporter is silent as to the religious observances and
the marriage festivities. They were not as vigilant and as
satisfying as are the skilled reporters of our day, who have the
imagination to weave a connected story and to give to us all the
hidden facts which we desire to know. Our reporters would
have told us how, when and where Ruth was married, what
kind of a house Boaz had, how Ruth was dressed, and so on,
whereas we are left in doubt on all of these points.

The historian does vouchsafe to give to us further information
on the general feeling of the people. They all joined in the prayer
of the elders that the lord would 'make the woman that is come
into thine house like Rachel and like Leah, which two did build
the house of Israel'; they prayed for Boaz that he might be more
famous and powerful; they prayed for the wife that she might be
a blessing in the house, and the husband in the public business of
the town; that all of their children might be faithful in the church,
and their descendants be as numerous as the sands of the sea.

In due time one prayer was answered, and Ruth bore a son.
Naomi loved the child and shared in its care. But Ruth said, 'The
love of Naomi is more to me than that of seven sons could be.'
Naomi was a part of Ruth's household to the day of her death
and shared all of her luxuries and her happiness.

The child's name was Obed, the father of Jesse, the father of
David. The name Obed signifies one who serves. The motto of
the Prince of Wales is 'I serve' (*ich dien*). It is hoped that Obed
was more profoundly interested in the problems of industrial
economics than the Prince seems to be, and that he spent a more
useful and practical life.[1] If the Bethlehem newspapers had been
as enterprising as our journals they would have given us some
pictorial representations of Obed on Naomi's lap, or at the bap-
tismal font, or in the arms of Boaz, who, like Napoleon, stood
contemplating in silence his firstborn.

---

1. Readers should note that this article was originally published in
1898 (Ed.).

Some fastidious readers object to the general tenor of Ruth's courtship. But as her manners conformed to the customs of the times, and as she followed Naomi's instructions implicitly, it is fair to assume that Ruth's conduct was irreproachable.

RUTH: THE DISCOURSE OF POWER
AND THE POWER OF DISCOURSE[*]

Ilona Rashkow

Few readers could dispute the overwhelming orientation of the
Hebrew Bible to the male world: while there are female characters, and there are even a few fragments of women's writings,[1]
the women in this text are exceptional. As Meyers notes, liberal
feminists and conservative traditionalists alike share a perception that the Hebrew Bible portrays women as secondary or
inferior to men in fundamental ways,[2] primarily because the
biblical source itself is largely a product of patriarchal societies
in which men dominated if not monopolized public discourse
and the civil and religious bureaucracies. The calamities of
Elimelech's, Mahlon's and Chilion's deaths in the book of Ruth
create a situation extremely unusual in Hebrew narrative:
women, not men, occupy center stage. As a result, it is the
female characters' discourse (56 of the 85 verses report speech
acts) which carries the narrative forward. This essay examines
the relationship of discourse and power in the Book of Ruth. In
doing so, I attempt to affirm the reality and significance of the

* Parts of this paper appear in ch. 5 of *Upon the Dark Places: Anti-
Semitism and Sexism in English Renaissance Biblical Translation* (Bible
and Literature Series, 28; Sheffield: Almond Press, 1990). I thank the publishers for their permission to use the material.

1. See A. Brenner, *The Israelite Woman: Social Role and Literary
Type in Biblical Narrative* (JSOTSup, 21; Sheffield: JSOT Press, 1985) for a
discussion of women poets and authors, particularly her analysis of
Song of Songs (pp. 46-56).

2. C. Meyers, *Discovering Eve: Ancient Israelite Women in Context*
(New York: Oxford University Press, 1988), p. 24.

female experience reflected and place it on a par with the male.

My methodology is discourse analysis. This type of analysis belongs to many fields, but it seems particularly appropriate for literary study. The literary implications of discourse have been developed recently, extending the discussion in linguistic circles about the relationship between gender, language and social structure to the narrative. Some scholars discuss the meaning of particular symbols when interpreting dialogue, the social and dialectical aspects. Other critics question the implications of using a symbolic medium at all,[1] recognizing that individual words can mean more than they seem to mean and do more than they seem to do.[2] This approach raises the larger issue of interpretation and the types of questions feminists ask of the text.[3]

Feminist critics do not speak of interpretation in any absolute sense, as if by challenging earlier, predominantly male exegesis we could be closer to the 'truth' or the 'real meaning'. Most literary theorists agree that reading is an activity which can never aspire to exactitude. Everyone brings cultural and personal contexts to the act of reading. From the ways in which one understands gender relations to the meanings of specific words, assumptions and beliefs 'bias' the reader; they operate as a kind of 'grid that obscures certain meanings and brings others to the

1.   See, for example, Anthony Wilden's comments ('Lacan and the Discourse of the Other', in J. Lacan, *The Language of the Self* [ed. and trans. A. Wilden; York: Delta, 1975], p. 230).

2.   According to Searle, in language the basic unit of communication is not the symbol, word or sentence, but rather 'the production or issuance of the symbol or word or sentence in the performance of a speech act' (J. Searle, *Speech Acts: An Essay in the Philosophy of Language* [London: Cambridge University Press, 1969], p. 16).

3.   As Jauss identified, the fundamental question posed by hermeneutics is why particular questions are posed and answered at a certain time and in a certain way (H.R. Jauss, *Question and Answer: Forms of Dialogic Understanding* [ed. and trans. M. Hays; Minneapolis: University of Minnesota Press, 1989], p. 51). One answer (contra Jauss) is that there is a subjective component built into the very process of question-formulation (questions themselves are, after all, interpretive frameworks).

foreground'.[1] In place of 'ideal, objective readings' there are only 'readings', each of which creates and is a creation of its context. To suggest that there is one 'proper' reading results in an authoritarianism feminist criticism rejects; in fact, in so far as feminist literary criticism is capable of being described, it operates by putting *everything* into question. One question discourse analysis asks of a text is 'who speaks in given contexts'.

Discourse is often viewed as a form of domination, with speech use an index of social values and the distribution of power. The converse of speech, silence, is equally meaningful since the literary character who is denied discourse often experiences narrative suppression as well.[2] Although Naomi may not be the focus of interest, she is certainly the central character in terms of discourse. The power of her speech emphasizes her initial bitterness and her desire for a literal 'return'[3] to Bethlehem. Once there, however, Naomi also wants a figurative 'return' to

1. S.S. Lanser, 'Feminist Criticism in the Garden: Inferring Genesis 2–3', *Semeia* 39 (1988), p. 77.

2. Ruth Bottigheimer discusses speech and silencing in a literary text on four levels: narrative, textual, lexical and editorial. The character who is condemned or cursed to a period of silence experiences narrative silencing in the plot; the distribution of direct and indirect or reported speech offers the potential for silencing a character at a second level, the textual level; silencing may also grow out of verbs used to introduce direct or indirect speech (certain verbs validate the speech that follows, while other introductory verbs mark subsequent speech as illicit); and the author or editor may comment on the text within the text (R.B. Bottigheimer, *Grimms' Bad Girls and Bold Boys: The Moral and Social Vision of the Tales* [New Haven: Yale University Press, 1987], p. 52).

3. One of the rhetorical techniques of biblical narrative is the use of keywords, and it is almost impossible to ignore the presence of שוב ('return'), and the similar sounding root ישׁב ('dwell') in relation to Naomi. Three times she counsels her daughters-in-law not to stay with her, and orders them to return (שׁבנה, 1.8, 11, 12). Orpah and Ruth tell Naomi that they will return (נשׁוב, 1.10) with her. Naomi reminds Ruth that Orpah returned (שׁבה, 1.15) to her people and her gods, and commands Ruth to do the same and return (שׁובי, 1.15). Ruth, however, tells Naomi that she wants to return (לשׁוב, 1.16) with her to Bethlehem. Outside the city gate Naomi meets the townswomen and tells them, 'God returned (השׁיבני) me' (1.21).

her community and lifestyle. Naomi's discourse enables the redemption of her property and facilitates her ultimate 'return'. Compared to Naomi, Ruth is given fewer lines of direct speech. As a result, Ruth's discourse reveals contextual assumptions, language use based on social or cultural behavior. In her relationship with Naomi Ruth is determined and assertive, but of relatively few words; with Boaz, Ruth maintains a higher level of formality but is quite articulate, almost too talkative. Ruth's discourse empowers her to replace marginality and insecurity by wealth and a more stable status. The power of Naomi's and Ruth's speech acts reverses their less propitious circumstances to a high level of success and social elevation.

Naomi's first speech act launches a lengthy conversation among the three travelers, Ruth, Naomi and Orpah (1.17-17). Naomi wants to return home and urges Orpah and Ruth to do likewise. לכנה שבנה ('Go, return') are emphatic sentence openers which express Naomi's emptiness. The double imperatives convey a sense of urgency. Naomi's intended destination for her daughters-in-law, 'each to her mother's house',[1] is striking given the overriding importance of 'father's house' throughout the male-oriented Hebrew Bible. In this context it is particularly unusual since widows normally return to their 'father's house'.[2] Naomi's discourse reveals an emphasis, rare in biblical narrative, on relationships between women, specifically mothers and daughters, rather than the customary emphasis on fathers and sons.[3]

---

1. 'Mother's house' is a rare term in the Hebrew Bible, occurring only three other times. In Song 3.4 and 8.2 it probably refers to the bedroom of a woman's mother as a safe site for lovers to rendezvous (cf. the parallel line in Song 3.4, 'the chamber of her that conceived me'). In Gen. 24.28, Rebekah runs to her mother's house to report her conversation with Abraham's servant seeking a wife for Isaac. A related expression, 'her house', is used of the 'Woman of Worth' of Proverbs 31 (in 31.21, 27). Cf. Meyers' essay in this volume.

2. See, for example, Tamar in Gen. 38.11; Num. 30.17; Deut. 22.21; Judg. 19.2, 3.

3. I. Rashkow, 'Daughters and Fathers in Genesis...or, What is Wrong with this Picture?' (unpublished paper presented to the SBL Annual Meeting, Kansas City, 1991).

While Naomi is concerned for the welfare of her daughters-
in-law, bitterness overwhelms her speech urging Orpah and
Ruth to remain in Moab. Naomi uses the term במעי (literally, 'in
my innards') in 1.11: 'have I yet sons במעי'. This expression
denotes emotions that are felt very deeply by men *and* women,
such as passion, deep distress or pity,[1] and generally is not used
to refer to reproductive organs. Naomi is doing more than
reminding Ruth and Orpah that physically she is no longer
capable of bearing children. Since technically there is no question of a levirate marriage (which depends on the issue from the
same father), Naomi is more biting in her sarcasm than she need
be if her only desire is to express concern for her two daughters-
in-law. Over and over she exhorts them to leave. She tells them
that she is barren and unrestorable. Her speech is five thoughts
which deal with having a 'man' and 'sons', and consists of two
rhetorical questions, two statements of fact, and a statement of
unlikely possibility:[2]

> Have I yet sons in my womb (במעי), who will be to you
> *husbands*?
> I am too old to be with a *husband*.
> Even were I tonight with a *husband*, and gave birth to *sons*
> Would you tie yourselves down without being with *husbands*?
> The hand of Yahweh is gone out against me (vv. 12-13).

The narrator reports in 1.14 that Orpah kissed her mother-in-
law, here a sign of leave-taking. Ruth did not, but rather 'stuck
with her' (דבקה־בה).

Ruth's first discourse in 1.16-17 defines her relationship with
Naomi: quiet determination. Naomi (in 1.15) refers to Orpah,
her people, and *her* gods. Ruth's response is startling and
emphasizes her assertiveness. Despite Naomi's almost overpowering authority, Ruth issues a command of her own. She
begins her speech by telling Naomi, 'do not press me to abandon
you', clearly expressing her ties to her mother-in-law. This

---

1.   See, for example, Isa. 16.11; Jer. 31.19; Song 5.4.
2.   The irony, of course, is that in the end what Naomi argues here as
impossible does happen: her husband and sons became the source of
Ruth's husband.

statement, rich in emotion, is unusual in this setting and is powerfully expressed.

The first verb, פגע, means 'encounter': either in a neutral sense, as in 'meet face to face', in a negative sense, 'encounter with hostility', or in the sense of 'encounter with a request'.[1] Although this verb is used 39 times in the Hebrew Bible, the usage in this narrative is particularly noteworthy since it is the only verse where פגע is used directly *by* a woman to refer *to* a woman's actions.[2] The second verb, עזב, is equally significant. עזב can be used in the sense of intentionally leaving something behind, as in ch. 2 where Boaz instructs his workers, 'Also let some fall for her from the handsful and leave them behind (ועזבתם) for her to glean' (2.16). עזב can also signify the idea of changing primary allegiance.[3] The most common usage, however, is the sense of 'abandon' or 'forsake', either a person or God.[4] It is this strong meaning of the word which Ruth conveys. What Ruth says to Naomi is, in effect, 'don't tell me to abandon you'. To emphasize her determination, Ruth repeats Naomi's own verb לשוב ('to return', v. 15), but with a difference. While Naomi uses 'return' to signify movement 'toward' ('your sister-in-law is returning to her people' [אל־עמה]), for Ruth 'to return' is to go 'away from' ('to return *from* going after you' [מאחריך]). Ruth is as adamantly determined to accompany Naomi as Naomi is opposed to her doing so. With carefully chosen words, Ruth states, 'where you go, I shall go', challenging Naomi's repeated 'go back'. Ruth's unspoken command is that Naomi must abandon all attempts to persuade Ruth to leave her.

Ruth continues her speech in 1.16 where she bluntly reminds her mother-in-law, 'your people *are* my people; your God *is* my God'. These clauses, in the present tense, leave no doubt that

---

1. See, for example, Exod. 5.3, 20; Jer. 7.16.
2. Even when Naomi uses this verb in 2.22, 'they will not meet [i.e. bother] you in another field', she is explaining the action of men, not using the verb form to relate to herself.
3. Gen. 2.24 is an interesting example, since it contains both דבק (in the sense of 'holding fast') and עזב: 'Thus will a man depart (יעזב) from his father and his mother and hold fast (ודבק) to his wife and they will be one flesh'.
4. See, for example, Prov. 2.17 and Judg. 10.10.

Ruth has *already* disavowed the solidarity of her family and the possibility of marriage and children; she has *already* abandoned her identity as a Moabite; she has *already* renounced her native religious affiliation. By telling Naomi, 'where you will lodge, I shall lodge', Ruth changes the action of the narrative. To confirm the seriousness of her intentions, Ruth swears an oath in Yahweh's name with a rhetorical flourish that exceeds even Naomi's soliloquy: 'Yahweh do thus to me and more also, because death will separate me from you' (1.17).[1] By one simple statement of God's name Ruth joins Naomi, her people, and her religion. Like Abraham who also left his family, country and faith to live in a new land (Gen. 12.1), Ruth has broken with family, country, and faith.[2]

Naomi recognizes the futility of objection. Ruth cannot be dissuaded. Literally, 1.18 reads that 'she [Naomi] saw that she [Ruth] was strengthening herself (מתאמצת)'—in effect, marshalling physical and mental resources.[3] Faced with such determination, Naomi 'ceased to speak to her [Ruth]' and withdrew into silence for the rest of the trip.

The chapter concludes with Naomi's speech to the women of Bethlehem. Her words resound with phrasing deliberately chosen for effect: 'Call me "Bitter" for Yahweh has greatly embittered me' (המר, literally, *'caused me* to be bitter'). Naomi tells the

---

1. Despite the frequent use of God's name by Naomi (eight times), by Boaz (five times), by minor characters and the narrator (five times), Ruth says God's name only once, and it is in this oath declaring her allegiance to Naomi. Although this is a typical oath formula, elsewhere in the Hebrew Bible the oath is spoken only by leaders about matters of state (by a king: 1 Sam. 14.44; 2 Sam. 19.14; 1 Kgs 2.23; 20.10; 2 Kgs 6.31; by a queen: 1 Kgs 19.2; by a prince: 1 Sam. 20.13; by a king designate: 1 Sam. 25.22; by a high priest: 1 Sam. 3.17; by an army commander: 2 Sam. 3.9; by clan elders: 2 Sam. 3.35). Hubbard raises the possibility that Ruth 'thereby speak[s] audaciously as a royal figure in anticipation of 4.17' (R.L. Hubbard, *The Book of Ruth* [Grand Rapids: Eerdmans, 1991], p. 119).

2. See P. Trible, *God and the Rhetoric of Sexuality* (Philadelphia: Fortress Press, 1978).

3. Hubbard makes the observation that semantically, ללכת אתה ('to go with her') is synonymous with הלכנה עמי (v. 11) but antonymous to מאחריך לשוב (v. 16) (Hubbard, *Ruth*, p. 121).

women that Yahweh 'testified against me', a metaphoric use of Israelite law[1] by which she portrays herself as a defendant in a legal action. Naomi has already been found guilty and punished but knows neither the charges nor the testimony against her. Naomi's silence towards Ruth which began on their trip back to Bethlehem continues even after their arrival. Trible suggests that the elderly widow is 'overpowered' by her sense of divinely-inspired calamity.[2] But perhaps Naomi's treatment of Ruth contains something more. Fewell and Gunn attribute it to embarrassment: 'the Moabite who stands alongside her embodies Naomi's (though in actuality Elimelech's) abortive flirtation with foreignness'.[3] Naomi's silence, as powerful as her words, seems to emphasize an alienation between the two women, and the discourse of power shifts to Ruth.

Ruth acts decisively, her speech acts direct and to the point. Having taken stock of the general situation, Ruth states her determination to address their poverty. First, Ruth must find food: 'I would go out to the field and glean among the sheaves'. Her method is to find a hospitable land-owner 'in whose eyes I shall find favor'. The construction of this verse (cohortative first person) establishes its meaning. In effect, Ruth is saying, 'Look, it's a good idea if...' Ruth is not asking Naomi's permission[4] but, rather, initiating the solution. Ruth, who at the end of ch. 1

1. See, for example, Exod. 20.16; Deut. 5.20; 1 Sam. 12.3; 2 Sam. 1.16; Mic. 6.3. Campbell distinguishes ב- עֱנה (testimony detrimental to the defendant) from ל- עֱנה (testimony favorable to him; E.F. Campbell, *Ruth* [AB; Garden City, NY: Doubleday, 1973], pp. 77, 83).

2. Trible, *Rhetoric of Sexuality*, p. 174.

3. D.N. Fewell and D.M. Gunn, *Compromising Redemption: Relating Characters in the Book of Ruth* (Louisville, KY: Westminster Press, 1990), p. 76.

4. Assuming that the particle נא here means, 'Please, I pray', some scholars (e.g. P. Joüon, *Grammaire de l'hébreu biblique* [Rome: Pontifical Biblical Institute, 1965], §114d), read this cohortative as a request for permission ('Permit me to...'). I read this as Lambdin does: the particle identifies the statement as a logical consequence either of a previous statement, or of the general situation in which it was spoken (T.O. Lambdin, *Introduction to Biblical Hebrew* [New York: Charles Scribner's Sons, 1971], pp. 170-71). Thus, this cohortative and the following one are not petitions for permission but declarations.

(1.22) returned *from* the fields of Moab, now (2.2) will go *to* the field in order to seek food and 'to find favor in the eyes of' someone.

Once in the field, Ruth approaches the overseer. She requests of him a privilege, permission to glean *and* collect grains from among the sheaves. Her action is unusual. Under the law, there is no need for the poor to ask permission to glean, but what Ruth wants goes beyond her rights. By enlarging her petition to include special benefits, Ruth presents the overseer with a request which he is not in a position to grant.[1] In this way, Ruth manages to be noticed by Boaz, and the overseer tells him that she 'stood from this morning until now'. The first part of Ruth's mission, to find a hospitable land-owner, is thus accomplished.

Although Ruth is of relatively few words in her dealings with Naomi, her dialogues with Boaz are formal and dramatic. Having waited for him to appear before beginning to glean and having been given permission to do so, Ruth 'fell on her face and bowed down to the ground' (2.10). This expression is used most often in connection with God, prophets and kings,[2] and Ruth's reaction is an exaggerated display of gratitude which calls attention to Boaz's superiority, particularly since the right to glean was already hers under the law.

Her first words to Boaz, 'why have I found favor in your eyes' (2.10), fulfill her promise to Naomi in 2.2 that she will glean in a field after someone 'in whose eyes [she] will find favor'. Ruth's choice of words in the second part of the sentence reveals her additional desire, that Boaz 'recognize me' (להכירני). Since this verb ('recognize' [often 'known before']; 'pay attention to') is used generally in the sense of literally 'seeing', her statement conveys the sense 'to give (me) more than a passing glance, to single (me) out'. The third part of her statement, 'even though I am a foreigner', confirms this. Since נכריה is primarily an ethnic term which designates someone from another group[3] with an

---

1. J.M. Sasson, *Ruth: A New Translation with a Philological Commentary and a Formalist-Folklorist Interpretation* (Baltimore: Johns Hopkins University Press, 1979), p. 47.

2. See, for example Gen. 17.3; Josh. 5.14; 2 Sam. 1.2.

3. See P. Humbert, 'Les adjectifs *zâr* et *nokrî* et la "femme étrangère"

even lower social status than the גר ('resident alien'; cf. לגור, Ruth 1.1),[1] Ruth's statement, literally 'you have noticed the unnoticed' or 'recognized the unrecognized', verbalizes Ruth's assumption of acceptance into Boaz's clan, perhaps even into his family,[2] even if Boaz is not yet cognizant of the fact. After Boaz explains that he had heard all about her actions, Ruth brings the conversation to a close, repeating yet a third time the phrase heard in vv. 2.2 and 2.10, that she may still 'find favor in his eyes'. The imperfect verb form (אמצא) acts both as gratitude for Boaz's kindness and, more significantly, as a wish for future positive dealings, the acceptance ('favor') of Ruth by her new community. Ruth's (not particularly) veiled desire to see Boaz again is expressed in her reason for gratitude: 'because you have comforted me and spoken to the heart of your maidservant' (v. 13). Although 'to speak to the heart' often means merely 'to speak reassuringly' to someone in distress,[3] it is used also to convey male–female love, to 'entice, persuade'.[4] Certainly, unless Ruth intends the expression as a *double entendre*, to mean both 'speak encouragement' and romantically 'woo, court',[5] her response is exaggerated, since all Boaz told her was to remain

des Proverbes bibliques', in *Opuscules d'un hébraïsant* (Neuchâtel: Secrétariat de l'Université, 1958), p. 115. The word is used of Ittai the Gittite (2 Sam. 15.19), the Jebusite city of Jerusalem (Judg. 19.12), Solomon's wives (1 Kgs 11.1, 8), and Israel's postexilic wives (Ezra 10.2, 10; Neh. 13.26, 27, and so on). In a few places, the term refers to someone who no longer belongs to the circle of family or clan (Gen. 31.15; Exod. 21.8; Ps. 69.9; Job 19.15).

1.　Because the former does not belong to the covenant people (Deut. 14.21) he or she enjoys no covenant privileges; that is, the נכרי can be charged interest on loans (Deut. 23.21) and forced to pay debts even in 'the year of release' (Deut. 15.3). Further, contact between the נכרי and Israelites is to be avoided (Judg. 19.12), probably to minimize the influence of foreign religious practices (1 Kgs 11.1, 7-8; Ezra 10.2; Neh. 13.23, 26-27).

2.　Sasson, *Ruth*, p. 418.

3.　See, for example, Joseph to his brothers fearful of revenge (Gen. 50.21), Yahweh to Jerusalem frightened of more punishment (Isa. 40.2).

4.　Gen. 34.3; Judg. 19.3.

5.　So C. Carmichael, '"Treading" in the Book of Ruth', *ZAW* 92 (1980), p. 256.

in his field to glean and to drink from the communal jars when thirsty.

The power of Ruth's discourse has drawn Boaz into her story. Significantly, Ruth has the last word. Indeed, her impressive remark leaves Boaz as speechless as her earlier one had left Naomi (cf. 1.16-18).[1]

When Ruth arrives home Naomi asks where she gleaned. Ruth does not answer the question directly; instead she tells Naomi with whom she worked, shifting attention from the location to the identity of her benefactor. Her discourse creates a turning-point in the conversation and in the narrative. As Hubbard states, 'One can almost hear Ruth slowly emphasizing each [word]—then pausing a pregnant instant before dropping the key word: *Boaz*'.[2] The name alters the scene's reality: Ruth's discourse has made Boaz part of Naomi's world.

Now Naomi's initial period of grieving and bitterness ends, and her speech acts reveal a talent for calculated action. Naomi muses on the meaning of Boaz's material kindness, and finds in it a promise. She creates and instigates a plan to have Boaz provide a permanent solution to their problems: redemption of her land. Naomi blesses Boaz for his actions and tells Ruth that 'the man is a relative of ours' (v. 20). Crucially for the continuation of the narrative, Naomi announces that Boaz is 'among our *redeemers*'. Naomi's voice engulfs Ruth's.

Naomi understands that Ruth's protection by Boaz is only temporary. In 2.21 Ruth relates to Naomi that Boaz told her to 'stick with my young men until the end of my entire harvest' (v. 21). Naomi offers Ruth stern, motherly advice. Addressing Ruth as '*my daughter*', Naomi tells Ruth that it is 'good that you go out with his young *women*' (v. 22), her counsel serving two purposes. First, Naomi wants Ruth to accept Boaz's offer; she is to work only in his field. Secondly, Naomi steers Ruth away

1. Cf. Trible: 'Things are once again not what they seem. Deference is initiative; initiative is reaction... Now the story does not censure Boaz for dereliction of duty, but it does subordinate him to the women. He has patriarchal power, but he does not have narrative power. He has authority within the story but not control over it' (*Rhetoric of Sexuality*, p. 176).

2. Hubbard, *Ruth*, p. 185.

from the male workers toward the female, avoiding potential romances with anyone other than the 'redeemer'.[1]

Not waiting for Ruth's reply, Naomi plunges immediately into exposition. First, she presents Ruth with reasons aimed at defeating any scruple and quieting any anxiety which might disturb her daughter-in-law. Naomi states that her main concern is to provide Ruth with a sense of security: 'My daughter, shall I not seek rest (מנוח) for you', subtly reminding Ruth of her prayer for her daughters-in-law while still in Moab, that Ruth and Orpah find security and rest (מנוחה) in the homes of new husbands.

Next Naomi gives Ruth explicit instructions to wash, anoint herself, dress, and go down to the threshing floor. The following stage in the plan, however, is the most daring. In fact, precisely what Naomi advises has been the subject of much debate: וגלית מרגלתיו, literally 'uncover his feet'. Two points are at issue here: the verb and the direct object. The verb גלה, used in this form, often means 'to uncover nakedness' for sexual purposes. Deut. 23.1, for example, states that 'a man shall not take the wife of his father, nor uncover his father's skirt'. Deut. 27.20 elaborates: 'Cursed is he that lies down with his father's wife because he uncovers his father's skirt'. The same expression also exists in later writings. In Isa. 47.1-3, the prophet speaks of a noble woman's degradation, in this case symbolic of Babylon, when her leg is uncovered, her nakedness is displayed, and her shame is exposed.

Secondly, the use of מרגלתיו, that which Ruth was to uncover, is ambiguous.[2] The problem with this verse is that this word in this

---

1. For Rudolph and Joüon the change from 'young women' to 'young men' poses a problem. They argue that the contrast is between Boaz's workers and those of someone else, not between Boaz's male and female ones (W. Rudolph, *Das Buch Ruth, Das Hohelied, Das Klagelieder* [KAT; Gütersloh: Gerd Mohn, 1962], p. 51; P. Joüon, *Ruth: Commentaire philologique et exégétique* [Rome: Pontifical Biblical Institute, 1953], p. 65). Verse 22, however, seems to convey both contrasts and makes their suggested textual emendations unnecessary (Rudolph: omit אחר ['other'] in בשדה אחר ['in another field']; Joüon: read masc. pl.).

2. W. Gesenius calls this form the plural of 'local extension', that is, an indication of a place or an area (W. Gesenius, *Hebrew Grammar*

exact construction is found only here and in Daniel 10.6, where
it is used under totally different circumstances. Since the term
'foot' is a common enough biblical euphemism for 'penis',[1] the
difference in Hebrew between 'uncover his feet' and 'uncover
his foot [= penis]' is subtle. In this context, and with an appropriate hesitation after 'uncover' (וגלית), could Ruth (or a reader)
miss the sexual intent implicit in Naomi's instruction? Naomi
quickly assures Ruth that any further 'action' in the relationship
would be up to Boaz. Apparently, Boaz is to respond to Ruth's
gesture with some instructions of his own!

Ruth's promise of compliance draws the scene to a close. Ruth
asks no questions, raises no objections, seeks no reasons.
Evidently, she understands Naomi's plan fully. Her simple
response ('All you have said to me [both overtly and implicitly] I
shall do', 3.5) confirms the arrangement and carries the story
forward.

Following Naomi's instructions, Ruth approaches Boaz while
he is asleep and uncovers his 'feet'. The story enters a new stage
as the 'traditional' roles of pursuer and pursued are reversed.
Structurally, the discourse in ch. 3 parallels ch. 2: dialogues
between Naomi and Ruth enclose the main scene, the dialogue
between Ruth and Boaz. Tension mounts. Ruth lies next to Boaz
who is asleep on the floor. He awakens, startled, to find a
woman at his feet. Although Ruth's honor is not uncovered, the
'skirt' of Boaz's robe and his 'feet' are. Ruth speaks with verbal
density: 'I am Ruth your handmaid; spread your wing over your
handmaid, for you are a redeemer' (3.9). Each of these words is
fraught with meaning.

In the first part of her answer, Ruth introduces herself as אמה,
the third of three progressively more familiar terms she has
used to describe herself to Boaz. At their initial meeting (2.10)

[Oxford: Oxford University Press, 1910], §124a-g). Gen. 28.11, for
example—וישם מראשתיו ('...and placed them "under" his head')—uses this
construction to describe the 'place' of Jacob's head. Trible concludes that
מרגלתיו in Ruth 3.4, 7, 8, 14 functions as a euphemism for the genitals
(*Rhetoric of Sexuality*, p. 199). Campbell views this usage as a rhetorical
device, an intentional ambiguity about just how much of Boaz was to be
uncovered (*Ruth*, p. 121).

    1.   Exod. 4.25; Judg. 3.24; 1 Sam. 24.4.

Ruth asked Boaz why he recognizes her, a foreigner. Three verses later, Ruth upgrades her status from foreigner to שפחה when she tells him 'you spoke to the heart of your *maidservant*', and reinforces her new status by telling him that 'I am not even one of your *maidservants*'. Now Ruth tells Boaz that she is his אמה, and again repeats this by telling Boaz to spread his wing (or skirt) over his אמה. While אמה is difficult to translate and to differentiate from שפחה, אמה is, according to several modern biblical scholars, appreciably higher on the social ladder than שפחה.[1]

Now Ruth departs from Naomi's script. Naomi had instructed Ruth that at this point Boaz would take the lead, and at the very moment one expects Boaz to 'instruct' Ruth, *she* directs *him* to 'spread the corner of your garment' (כנף) over your maidservant', its sexual connotations surpassing even those of Naomi's speech. The *double entendre* here is that of Deut. 27.20, 'Cursed is he who lies with his father's wife, because he has uncovered his father's skirt (כנף)' (quoted above). In Deuteronomy, כנף is a euphemism for the genitals, either those of the wife or, perhaps more likely (given the nature of a כנף as an 'extremity'), those of the father. Naomi has instructed Ruth to 'uncover' Boaz's 'feet'. Having done so, Ruth's discourse invites Boaz to 'cover' her with his כנף. Clearly, as Gunn notes, a euphemistic meaning ('penis') seems to fit this context extremely well.[2] Boaz is in a position to redeem the land formerly belonging to Elimelech, and Ruth reminds him that he is 'a redeemer'. Ruth's powerful discourse forces Boaz to act. What subsequently happens is then conveniently masked by the all-purpose verb שכב ('lie down, lie with, sleep with').

Naomi greets Ruth's return with an excited but enigmatic question, 'Who are you?' (3.16), the same question Boaz had asked Ruth (3.9). Normally, this question seeks someone's

---

1. Cf. A. Berlin, *Poetics and Interpretation of Biblical Narrative* (Bible and Literature Series, 9; Sheffield: Almond Press, 1983), pp. 88-89; Campbell, *Ruth*, pp. 101, 123; Sasson, *Ruth*, pp. 53, 81; E.M. MacDonald, *The Position of Woman as Reflected in Semitic Codes of Law* (Toronto: University of Toronto Press, 1931), p. 62.

2. D.M. Gunn, *The Fate of King Saul* (JSOTSup, 14; Sheffield: JSOT Press, 1980), pp. 153-54, n. 5.

identity,[1] but not in this context. Since Naomi addresses Ruth as 'my daughter', she recognizes the arriving figure despite the darkness. And, unlike in 3.9 where Ruth replies with her name, here she provides Naomi with a report of Boaz's actions. Although the question can be understood literally, Ruth interprets the מי contextually (that is, 'Who [in status, in situation] are you?'). Based on the circumstances, Ruth understands Naomi's words to be a request for a report on her meeting with Boaz. Paraphrased, Naomi asks 'how do things stand with you', 'are you his wife or not?'[2] Since meaning is a function of the *context* in which linguistic communication is performed,[3] 'who are you?' in this situation means 'did my plan succeed?'[4] Due to the power of Ruth's discourse, the answer is an emphatic 'yes!'

Events have now come full circle. Ironically, the verbose Naomi is silenced by the women who greeted her return to Bethlehem. As Hubbard points out, 'in 1.19-21 [the women] listened while Naomi lamented; here she listens while they rejoice'.[5] Naomi's bitter discourse closed ch. 1, but the exuberant words of the townswomen close the narrative.

1.　Gen. 27.18-19, 32; 1 Sam. 26.14; 2 Sam. 1.8.

2.　According to Moshe Greenberg, covering a woman with a garment expresses 'acquiring' her, since it is understood that henceforth the woman will be covered to all except her husband (*Ezekiel 1–20* [AB; Garden City, NY: Doubleday, 1983], p. 277).

3.　As Schmidt describes, discourse is not 'a set of signs with a fixed meaning' but rather a 'dynamic system of communicational "instructors" with a variable meaning-potential which is defined by specifying co-texts and contexts' (S.J. Schmidt, 'Reception and Interpretation of Written Texts as Problems of a Rational Theory of Literary Communication', in *Style and Text: Studies Presented to Nils Erik Enkvist* [Stockholm, 1975], p. 401). Thus, meaning is created not only by decoding signs but by contextual assumptions requiring inferences about language use.

4.　Cf. Sasson, who reads מי as a genitive, 'Whose wife are you?' (*Ruth*, p. 100) and G. Gerleman, who reads it as 'a pure interrogative particle', hence 'Is it really you?' (*Ruth: Das Hohelied* [BKAT, 18; Neukirchen–Vluyn: Neukirchener Verlag, 1981], p. 33).

5.　*Ruth*, p. 276.

Brenner notes that the book of Ruth shares a common theme with many of the patriarchal narratives, 'the reversal of feminine fortune'.[1] Discourse analysis helps explain why. Ruth and Naomi know what they want and go after it. Their discourse is that of power; the power of their discourse is that they succeed.

1. A. Brenner, *Ruth and Naomi: Literary, Stylistic and Linguistic Studies in the Book of Ruth* (Hebrew; Tel Aviv: Afik Sifriat Paolim/ Hakibbutz Hamenchad, 1988), pp. 40-42; also the article in this volume.

HEROISM AND PROPER NAMES, OR THE FRUITS OF ANALOGY[*]

Mieke Bal

Balancing the Tension

Once the underlying passivity and fears of impotence of heroes like David the Great and Samson the Strong are plausible, and once the procedures of ideological transformations as they are displayed in both scholarly and popular reception are outlined, the insecurity in patriarchal heroism can be studied in its artistic figuration. It is time to examine in more detail the typical narrative art of the biblical love stories and the way that art exposes specific attitudes toward sexuality. Such a study cannot be comprehensive and there is no need for it to be. My aim is not to describe biblical narrative art and differentiate it from modern Western literature as, for example, Robert Alter does;[1] rather, I wish to point to the ideological changes brought about by these differences insofar as the relations between the sexes are concerned. Therefore I will analyze only one feature that I consider basic: the construction of the characters.

Literary characters, as representations, as images of the culturally valid view of the subject, have the property of displaying, in condensed form, the problematics inherent in that view. A specific and in some sense alien tension between analogy and chronology is characteristic of biblical love stories. It is that very tension which facilitates the evolution of the myths from one culture to another. Understanding of that tension from within is a first condition of its neutralization.

[*] This article is taken from M. Bal, *Lethal Love: Feminist Literary Readings of Biblical Love Stories* (Bloomington: Indiana University Press, 1987), ch. 3, pp. 68-88.

1. R. Alter, *The Art of Biblical Narrative* (New York: Basic Books, 1981).

In this chapter, the construction of characters in the book of Ruth will be approached from the point of view of the function of proper names. That construction is dependent on a device that falls under the general heading of *analogy*. The proper name and its narrative function reveal, however, the fact that analogy can work only within a concept of chronology. The interdependence of both allows only relative differentiation. They are delicately balanced, and a fruitful understanding of text and reception is based on a flexible view of their dynamic relation. Once the importance of analogy as a function of typically biblical metatextuality is established, the limits of too strict a thematic reading must be demonstrated. To that end, the same device will be considered from the point of view of a dialectic of chronology in chapter 4.[1]

In the book of Ruth, characters can only be heroes insofar as they resemble one another. At first sight, this collective heroism is alien to our notion of individualism, but it becomes self-evident as soon as the use of the text in Jewish liturgy is brought into consideration. Using the terminology of modern literary theory, I wish to show that this mode of reading is not as radically novel as it may seem. The document of reception that serves as a starting point is, this time, a piece of creative writing. It will not demonstrate ideological misreading as did the rewritings in the previous chapters.[2] The case is more complex. As I argued earlier, distortions are unavoidable, but the particular orientation they choose is relatively optional. Victor Hugo's poem features here the possibility of ideological variation: although his poem is not without connections to the general modern view of sexuality, it is based on aspects of the biblical book that have remained unnoticed in Christian reception, buried as the story has been under morality and the need for male, individual heroism.

1. Bal, *Lethal Love*, pp. 89-103 (on Gen. 38).
2. Bal, *Lethal Love*, pp. 10-36 (on 2 Sam. 11) and pp. 37-67 (Judg. 16) respectively.

Starting from a Detail

Sa barbe était d'argent comme un ruisseau d'avril
Sa gerbe n'était point avare ni haineuse
Quand il voyait passer quelque pauvre glaneuse:
'Laissez tomber exprès des épis,' disait-il.

His beard was silver like a spring brook
his sheaf was neither miserly nor spiteful.
When he saw some poor gleaner passing by
he said: 'drop ears on purpose'.

Hugo's poem, which is part of *La légende des siècles* (1859), uses the story of Ruth in an evocation of an old man's mysterious experience of love on a peaceful summer night. In an attempt to make the elements of the story more general, Hugo interestingly reverses the perspective. Thus he draws attention to a reversal in the text itself.

The quoted verses are the best-known lines of Hugo's poem 'Booz endormi'. They have been commented upon by Jacques Lacan and, subsequently, by Anne Uebersfeld and Michel Grimaud.[1] The first feature of the poem that strikes the reader is the choice of the male character as the protagonist. In most commentaries on the book of Ruth, Boaz is interpreted as the *destinateur*: it is the generous Boaz, who, from the height of his position as a rich man, allows the 'pauvre glaneuse' Ruth to reach her goal, so well deserved: a place of her own, under the roof of some rich man.

Lacan, in a most convincing metatext, directs attention to the fundamental negativity of Hugo's poem, in which the pro-claimed generosity of the man is questionable: 'His explicit generosity is reduced to less than nothing by the richness of the sheaf which, taken from nature, is ignorant of our reservations and rejections'.[2] And Grimaud writes in his commentary on Lacan, 'Indeed, one of the aspects always neglected in readings

1. J. Lacan, *Ecrits* (Paris: Seuil, 1966); A. Uebersfeld, *Le roi et le bouffon* (Paris: José Corti, 1974); M. Grimaud, 'Sur une métaphore métonymique hugolienne selon Jacques Lacan', *Littérature* 29 (1978).
2. Lacan, *Ecrits*, p. 507.

of "Booz" is the intensity of the affirmations of impotence'.[1]

It is difficult indeed, to close one's eyes to the sexual meaning, and this in a negative sense, of the verse in which Uebersfeld[2] sees a paradigmatic example of the shift from metonymy (Boaz and the sheaf he possesses) to metaphor (Boaz and the sheaf he *is*). I would suggest that synecdoche is the means of this transition. It is only because Boaz considers the sheaf as a significant part of himself that it can take its metaphorical meaning.

The fabula of the book of Ruth is well known: on the advice of Naomi, her mother-in-law, Ruth goes in her finest dress to try to seduce Boaz into a marriage that would protect both impoverished women from misery. The seduction attempt is incredibly outspoken and daring: by night, the young widow takes her place in Boaz's bed, uncovers his feet (if not 'worse': the Hebrew word is ambiguous and also means 'testicles'[3]) in order to 'lay by him'. Even the most moralizing and orthodox commentaries refrain from attempting to 'cover up' the sensational story and engage in a more promising strategy: they try to defend Ruth's move as understandable, to naturalize it and thus to make it morally acceptable.

Lacan and Grimaud, both sensitive to the old Hugoesque Boaz's anxiety, his fear of dying childless, are interested in the *displacement* in the tenth verse of the French poem ('sa gerbe n'était point avare ni haineuse'), which transforms the shocking metaphor into an innocent metonymy, without entirely succeeding in the repression of ambiguity, still preserved in the possessive adjective 'sa'. *Displacement*, that fundamental figure of Freudian rhetoric and that most efficient tool of censorship, is manifest not only on the microstructural level of this verse and its rhetorical figure of speech. In this chapter, I want to deal not with the displacement the poem contains, but with the one it *constitutes, is*, and this in the most concrete sense of the word. Thus the transition from metonymy via synecdoche to metaphor characterizes not only Hugo's verse but also its relation to the biblical book and even, as will become clear, the composition of

1. Grimaud, 'Sur une métaphore', p. 103.
2. Uebersfeld, *Le roi*, p. 587.
3. Cf. Rashkow's article in this volume.

the book itself. Indeed, compared to the biblical book, Hugo's poem is the result of the maximizing of a detail, a telephoto effect. The detail is a short fragment of the seduction scene (Ruth 3.6-15). The enlarging which, as with any synecdoche, necessarily entails displacement, is two-sided. First, the poet picks out a secondary character to make him the protagonist of his version of the fabula. Second, the detail he picks in the whole scene is a motif that is hardly explicit, the one of v. 10: 'Blessed be thou of the Lord, my daughter: for thou has shewed more kindness in the latter end than at the beginning, inasmuch as thou followest not young men, whether poor or rich'.

As opposed to nonliterary metatexts, that is, theological commentaries or works of literary scholarship, the poem stresses feelings that this verse only touches upon: Boaz's fear of old age, of losing his sexual potency and attractiveness, of being incapable of changing his sad situation as a childless widower. In the poem, the enormous oak that, in his dream, grows out of his belly, loaded with posterity, constitutes the image, moving in its directness, of the rich man's worries. From that point of view, Ruth's approach is a stroke of luck that he would not have dared to hope for and, indeed, he is most grateful to her for she will help him out of *his* misery. The whole development of Hugo's poem comes out of this verse, as vital for the poem as is the oak for Boaz. Not only, then, does Hugo displace emphases; he totally reverses the perspective. He changes the story of Boaz's generosity into that of Ruth's generosity, and he changes the very meaning of the concept: while Boaz gave what he possessed, Ruth gives what she *is*.

Two assimilations produce Hugo's figuration of Boaz's dream. In the Christian exegetic tradition, a confusion often exists between Boaz's and Jesse's tree. This can be seen, for example, on the windows of the Chartres cathedral. A second confusion, for which Hugo may not have had any source, is the one between this tree and another 'erection', the ladder also seen in a dream, by Jacob. The condensation is revealing, based as it is on dreams of election, ascension and posterity as one and the same issue. Hugo's representation of Boaz's dream of potency enhances the conception of individual male success as a position in history. At the same time, it opens up the difference between what one *is* and where one *stands*, between one's position in analogy and in chronology, which ultimately differentiates between the book as a love story and as history.

Even the most feminist of commentaries, Phyllis Trible's classic analysis,[1] does not account for the problematic aspect of v. 3.10 in terms of coherence. Indeed, Trible's interpretation stresses, like most scholarly metatexts, the idyllic side of the book of Ruth, with which the quoted verse is so violently in contradiction. On the other hand, works of art conceived after this source text give a more interesting account of possible readings. Hugo's poem is not the only one. We know Rembrandt's painting *The Jewish Bride*, which is sometimes claimed to represent Ruth and Boaz. Here, Boaz is depicted putting his hand on Ruth's breast, an obviously sexual gesture. Instead of sticking to a paraphrasing critique of the text, which cannot go beyond overtly stated meanings, according to which Ruth's happiness in finding a solvent husband is the well-deserved price for her devotion to her old mother-in-law, and according to which, consequently, Boaz remains a pale figure as the *destinateur* in the background, and can easily be recuperated as prefiguring Christ, it seems more interesting first to take the status of the book seriously. The book of Ruth is an institutionalized *metatext*, which was meant to be read at specific feasts and to comment upon the Torah.

Commenting upon Ruth, Hugo provides a cue to take the story as comment upon the Torah. If in Hugo's version the female name has disappeared from the title, we should not mistake that change, for that displacement helps to illuminate another displacement, of which the last half of 3.10 only displays a trace. Displacing the displacement, then, Hugo reinstates the repressed side of the text, which is its metatextual function in the first place. The question then arises: what is the content of the commentary that the book is supposed to give?

In 3.10, there is a kindness (*ḥesed*) at stake. The word is an understatement—most translations give 'generosity'. The kindness alluded to is a kindness 'in the beginning'. There is a first

---

1. P. Trible, *God and the Rhetoric of Sexuality* (Philadelphia: Fortress Press, 1978).

kindness, and then there is a second kindness, evaluated as greater. The latter kindness, and thus the best one, is Ruth's courting of Boaz. The first one, discussed several times already, is spoken about for the first time at the end of ch. 1: 'And Ruth *clave* unto her' (1.14). Now, this verb is a very strong one. It is used in Gen. 2.24 to say that man will cleave unto his wife. It is exclusively used with a male subject, in reference to the matrimonial bond. Also, it is active, signifying the free choice made by a subject to renounce freedom in favor of another being. With these features of the verb in mind, it is easy to evaluate as an instance of censorship the translation of the *Alliance Biblique Française*, which runs, 'Mais Ruth refusa de se séparer d'elle', where the verb 'refuser', by its inherent negativity, undermines the subject's position as active, and its action as positive adherence.

Ruth's faithfulness to Naomi or, we may say more directly, her *love* for Naomi, is praised several times, and by Boaz himself in 2.11-12. Her generosity, compared with which this legendary love almost vanishes, consists, according to Boaz, in her not 'following young men'. The scandal of the comparison is more audible in the artistic sensibility of both Hugo and Rembrandt than in the censored rationalism of scholarly metatexts or in 'purified' rewritings like children's Bibles. Ann Edwards, for example, replaces the comparison with a sheer juxtaposition: 'For you have not looked at the young men, rich or poor, and you have remained with your mother-in-law'.[1] The Hebrew technically allows, of course, a juxtaposition, but juxtaposition itself easily signifies a comparison. It is, however, impossible not to take this scandal into account, because without it the verse simply does not make sense. I would even go so far as to assume that either the comparison *is* strikingly scandalous or the verse is a corruption of the text. Even the most moralistic metatexts have not gone that far.

Let us take the hypertrophy of the detail and relate it to the text, on the one hand, and to Hugo's metatextual reversal, on the other. It is, then, a *symptom*, in both Peirce's general and Freud's specific sense. The displacement is a displacement of

---

1.   A. Edwards, *A Child's Bible* (London: Pan Books, 1969), p. 196.

a displacement. We will shortly see how the texts on which Ruth comments form a chain of samples of sexual relations that Ruth criticizes and represses in the same move. Thus the meta-textual aspects of the book hide their own revolutionary import, allowing, without forcing it, a patriarchal reception. What is revolutionary is, as I will argue shortly, the possibility of the construction of Boaz as a hero through metatextual identification with female characters. This construction, which we will now turn to, operates through the narrative exploitation of the proper name.

Narrativization of the Proper Name

More often than not, biblical names have a meaning. If they do not have one, they are assigned one in the text's afterlife. Far from being purely deictic, like names in today's Western culture, they have a specific meaning that integrates the character into its life, and that can also imprison it there. The name *Orpah*, for example, given to the character of contrast who in Ruth 1.14 follows the advice of her mother-in-law to privilege the reality principle and return to her family in order to find a husband among her own people, means 'back' or 'neck', and is explained by Midrash Rabbah 'because she turned her back'. Hence the meaning that became standard: 'the one who turns the neck'. Not only is the name in such cases so well adapted to the character that we could say that it is iconic rather than symbolic, keeping its indexical aspect, it is also narrative. For, far from describing just a feature of the character, it tells its action—an emblematic action, indeed, which thus becomes predictive, but which remains narrated action. This entails the problem of chronology and its relation to analogy.

Receiving the name, the little girl is not yet 'the one who turns the neck', but she is already defined as such. She is subjected to her name, determined by it. It is because she has this name that she will remain her whole life 'the one who turns the neck', until history will finally allow her to do what is expected from her. Lacan would have here a good example of his concept of the subject subjected to the symbolic order as early as before birth, by the proper name. The model, of which Orpah is our paradigm case, also contains a statement on narrative discourse. In biblical culture, the word and the thing are not separated, and we do not need to insist on the importance of the verb for the creation of the world that Yahweh wished to be so thoroughly semiotic. The narrative order articulates and models this world, and Orpah, charged with her narrative role as abandoner and her semantic content as the opposite of Ruth the faithful, has no way of defending herself against the destiny that order assigned to her by analogy.

Things are not always so fatal. The character is not completely defenseless against the name. Naomi the sweet, for example, bitter because of the accumulation of misery that befalls her, chooses the name of Mara the bitter one, deciding to call things by their names. History may dominate the subject; at least the latter can face the situation, assume the focalization of its own life. But Naomi, however justified her decision may seem at the moment she makes it, does not take the narrativity of her name into account. For within the narrative order, it is the case that if she has the name of Naomi the sweet, that is because, sooner or later, she will be Naomi the sweet. The name, which seems to have become irrelevant at a certain point, has not lost its predictive force.

Summarizing the lives of characters, names interpret them. Among all the events that could befall Orpah, it is her separation from Naomi—the choice it implies and the elimination of the character from the book when she turns her neck, disappears from Naomi's life—that the name reveals. The character is summarized by her name; so is the text devoted to that name.

In the case of Naomi, chronology corrects analogy. History corrects the character who had not enough faith in her name. Hence, there is a metatextual aspect in proper names. It is related to their iconic aspect: it operates through it. In modern literature, we have cases of semanticized names. The meanings we have seen in the names of Bovary and Homais, the 'barres raides' in the name of the husband Desbaresdes in *Moderato Cantabile*, are elements of a significant semantic network. But as distinct from those cases, aspects of names in Ruth *tell*. And since they can only tell the crucial, determining action, by which the destiny of the character is summarized, the bond they make between chronology and analogy comes close to what the French call a *mise en abyme,* a microstructure that contains a summary of the overall fabula in which it functions.[1] To use Shoshana Felman's terms, when she deals with the idea of paternity, 'It is a promise of proper *meaning* and of *proper name*'.[2]

Boaz's name means the powerful/potent. Naming him so, the text comments upon its own fabula from a point of view that is opposed to Victor Hugo's. But Hugo deals with names differently. He integrates the names of his characters into another network, which has a complexity of its own. He picks the name of the male character for his title. Now, the book of Ruth is one of only two books in the Hebrew Bible that have women's names as their titles. Should we suppose that Hugo the male could not stand all this attention being given to the woman? Not at all. For he adds the word 'endormi', as if he wanted both to draw our attention to the hypertrophy of the woman in the biblical context in which she otherwise has a definitely minor role to play, *and* to suggest an interpretation for it: it is *because* Boaz is sleeping that the woman can take this initiative. Boaz the powerful/potent is, in fact, Boaz the sleeper, the weak, the impotent. The sleep of the male is seen as a *sine qua non* of woman's access to her femininity.

The textual problem raised retrospectively by Hugo's meta-text is symmetrical with the other textual problem of the book of Ruth, found in the middle of ch. 4, vv. 11 and 12. This detail is part of the narration of a scene that goes from v. 1 to v. 12 and that is the only scene of the book in which there is no woman. In this passage, proper names are used in another way, with more explicit metatextuality. It is probably not by coincidence that the problem is even constituted by the proper name. The contrast between this scene and the previous one is systematic. There, the

1. See L. Dällenbach, *Le récit spéculaire: essai sur le mise en abyme* (Paris: Seuil, 1977); M. Bal, *Femmes imaginaires: l'ancien testament au risque d'une narratologie critique* (Utrecht: Hess; Montreal: HMH; Paris: Nizet, 1986); A. Jefferson, '*Mise en abyme* and the Prophetic in Narrative', *Style* 17.2 (1983), pp. 196-208.
2. S. Felman, *Le Scandale du corps parlant: Don Juan avec Austin ou la séduction en deux langues* (Paris: Editions du Seuil, 1980).

fabula was played out during the night, in the warmest intimacy, in Boaz's bed. Here, the sequence is in public, at the city gate, the place of jurisdiction—the place, too, that separates the female from the male domain. It is the entry point of the city. The action consists of a trial, the trial by which Boaz will legally acquire Ruth; men's business exclusively, while the object, the price at stake, is a woman.

Jurisdiction is basically a commentary on the law, hence the metatextual character of the scene. In this process, the elders of the city evoke a few proper names, the narrative content of which stretches far beyond the occasion for which they are summoned. We can even assume that the knowledge that the elders (in other words, the authorities) can possibly have of the motive for the allusion is insufficient to justify it. For the only motive can be analogy: the presumed iconicity between the cases evoked and the case at stake. I quote the problematic verses:

> 11 The Lord make the woman that is come into thine house like Rachel and like Leah, which did build the house of Israel...
> 12 And let thy house be like the house of Perez, whom Tamar bare unto Judah, of the seed which the Lord shall give thee of this young woman.

Let me first draw attention to the fact that the use of the proper name is not only more explicitly metatextual but also more explicitly narrative. For the name goes with the narration of actions of which the evoked women are the subjects: in other words childbearing, realizing the dream of the enormous oak. Building the house of Israel: the Hebrew Bible being, to some extent, entirely consecrated to that construction, we come close to a totalizing *mise en abyme*, which would contain not only the texts directly alluded to (Gen. 30 and 38) but the Torah as a whole and even, by extension, the Bible as a whole, including the past and future fabulae it contains. The difference between analogy and chronology is almost ruled out.

The textual problem raised is the irrelevance of the two evocations. 'Rachel and Leah' form a strange doubling of the woman Ruth. We shall have to examine their case in order to understand to what extent the elders are rather over-relevant.

The allusion to Tamar is overtly painful. She bears her son Perez to the old Judah, her father-in-law, and the role of the male in that story is far from edifying. To evoke her to the old Boaz, anxious to possess a young woman legally, in obedience to the rules of the society, in spite of the insecurity he had expressed to her only the previous night, seems a displaced and indiscreet allusion that is not very reassuring. It is difficult to imagine that the elders, who are so much in favor of the solution Boaz proposes, would deliberately try to hurt him.

There is a third name in this scene, the thrice-pronounced name of Moab, Ruth's country. This country is no other than the country of Moab, the son of Lot whom Lot engendered with his own daughter, unaware and during his drunkard's sleep. We will have to return to that synecdochical name too. Together, the names evoked in this scene form a series that is indeed narrowly tied up with 'the building of the house of Israel', with the relations between the sexes and procreation. Taken together, the names form a *mise en abyme par excellence*: the *mise en abyme* that, instead of proposing one interpretation, as is usually the case, offers all possibilities.

Since the problems evoked have to do with narrative subjects, with social life and unconscious allusions, I will briefly follow the three lines such an account suggests: narratological, historical, and psychoanalytical analyses.

In Search of the Subject

It may seem useless, in a text where the female character is appointed heroine as early as the title itself, to try to account for her place in the subjectivity of the text. The structure of the latter is less simple than it seems at first sight, however. For the overall subjectivity in a text is not accounted for solely by the one character who is the hero or heroine. The number of speeches allotted to each character in the book of Ruth is tallied in Table 1. Obviously, there is no self-evident reason to privilege Ruth. Naomi speaks often, and the order of speech acts shows that she takes the initiative, while Ruth reacts. Ruth executes Naomi's projects, if in a somewhat autonomous way. In the middle section Boaz takes a few initiatives, too. His addresses belong to the public domain: he speaks to the elders, to his employees, and he speaks privately and publicly to Ruth. The collective speakers are remarkable. Their function is thoroughly social. They react to and comment upon events, representing, as does the chorus in classical tragedy, public opinion. The first 'collective speaker' consists of the inhabitants of Bethlehem who verbalize, in the interrogative form, Naomi's pain, revealing— but interrogatively—the contradiction between the name and the character, thus between the word and the thing, a contradiction that is inconceivable. Therefore, Naomi does not accept being publicly named as something that she is not.

In the last chapter there are two distinct collective speakers, each speaking twice. First the elders speak, then the neighbors of Naomi. They are the last quoted speaker; they have the last word.

Table 1
Number of Speeches per Character per Chapter

	ch. 1	ch. 2	ch. 3	ch. 4
Narrator	3	7	3	7
Naomi	4	4	2	0
Ruth	2	5	3	0
Boaz	0	5	3	4
Redeemer	-	-	-	3
Collective Speaker	1	0	0	4

In the action of this book, focalization is at stake. How are we to see Naomi's situation? We have noticed already that she corrects the view expressed by her name. How are we to see in the first chapter the situation of her daughters-in-law? Three visions are given, implicitly or explicitly. Naomi gives her evaluation first; the two women oppose hers; finally, Orpah takes over Naomi's view, while Ruth perseveres. Boaz, when he first sees Ruth, asks for information about her. When the information is positive, but only then, he takes on himself the favorable view of Ruth. How are we to see Boaz's project? He asks the elders. He does not know that Naomi has given her view already and that he is left merely to act it out. The two middle chapters contain many questions, wishes, promises. If

Naomi is once mistaken about her own life, Ruth never is. Boaz is not either, but for another reason: as we have seen, he develops his view as derived from the public view. However, as supreme proof of his subjective power, he dares add one view of his own: the one expressed in 3.10.

So far the textual subjectivity has been shared mainly by two elder characters, Boaz and Naomi. Ruth's subject position, however autonomous it sometimes seems to be, is formally derived from the two elders. Naomi is privileged; her activities frame those of Boaz. The analysis of the fabula does not add much to this picture. Actions are neatly separated, and each character has his or her share. Naomi takes initiatives in the private domain, Boaz in the public sphere. It is striking, however, that Boaz's initiatives need social support from other subjects. After his first encounter with Ruth he asks for information about her, as if he wants to make sure that any eventual move on his side will be sanctioned beforehand. The trial at the gate exemplifies this need. Naomi's and Ruth's behavior is opposed to Boaz's: they brave public opinion.

Here the evocations by the elders intervene. Speakers of authority, they carry out the performative act of wishing, a lighter form of promise—lighter precisely in terms of its lack of authority. The elders, however powerful they may be, cannot completely determine what the subject Ruth will do or be. They do not master chronology but do something else instead. They evoke by analogy three other women, subjects of the building of the house of Israel, thus sanctioning a sexual practice in which the power of the male is overruled by the female subject.

This brief analysis of narratological subject positions emphasizes the following points. Subjectivity is not, by priority, assigned to Ruth. Naomi has a place of honor, but not exclusively. There is repartition, the different domains of life being functions of that repartition. Boaz is as important a subject as Naomi, but he is less autonomous. He needs help. Surprised by Ruth's unexpected presence, he 'is afraid' (3.8). We can see a fairly spectacular sign of the derivative nature of his power in the fact that, in spite of his awareness of the return and misery of his kinswoman Naomi, he does nothing to help her.

Ruth reaches full textual subjectivity in the metatext only. The metatext is prospective, in the performed wish that can be realized in the future only, and that precisely will not be realized. For the child Obed that she will bear will be born to Naomi. At the same time, the wish is retrospective, in the equation it establishes between Ruth and the three women of the past. This double temporal aspect is significant: the present is lacking.

In Search of Foundations, or the Subjects versus the Law

In order to evaluate Boaz's subject position as compared with that of the other characters, we have to take a look at the institution to which he addresses himself in his insecurity: the law. The law functions as the center of the different social and economical problems around which this fabula is turning, and if one wants to avoid anachronistic interpretation, this situation cannot be ignored. The law specifies the relations between the characters, first of all between male and female, but also between generations, and it sets the limits to individual freedom. The very fact that those limits are thematized is a sign; it gives evidence of a specific attitude toward legitimacy and transgression.

The law, the institution in relation to which the subject establishes itself (Lacan), is at the same time the paradoxical institution that both sets the limits to subjectivity and, by its fundamentally *intersubjective* nature, *subject* to interpretation by *subjects* who are *subjected* to it, designs the limits of its own (pseudo-) objectivity. It represents the performative acts of interdiction (of transgression) and of promise (of social intersubjectivity), both turned toward the future; it also represents the constative act of *stating* (transgression in the past). Once more the present is lacking, and when the present is lacking the subject is alone.

That the problem raised in this text is social in the first place is already obvious when we consider the systematic opposition between the characters. Ruth is badly off: she is a woman, a widow, a foreigner and childless. Her tribe lives in hostility with the Jews (Num. 25). Naomi is not a foreigner, but she is a childless widow, and too old to change that situation. At the other side of the opposition we have Boaz. He is a male, rich, and he lives on his own land. He is an ideal citizen: constantly aware of morality (2.11; 3.12-13), of law (4.1-12) and of formal justice, he may qualify, with only a little anachronism, as an *honnête homme*. Ruth's and Naomi's problems are economic. Boaz represents the possession that is opposed to their hunger (his sheaf). But their problems are chronological as well, in that the line of history is threatened by their childless widowhood. Boaz, as we have seen, has the same problem, and so the neat opposition is broken. This unevenness provides an entrance into the problem, a 'breach toward a latency', as Delay phrases it in his study of Gide,[1] which develops around the tension between laws. Indeed, there is a tension between the letter and the spirit of the law. Each one of the main characters has a problem to settle with the law. Let us see how they choose their approaches.

The first conflict is mentioned in 1.16. Ruth defies Yahweh himself. In Deut. 23.2-4 her tribe had been excluded from Yahweh's congregation unto the tenth generation. There is a double motive for this exclusion. In Deuteronomy it is said that the Moabites had not fed the Israelites when they were starving in the desert. But in Num. 24.1 a second reason is given: the sons of Israel had relations with the daughters of Moab: 'illegal cleaving', we could say. Fortunately, Yahweh will take Ruth's side. For in spirit she *is* a daughter of Israel. She deliberately chooses the insecure position of a foreign widow out of solidarity (*ḥesed*) with her mother-in-law, who advises the opposite. Thereby she earns the right of transgression, so that the laws of Israel do apply to her, as we see in 4.5.

The second tension between law and legitimacy is more problematic. It is the tension between the law of *gô'ēl* and the law of levirate marriage. The law of *gô'ēl* obliges the closest kinsman of an impoverished woman to redeem the land that that person is forced to sell. The law provides a sort of social security, and is at the same time a means of preventing alienation of property from the family. The law of levirate marriage obliges the brother of a dead man to marry the widow if she has no children. This law has two sides to it, as well: it protects the widows and, probably in the first place, insures posterity for the

1. J. Delay, *La jeunesse d'André Gide* (Paris: Payot, 1973).

dead, for the child born of that union will be named after the dead. This law is thematized in Genesis 38 and will be discussed in the next chapter.[1]

In 4.6 the unnamed kinsman refused to marry Ruth, though he had been ready to redeem the land. Juridically speaking, this man is in the right, for he is not her brother-in-law. The confusion of both laws would be a transgression of another law, the one of Deut. 22.2 and following: the law against illegal 'cleaving'. The not very clear relation between the law of *gô'ēl* and the law of levirate (Lev. 25.23 and following, versus Deut. 25.5) would make the man transgress the taboo of Deut. 22.22 and following and that of Deut. 23.2. The cheap moralism of many commentaries that blame this man for being interested only in acquiring land and pursuing his personal interests points to the evolution from biblical to Christian attitudes. It hides the deeper problems involved. For again, the apparent opposition between the two characters, Boaz and the unnamed man, goes together with resemblance. As Hugo shows us in his account of 3.10, Boaz also has an interest of his own. Being already rich, the interest is just different. Secondly, Boaz *wishes* the unnamed man to refrain from his right as *gô'ēl*. That wish is the very reason why he does not call him by his name: he wants him, at all costs, not to marry Ruth, not to enter into the legal system in which subjects have intersubjective names. Also, he does not give all the information right away. Thirdly, since the man seeks, like Boaz, to establish his subjectivity in the law, there is no reason to blame the one rather than the other. Like a mirror image of Orpah, he obeys the reality principle. If he is to blame, it would be at most for being a little formalistic, like one of those people who in meetings are eager to talk about rules and procedures in order to delay the fearful moment of dealing with the matter at hand. If he were to be completely wrong, there would be no tension in the story, which would then be a simplistic story of the victory of good over evil. Moralism hidden in an idyll—that is what most commentaries make of it. Thus they destroy it. For if there is tension, it is *because* this man is right. It is because, indeed, Boaz is in danger of transgressing

1.   Bal, *Lethal Love*, ch. 4 (on Gen. 38), pp. 89-103.

the law of Deut. 22.2. The ambiguous scene on the threshing floor, which Hugo's poem emphasizes, is the climax of that tension. What happens there is not only that Ruth uncovers Boaz's feet and/or sexual parts, that Boaz wakes up and is afraid, that he asks the woman at his feet *who* she is, and not, as in 2.5, *whose* she is, but also that he praises her, being full of gratitude to her for choosing him and not a young man who, not only rich but even poor, would in Boaz's eyes be far more attractive to her than he is.

The tension between the two laws is inherent in the two domains they cover, which are not unrelated. *gô'ēl* is the law of the possession of land; levirate law concerns posterity. These two aspects constitute history. That they do is exactly one of the messages that the book of Ruth, where they are constantly mixed, delivers.

When Naomi leaves her country during the period of starvation, for example, she has children (she is 'full'), but she has no food. In Moab, the country of fertility, but also the country of promiscuity, she receives food but loses her children. She returns 'empty'. Back in Bethlehem, she has nothing. The strictly illegal combination of *gô'ēl* and levirate, the law of land and the law of persons, restores both to her. Thus history moves on again, after a threat of stagnation. Therefore law and justice, of which the latter is metatextual in relation to the former, are so crucial in this text. Therefore the trial at the gate has to be held as the trial between law and legitimacy.

The testimony of the elders provides Boaz, the perfect citizen, the weak subject, with the indispensable support he needs to dare to transgress the law while at the same time allowing him to find the foundation of his very transgression in the law. The trial is a try-out of law itself.

We can summarize this whole field of problems in five motifs, expressed in key words, each of which brings up a social domain as regulated in some law (Table 2). The relations among all these motifs are brought to light in the scene of the trial:

| trial | testimony | justice | jurisdiction |

All the problems of the concerned subjects will be solved in this event: the sexual problem of Boaz will find a solution in the

solution to the economical problem of Naomi, so that together
they can set history in motion again, the history of 'the building
of the house of Israel'.

Table 2

Motif	Key Word	Social Domain	Law
same/ different	to leave/ to return	'international' relations	cursing Moab (Deut. 23.2-4; Num. 25.1)
possession	land	economy/ history	gô'ēl (Lev. 25.23)
posterity	child	demography/ history	levirate (Deut. 25.5)
morality	cleaving	sexuality	law against promis- cuity (Deut. 22.2 and following)
hunger	empty	economy	gô'ēl

The Unconscious Performing Speech Acts: Symptoms

The slightly misplaced combination of laws can be considered as
one of those involuntary signs that Peirce calls symptoms, and at
which Freud addresses the very pointed question: symptoms of
what? In Peirce's logic, the distinction between symptoms as
involuntary signs, and signals as signs of which the sender is
aware, seems almost a Freudian slip. Why does it matter within
Peirce's typology of semiotic aspects whether or not the sender
knows? Freud, who is more concerned with the motivations of
symptoms, since only by working through those motivations
could he cure them, asks the question that Peirce could have
asked, had he gone beyond logic. His logic would have gained in
consistency, since the displacement of accents between sign and
interpretant would have helped to differentiate further between
his other types: icon, index and symbol. We can only dream
about an encounter between these two geniuses, Peirce and
Freud. As it stands, symptoms remain problematic, especially in
texts, where there is no sender to examine. If we agree to

replace the sender with textual habits, we may arrive at some intuitions about how the two concepts of the symptom would be able to interact. We will, then, start at those signs which are characterized by the encroachment of the 'a-normal' into the 'normal'. They are abundantly present in Ruth, and first of all in the mixture of laws.

There are other 'mixtures', transgressions of clear limits, like the one between the public and the private that Ruth so blatantly transgresses when she goes back to the field where she had been gleaning the day before, only to go to the center of the field, the threshing floor which, by a strange mixture, is also Boaz's bed. The trial at the city gate, at the entrance to the female domain, where two men debate the question of who dares to take the woman, is the *place* of the mixture. It is possible to assume that the mixtures are based on an unconscious feeling of resemblance, of analogy between two items that have been mixed up, so that the symptom can be said to be based on a form of *iconicity*.

There are also slips, *lapsus* in the classical sense. We can speak of a *lapsus* whenever a word is attributed to a woman that is 'normally' exclusively attributed to a man. We have already noticed the case of the verb 'to cleave' (1.14), 'normally' used in relation to men and referring to heterosexual relationships. A slip that is also generally noticed, but left unexplained, is the one in 4.17, which is symmetrical to the former. Here again a word is 'inadvertently' attributed to a woman: 'There is a son born to Naomi'. A *lapsus* of this kind stresses the tension between arbitrary and motivated signs; thus, it questions the *symbolic* (in the Peircean sense). The expression is 'normally' reserved for the father. What social convention calls 'normal' is supposed to be the domain of the symbolic in the Peircean sense. One remembers the Alsatian woman who found the word 'Käse' so much more 'natural' than 'fromage'. Using words in an 'unnatural' way, assigning them to the 'wrong' subjects, is bringing the indexical bond between the word and the group that 'naturally' possesses it to the fore. This latter bond is then exposed in its arbitrariness, on a different, less innocent level than the arbitrariness of the linguistic sign. This arbitrariness of indexical monopoly is the basis of linguistic classism.

A third group of symptoms consists of *allusions* that seem to be misplaced. They are *indexical* to a larger extent than they seem to be; thus, they question the distinction between analogy and chronology. The allusions—to Rachel and Leah, to Tamar, to Moab—all refer to an earlier phase of the 'building of the house of Israel'; hence they extend the fabula's chronological span, including past phases. They are also *wishes* and thus include the future. On another level they are, however, basically analogical. It is through the analogy between the comparant and the compared that the chronological extension is possible at all. When taken together, a new chronology will establish itself. As we will see shortly, the analogies show differences, and the assessment of the differences produces the unconscious chronology of the different phases of repression of women.

The retrospective allusions, the comparisons between Ruth and other women, illuminate a paradoxical phenomenon: a collective unconscious. For the elders can hardly be supposed to be intent upon hurting the very Boaz whose project they overtly applaud; yet they display a rather painful insight into what happened, without having any factual knowledge. We have seen the same intuitive knowledge displayed by Joab;[1] the ideology adopted here is, however, different. Social subjects as the elders are, they do not represent the law itself. They can only refer to it; they can say how they interpret it in relation to Boaz's inter-pretation. Collective speakers, they speak about the law; they *are* not the law. Their discourse is metatextual in principle. Thus they testify 'juridically' but also linguistically to the inescapably (inter)subjective status of legal foundations.

What is 'wrong' with these symptoms of which the elders are the speakers? The first allusion consists of a doubling of the female subject. Ruth is compared to both Rachel and Leah. The case of these two wives of Jacob is significant. Hugo responds in several ways to this allusion. The confusion between Boaz's dreamlike nocturnal adventure and the dream of Jacob's ascen-sion becomes more interesting at this point. The analogy rests on the conflation of the sexual aspect of the one and the ambition of the other. Thus, Hugo rewrites the philosophy of

1. Bal, *Lethal Love*, pp. 32-33.

history as he sees it—giving women and sexuality the credit of indispensability. We have reason enough, then, to take a closer look at the case of Jacob's wives.

The fabula is well known: Jacob wants to marry the beautiful Rachel. He labors seven years in the service of her father, Laban, who happens to be his uncle, and at the marriage the veiled bride turns out to be the ugly Leah, substituted for her beautiful sister thanks to the invisibility of the veiled face. Jacob has to labor seven more years to deserve his beloved. This split between love and fertility, which is also that between sexuality and maternity, is only too well known. Rachel complains about her lack of children, and Leah complains about the absence of the husband, the lack of love.

The problem is solved when the two women manage, in a collaboration that materializes entirely without their husband, to conquer each other's shares by abandoning their privilege. Leah gives her sister the fruit that fertilizes (cf. the fruit of the tree that gave sexual knowledge in Genesis 2), while Rachel sends her the husband. This encouraging story rests on the efforts the two women accomplish to break out of the narrow limits set by their father and husband. The exchange is thus thoroughly subversive. The elders, in Ruth, comment upon that story by acknowledging afterwards the rightness of the women's subversion when they equate Ruth to the position of Rachel and Leah together. The equation $1 + 1 = 1$, which restores the unity of the two aspects of femininity that were separated by the men, also illuminates Boaz's position. For if, as Lacan rightly points out à propos of Hugo's poem, he was worried about his lack of posterity—his symbolic castration that Hugo adds to the story—the dream of the great oak reveals Boaz's worries about sexual impotence as well. The comparison displays not only the legitimacy of feminine subversion, but the interest man has in accepting it as well, even the interest he has in participation. Slowly, a conception of 'collective heroism' comes to the fore. A new form of hero, different from both the filial and the paternal hero, emerges here.

But there is more. There is a second woman in this case as well and, further, there is a second comparison. The second woman in the Ruth story is Naomi. The solidarity (*ḥesed*) between Ruth and Naomi gives social security and posterity to the one by means of the sexuality and fertility of the other: Obed is born unto Naomi. Beauty and fertility go together in the same woman. To what extent is the *ḥesed* in this case comparable to the one between the two wives of Jacob? Boaz, as we have seen, admits his old age when he compares himself to the young man. His legalistic 'trick' consists of extending the levirate law to the next generation. Indeed, he is not Ruth's brother-in-law, for he is not Naomi's son; but he may be Naomi's brother-in-law, her husband Elimelech's brother. And then, in marrying Ruth, he marries Naomi a little too, while also identifying with her. For unto her clave Ruth. That is why the neighbors can say: to Naomi a son is born.

Now, there is still the second comparison. It is more complex than it would seem. For there are again two names, this time a male and a female name. The subject to whom Boaz is compared, Perez, is presented as the object of a female subject, Tamar, who bore him unto Judah. The case is highly dubious and close to illegality, if not illegitimacy. Perez, in his turn, is like Jacob, the male subject of the first comparison. For they were both born as the 'officially' younger one of twins but illegally took the place of the firstborn.

Leah had been veiled in order to gain access to sexuality. Symmetrically, Tamar was forced to veil herself in order to get her due: a child, by the desire of Judah who, like Boaz, was mistaken about generations. Tamar bears Perez unto Judah, thus correcting the latter's fault. For Judah tries to protect his younger son from the contact with the woman, which he judges lethal, and is thus about to stop the continuity of history. So Tamar corrects a fault committed against woman, for the sake of patrilinear history. While Rachel and Leah correct the fault of the split between the two aspects of femininity, Tamar corrects a more archaic fault against woman, which is even more destructive: the fault of being afraid of her, and of institutionalizing that fear, that *horror feminitatis*. But there is still Perez. As the son of his mother, he is a transgressor of rules. His name means 'break'. Breaker of rules, he represents also the 'brèche vers une latence' of the cure. Boaz the perfect citizen is compared to him. How can he be compared with the fruit of Tamar's wit and

Judah's double standard? Integrating the two laws, Boaz is transgressing as well. In ch. 3, he is still dominated by the sexual standard of Judah and Lot: he is tricked by the woman during his alibi-sleep. This is the third, still more archaic fault committed against woman: the denial of responsibility. He does not yet recognize or acknowledge Ruth, and he is afraid of being confronted by her. He misses the acknowledgment of the woman, like Judah and like Lot, of whom three times it is said that he did not know what he was doing, what happened to him. In ch. 3, Ruth cannot but be the veiled woman, unacknowledgeable, who is denied the status of intersubjective subject by her sexual partner.

As we will see, the success of Tamar's action is precisely there: in the acknowledgement by the father of his own fault. Tamar, says Judah, has been more *just* than he. The comparison, then, raises the problem of the relation between charity and justice, between gift and due. When Boaz goes to court at the city gate, he identifies with Perez the transgressor of rules, son and grandson of Judah, who is like himself a mediator. Boaz becomes the mediator between generations, sexes, classes and people, between law and justice, the public and the private, economy and history. Assuming this position as a mediator, participating in collective heroism, Boaz constitutes himself the gate he wished to enter.

The three proper names alluded to in Ruth, and in particular in the court session that gives a statement about the fabula by interpreting it, form a coherent series. Moab, Ruth's country, Lot's son, symbol of fertility as well as of promiscuity, is also the symbol of nonreflective sexuality, where the subject-position is refused so that no relation between subjects is possible, but only action of a subject on an object. If Ruth deserves the right to be subject to Israelite law, she does so by bridging the gap between nonreflective and self-conscious sexuality. She 'turns her neck' to her archaic tribe by correcting its practices. Rachel and Leah manage to go even beyond that: they conquer a whole feminine subjectivity, and Tamar proves that their case is right.

The metatexts that state that Boaz is practising charity miss the point of the word *ḥesed*, the meaning of which Tamar shows to Judah: justice rather than charity, due rather than gift. If

Boaz is a hero, it is because he dares to assume the point of view of the woman, because he has understood that it is in his interest to do so. He accepts being reflected, by the *mise en abyme*, in a female role. Nonreflective as he is in ch. 3, like Judah and Lot, he becomes shrewd like Tamar in ch. 4. Acknowledging his position of a subject that needs the other to be accomplished as such, he is able to identify with Naomi, she to whom the child is born. Thereby, he earns the place that is reinstated for him in the final genealogy—or is it just the male line that takes over at the end?

The series of transgressing women tells a story by analogy, dispersed among several episodes but still coherent: 'the continuity of history, or how to admit love'. In other words: the building of the house of Israel, against all odds, against fearful fathers. Together the three fabulae alluded to become the *mise en abyme* of the history of Israel, paradoxically represented in an antichronological figure that fills in the unavoidable lack of the *present* in any chronology.

Reflecting Reflection

Boaz's awareness of the indispensable part of women in history and in his own life, which he wishes so badly to insert into history, represents the fruit of reflection as a daring act. It also represents the entrance into the symbolic order that is so full of other subjects. The meaning of the one character that Boaz is could not be understood without the interaction, through the symptoms I have analyzed, with the other characters. That this growing intersubjectivity is signified in the first place by the proper name seems consistent with the Lacanian account of this passage, which others would perhaps call a rite of passage.[1] The proper names whose intertextual and intratextual interplay we have been following for a while end up as partaking in one of the most knotty figures of contemporary narratology, the *mise en abyme*. Why is this little figure of analogy so fascinating, for critics as well as for writers and readers? Its status as trouble-maker, as disturber of chronology, as interrupter of the neat

1. See e.g. A. van Gennep, *The Rites of Passage* (trans. M.B. Vizedon and G.L. Caffee; Chicago: University of Chicago Press, 1960).

linearity of narrative, makes it especially attractive for the purpose of this study. Moreover, it is a privileged concept, in that it has been subject to extensive elaboration in different disciplines: art history, narratology, philosophy (Derrida), semiotics; it has attracted reflection and predilection from writers (Gide, Leiris, Ricardou) and, through the metaphor used to describe it, the mirror, it touches upon Lacanian psychoanalysis.

The mirror has the attraction of a paradox. The notion on which the mirror metaphor is based is that of *reflection*, which is in its turn paradoxical. Language is the source and the means of this paradox. It is anchored in the process of self-identification in which the Lacanian mirror stage is a decisive phase. The dramatic confrontation with the *same* by the perception of the *different* is staged in the *mise en abyme*. The identity is constructed by a dialectic between the unique and the identical. The *mise en abyme*, then, is unique in that it tells metatextually its own version of the fabula, its own story, by repeating the fabula. The figure integrates the mirroring between the imaginary and the symbolic reflection. In the mirror, the subject recognizes itself as a topic, by the mutual focalization of the mirroring and the mirrored subject. In intellectual reflection, the speaking/ thinking subject reflects on its own status, thus becoming in its turn an object, radically different.

The most serious flaw of Lucien Dällenbach's important book on the *mise en abyme* is the absence of any reflection on the status of the *mise en abyme* as a sign. However, if it is not a sign, it cannot be, for then it could not function as a reflection. But if it is a sign, it has to be delimited, and there resides the problem as well as its interest. The problem is, again, two-sided. One of the characteristics of the *mise en abyme* is its virtually endless regressive potential, which so fascinates Leiris in the Dutch cocoa box. This movement destroys any possible linearity of the text. Not only is it impossible to follow the chronology any longer as soon as a *mise en abyme* arises—it arises in order to interrupt it—but also, the limits between the whole and the part, between the text and the metatext, become problematic. For the figure imposes its unique version of the fabula and thus disrupts the version we were reading at the moment it intervened. The status of the detail is thus called into question.

In that respect, the so-called *mise en abyme éclatée*, the frag-mented *mise en abyme* that consists of the dispersed elements of a previously assumed *mise en abyme* throughout the whole text, reflects in its turn the effect of *mise en abyme* as a general *mode of reading*. In other words, after the scene of the trial we will have to turn back, following the etymology of the word 'reflection': *to turn our necks* and return to Orpah. We will, then, have to follow the two women once more to the country of Moab, where they will have to return in order to provide us with the elements of reading that the process presupposes. If perfect analogy, reflection, is an illusion, so is chronology.

Afterword

In the years that have passed since I wrote this essay on Ruth, my interests have shifted more strongly than they already had from narratological concepts to their productive use in a social perspective, from solely verbal texts to a perspective that takes the visual dimension of culture more to heart, and from the Bible to Rembrandt. Those shifts make me feel slightly alienated from the essay today, but they do not make me resist a reprint.

The most central shift, however, does make me feel a bit uncomfortable with the reprinting, and that is an increasing semiotic scepticism. In the analysis of Ruth I have made a case for a stable interpretation of certain words which could thereby become key words. The interpretation of *ḥesed* is the most obvious example. Today I would still want to propose that strategy, for I still believe it helps to be attentive to a sense of equity and shared interest in the text. This in turn leads to an interpretation which is much more down-to-earth than the lofty one which turns on charity. Charity is always entangled with domination and even contempt, and I feel strongly about avoiding unnecessary condescension. It is also, I think, anach-ronistic to place Ruth in a context that is closer to the nineteenth century than to ancient Israel, and closer to Christianity than to Judaism.

However, if I were to rewrite the essay today, I would surely want to qualify the tone of that argument. In light of my cur-rent persuasion that meaning is much less stable, much more versatile than I am suggesting in the essay, I would empha-size the strategic motivation of *my* insistence on those partic-ular meanings of words. I do not think such a relativization diminishes the strength of my argument; on the contrary, I think it strengthens my case for a reading that alienates from traditional readings while opening up other visions.

Needless to say that I would also, today, acknowledge the numerous new contributions to feminist biblical interpretation, and those devoted to Ruth in particular. But that, I suppose, is the fate of all reprintings: one stays hopelessly behind.

November 1991

NAOMI AND RUTH[*]

Athalya Brenner

I

Many readers and commentators have noted that Naomi and Ruth[1] 'belong together and cannot be separated', and that 'the one would be nothing without the other'.[2] On the other hand, it has been suggested that the source of the story may have been 'a family saga, perhaps a straightforward story of the return of the widow Naomi and her levirate marriage...or that of her daughter-in-law Ruth'.[3] The purpose of this article will be to try to explore the second possibility—namely, that the book of Ruth is composed of two still-distinct strands, a Naomi story and a Ruth story; that each of the two strands originally belonged to a separate, although parallel, folk-tale or novella; and that the seams which combine them are still discernible.

II

In its present form, the book of Ruth contains several difficulties which cannot be easily dismissed. Even if we exclude the final genealogical passage from our discussion (4.18-22),[4] there is still

* This essay first appeared in *VT* 33.4 (1983).

1. The spelling of biblical names follows that of the NEB.
2. O. Eissfeldt, *The Old Testament: An Introduction* (trans. P.R. Ackroyd; Oxford: Basil Blackwell, 1965), pp. 481-82.
3. J. Gray, *Joshua, Judges and Ruth* (Century Bible; London: Nelson, 1967).
4. Many scholars think that this passage, whose style is obviously different from the rest of the book, is an appendage. For details cf. the

the problem of the passage which tells of Obed's birth (4.13-17). Although Ruth is the one who marries Boaz and gives birth to a son and heir, Naomi is 'redeemed'. Her daughter-in-law is described as the agent of redemption, but not as the chief beneficiary (vv. 14-15).[1] From this point onwards Ruth is never mentioned, and Naomi is depicted as the child's nurse or adoptive mother (v. 16).[2] This seems strange while—presumably—the real mother is alive and well. The new-born is proclaimed to be Naomi's son by the neighbours involved in the naming ceremony, while Ruth (who was formerly named the biological mother) is completely excluded (v. 17); and the original, suitable name for the baby—as has been suggested by several scholars—should have been 'Ben Noam' or a similar form derived from *n'm*, after Naomi,[3] rather than the present MT Obed.

Furthermore, Naomi and Ruth share the dominant role of the chief heroine or, rather, are placed in this position interchangeably. Let us follow up this statement chapter by chapter. Naomi is undoubtedly the central figure in ch. 1. In her capacity as acting head of the unfortunate family, she is the one who initiates the homecoming as well as the attempt to separate herself from her daughters-in-law. Ruth's loyalty to her is superbly touching; however, this does not elevate Ruth to a superior position. The Bethlehem women make a great fuss over Naomi, while Ruth is neither introduced nor referred to. On the contrary, Naomi categorically states that she is an empty vessel (1.21), a widow without hope. No mention is made of Ruth as a present or future means of consolation and change. Her silent

---

standard introductions to biblical literature and commentaries ad loc. For a discussion and summary of the problem see also J.M. Sasson, *Ruth: A New Translation with a Philological Commentary and a Formalist-Folklorist Interpretation* (Baltimore: Johns Hopkins University Press, 1979; The Biblical Seminar, 10; Sheffield: JSOT Press, 2nd edn, 1989), pp. 178-87.

1. Sasson, *Ruth*, pp. 162-63.

2. Hebrew *'ōmenet*, which is far from clear. Cf. BDB, KB, Gray (*Joshua, Judges and Ruth*), Sasson (*Ruth*), and P. Joüon, *Ruth: commentaire philologique et exégétique* (Rome: Pontifical Biblical Institute, 1953) for this verse.

3. See, for instance, Gray, *Joshua, Judges and Ruth*, p. 404.

presence is briefly alluded to at the end of ch. 1 only (v. 22), within a verse which abounds in problems of both syntax and contents.[1]

In ch. 2 the situation dramatically changes. Ruth, hitherto the more passive and definitely secondary figure, is at the centre of the stage: she takes the initiative and starts acting independently. She dutifully shares her plans with Naomi, and the latter expresses her consent but remains inactive. Now the tables are turned: Naomi is mentioned incidentally to Ruth, not vice versa (2.6, 11-12); and is not referred to again until the end of the scene (v. 18), when Ruth comes back a victorious breadwinner. Even then Naomi remains no more than an adviser (vv. 19-20). Ruth manages to look after herself and her mother-in-law until the end of the harvest season without further instruction. Furthermore, Naomi has no part in Boaz's elevation of Ruth to be a 'handmaid', that is, family retainer (vv. 8ff.).

In ch. 3 Naomi continues where she left off (ch. 1). Her idea for solving her problem, which is also Ruth's problem, is well thought out. Ruth accepts her guidance and carries out her directives without a murmur (vv. 6ff.), and the seduction scene is executed in a suitably effective manner. While it is true that Ruth occupies the centre of the stage, she nevertheless—and in contradistinction to her previous mode of behaviour (ch. 2)—follows Naomi's scheme. Naomi's land is then redeemed,[2] and the change in her personal fortune attracts more attention than Ruth's (4.13-17; and see above). One gets the impression that, whenever both women are in public together, Naomi's position is more dominant (as befits their family relationship); in private, on the other hand, they exchange roles: at times Naomi is the leading figure, at others Ruth.

How can this state of affairs be explained? It can be argued that this type of thing does happen in 'reality'. A person may either act overtly in order to further his or her aims, or he or she may choose a covert mode of behaviour, for example, to manipulate other people into doing his or her own work for him or

---

1.   Joüon, *Ruth*, pp. 45-46; Sasson, *Ruth*, pp. 36-37.

2.   For the redemption problem see the summary in Sasson, *Ruth*, pp. 138-39 with literature cited and evaluated.

her. In both cases actor and acted upon, manipulator and mani-
pulated, may derive equal or similar benefits from the results of
their shared action. Hence, they may agree to exchange roles—
either deliberately or else spontaneously, consciously or uncon-
sciously—for their mutual benefit. To this line of argument we
might answer: in this instance we are dealing with fiction, not
with 'reality'. In fiction, more so than in 'real' life, this kind of
role-exchange has to be not only plausible (and necessary to the
advancement of the plot), but also essential. Otherwise, why
employ such a clumsy device? So, is this see-saw movement
between the two women essential to our story?

One imagines that the portrayal of Ruth as a more dominant
character, together with an ending which posits her as the
centre of attention and a prologue which establishes the special
relationship between the two women, would convince us equally
well. If so, there must be another principle behind the present
structure of the book.

At this point we should perhaps refer back to our initial
notion, namely, that Naomi and Ruth are inseparable, and ask:
in what way do these two women belong together, so much that
one is nothing without the other?[1] One possible answer sees
them as the two faces of the same Eve, a composite figure which
embodies two separate aspects of the same entity. These are
youth's hopeful femininity on the one hand and aged, spent
womanhood on the other. A similar concept underlies the
ancient Greek Demeter–Persephone myth. This myth, to be
sure, is partly analogous to the story of Naomi and Ruth, but
also differs from it on a number of counts.[2]

---

1. Cf. the beginning of this article.
2. Demeter's chief concern is to be reunited with her daughter who,
for her part, remains childless. Indeed, once the annual reunion
between the two is arranged and accomplished Persephone has no need
to become a mother herself: she can remain a perpetual child at her
mother's side, at least for six months at a time. Naomi, on the other
hand, worries about Ruth's childlessness, and Ruth's eventual motherhood serves to redeem them both. The emphasis on motherhood is the
core of woman's existence in youth as well as in maturity. However,
because both Greek and Hebrew stories (one a myth, the other a non-
mythic tale) are linked to the cereal harvest, and because both of them

The suggestion that our book of Ruth is a mythic narrative, or that it contains straightforward allusions to a myth of dual femininity,[1] seems unwarranted by the text. Yet, neither Naomi nor Ruth seems to be a full, 'round'[2] figure in her own right. If we accept the notion that they both exemplify the principle of femininity—albeit in two distinct stages of its development— then the division of labour, initiative and reward between them is plausible, for the only difference between the two sides of the same coin (the elder woman and her younger counterpart) is their age.

What can we say against this line of interpretation? Its psychological, Jungian slant is self-evident. Even though it has the above-mentioned partial parallel in Greek literature, the analogy is far from complete or satisfactory. No literary connection (as differentiated from similarity of theme) for the two can be traced or established. The psychologists would probably respond by saying that no literary links need be proven since we deal here

feature an older and a younger woman who have a mother–daughter relationship, the analogy between them has been pointed out often enough. See M.H. Jameson, 'Mythology in Ancient Greece', in S.N. Kramer (ed.), *Mythologies in the Ancient World* (Garden City, NY: Doubleday, 1961), pp. 251-52; E. Neumann, *The Great Mother: An Analysis of an Archetype* (trans. R. Manheim; Princeton, NJ: Princeton University Press, 2nd edn, 1974 [1963]), pp. 307-309 and other index references to Demeter and Persephone-Kore. Cf. also M.C. Astour, *Hellenosemitica* (Leiden: Brill, 1965).

1.   To the best of my knowledge, the fullest 'psychological' treatment of Ruth is—unfortunately—an unpublished one. This is a dissertation written by Dr Y. Kluger, who is a practising Jungian analyst, and presented to the Jung Institute in Basel. My thanks are due to Dr Kluger for letting me read his manuscript.

2.   This famous term was coined by E.M. Forster. In his old but still valuable contribution to literary criticism, *Aspects of the Novel* (New York: Harcourt Brace Jovanovich, 1954) he defines (in ch. 4) a *dramatis persona* as 'round' if he/she can surprise us convincingly, while still remaining plausible. If it does not, or if its plausibility becomes impaired, then it is a 'flat', one-dimensional or symbolic figure. To my mind, the changes of initiative and role between Naomi and Ruth are not adequately grounded in the narrative (as it now stands); hence, the figures themselves are far from 'round'.

with primary archetypes, and archetypes are commonly stored within humanity's collective memory. Still, more than a general notion of similarity must be established if the principle of the two faces of femininity is to be applied to our book. And finally, no similar motif is to be found within the Hebrew Bible itself. (Naturally, this last argument cannot be considered a conclusive piece of evidence but only a supplementary one.)

III

Recently, a new commentary on the book of Ruth has been published by Jack M. Sasson (see above). One of the more interesting features of this commentary is Sasson's application of modern ethno-poetic criteria to the analysis and interpretation of the *dramatis personae* and plot. He supplies Propp's categories of the *personae*,[1] which are applicable to fairy tales as well as to folk-tales. Accordingly, the book of Ruth is examined as if it were a folk-tale.

Propp's list includes the following figures (which, in his opinion, are common to all or most tales of the types just mentioned): (1) Villain, (2) Donor (provider), (3) Helper, (4) a. Sought-for Person, or b. Father, (5) Dispatcher, (6) Hero (seeker or victim), (7) False Hero.[2]

If this list be applied to the book of Ruth, says Sasson, the three primary figures (whose influence on the development of the plot is the most crucial) are those of Naomi, Ruth and Boaz. Naomi is then the Dispatcher who sets the Heroine Ruth on her quest and, ultimately, draws most of the benefits from this quest.[3] Boaz fulfils more than one role: that of the Donor (ch. 2),[4] and that of a 'new Hero, inasmuch as [he is] the Hero's Helper'.[5] The Sought-for Person is the *gô'ēl* (Ruth's/Naomi's offspring), while the False Hero is the *pᵉlōnî 'almōnî*.[6]

1. V. Propp, *Morphology of the Folktale* (ed. L.A. Wagner; Austin, TX, 2nd edn, 1968), pp. 74ff.
2. Sasson, *Ruth*, p. 201.
3. Sasson, *Ruth*, pp. 201-202.
4. Sasson, *Ruth*, p. 205.
5. Sasson, *Ruth*, p. 211.
6. Sasson, *Ruth*, p. 202. The complete analysis of character roles and

Although Sasson's approach is undeniably novel and attractive, it has its weaknesses. An initial 'state of lack' features instead of the 'villainy', which is well within Propp's scheme.[1] However, Boaz's activities must be analysed, within this frame of reference, in terms of at least two different roles—which is not impossible, but rather complicated and potentially misleading. Even more important is the fact that the chief difficulty—the apparent exchange of roles between Naomi and Ruth at various points in the plot—is not satisfactorily removed. Sasson explains Naomi's pronounced gain (ch. 4) from Ruth's actions (which she has instigated, ch. 3) by the general observation that the Dispatcher is the person who ultimately benefits the most from the Hero's toils. This is, indeed, quite true. Nevertheless, it does not clarify the literary necessity for Ruth's assuming of the initiative without having been dispatched (ch. 2). Nor does it justify the complete lack of reference to her at the end of ch. 4. Even though Naomi is the appropriate chief beneficiary of the plot, must her daughter-in-law be ignored altogether? It seems, therefore, that on these two counts our story, as it stands, does not wholly conform to Propp's scheme.

Similarly, Sasson's analysis of the movement forward and the functions of the plot could be criticized too. By describing the action in Propp's terms Sasson still does not account for the partial confusion between Ruth and Naomi. Propp allows for the repetition of one plot element and the movement ('function') resulting from it—namely, an initial act of villainy or a state of lack which sets the tale moving. In our case the first lack is Naomi's (ch. 1), the second Ruth's (chs. 3, 4) but Naomi's too (ch. 4). Sasson says that, in the second instance, 'The lack...is that of a husband for Ruth'; and adds (in brackets): 'This lack should not be confused with that of Naomi, the Dispatcher, the fulfillment of which will allow the tale to come to an end'.[2] According to this description Ruth's lack—later satisfied by Boaz—is that of a husband, while Naomi lacks a son and

plot functions, to which I shall refer presently, is to be found on pp. 203-204.

1. Sasson, *Ruth*, p. 203—Propp's junction viiia.
2. Sasson, *Ruth*, p. 207.

sustenance.[1] It seems to me that these fine distinctions are not borne out by the text. Initially, both Naomi and Ruth lack food, husbands and heirs.

Ultimately, both achieve a reversal of the problem of livelihood (not only Naomi); and there is no clear-cut distinction as to whose child the new-born is: it is as if he belongs, directly and simultaneously, to both of them. Again, in my opinion the difficulty is not resolved by stating that the Dispatcher always benefits by the Hero's actions. Benefits, yes, but—as in our case—to the point of supplanting the presumed Heroine, while at the same time exchanging roles as well? This difficulty is sustained even after the application of Propp's method. Perhaps we should turn now to another avenue—that of a historical analysis. As such, my hypothesis does not contradict Sasson's application of Propp's scheme, but merely seeks to supplement it at its weaker spots.

IV

My working hypothesis and starting point is that, once upon a time, there existed two (oral?) tales. Both tales shared a common main theme, a theme which is well known from patriarchal and other stories: the reversal of feminine fortune (a destitute/barren woman becomes the mother of a hero/important person). Both tales originated in the same geographical (Bethlehem of Judah) and social (the Judahite Perez family)[2] milieu. In each of these supposedly local family traditions we can discover a convergence of various themes which are found elsewhere too—in the Torah and the Former Prophets.[3] In other words, the topic and structure of the two tales were similar, although they differed in details of plots or sub-themes. In each narrative

1. Sasson, *Ruth*, pp. 208-209, 213.
2. The genealogies of the tribe of Judah, with the descendants of Perez among them, are mentioned in the following places: Gen. 38.29, 46.12; Num. 26.20; Ruth 4.12, 18ff.; Neh. 11.4-6; 1 Chron. 2.4-5, 4.1ff., 9.4ff.; Mt. 1.2-6.
3. Such as in the stories told about the Matriarchs (Sarah, Rebekah, Leah, Rachel) and their handmaids; Samson's mother; and Hannah (Samuel's mother).

only one of the two leading women (Naomi and Ruth) featured as the sole heroine. Let us call the Naomi story 'Variant A' and the Ruth story 'Variant B', and attempt to reconstruct them side by side.

	A. The Naomi Story	B. The Ruth Story
Heroine	Naomi (Judahite).	Ruth (foreigner; link by marriage).
Marital status	Elder widow, bereaved mother, in exile.	Young and childless widow, in own home-land.
Economic position	Destitute, but still has some land in Bethlehem.	Destitute—no land, no apparent source of income, no protection.
Starting point	Return (alone from Moab to Bethlehem).[1]	Spontaneous migration[2] from home-land to the unknown—dead husband's land.
Expectations	Reversal of fortune (to previous position of wife and mother).	Change—reunion with late husband's unknown family.
Additional difficulties	Long absence.	Lack of recognition and connections.
Plot	Naomi comes back, is recognized; still has title or rights of sorts to family's land, and must be redeemed or	Ruth appears at the unknown land. Using courage and initiative, she manages to introduce herself to

1. Cf. the same starting point in the patriarchal 'reversal of fortune' scheme (within the framework of the divine promise), viz. famine–exile–apparent loss of hope–reversal–return.

2. A voluntary migration, not even dictated by a divine command (Cf. Abram, Genesis 12). This is a completely new theme, the opposite of the negative 'foreign woman' theme that we find in Proverbs 1-9 (if, indeed, the phrase 'foreign woman' here refers to someone from a foreign land), the Deuteronomic writings, and Nehemiah.

	released from ties. She calls on Boaz,[1] who redeems her and her land after discouraging the other *gô'ēl*. A son is born, family line and estate are retained and Naomi's fortune fully reversed.	husband's family and become a retainer.[2] She seduces Boaz, thus securing a husband and later an heir, and redeeming her late husband's line and—possibly—land she has not heard about until coming to Bethlehem.
Outcome	Satisfactory solution.	Satisfactory and surprising.
Main themes	Reversal of fortune (status and land). The older woman is reinstated and becomes a mother.	Reversal of fortune. A young, defenceless widow becomes a foremother of a dynasty. A stranger joins Judahite society and religion voluntarily, and becomes integrated through her wit, efforts, looks and faith.

After having reconstructed the two hypothetical tales, we should note the following considerations:

1. Variant A (Naomi) is closer to the patriarchal and other exceptional birth stories (Samson's mother, Hannah) than B, for the latter contains fewer themes of the types recurrent in the former and its parrallels.

2. Variant B introduces favourably a relatively new theme: the integration of a foreign young woman into Judahite society.

3. In both stories the 'happy ending' serves to reinforce the existing social order.

4. Some of the items which appear in each of the variants are either similar (childlessness, destitution, later marriage and birth) or else compatible (knowledge about the heroine's right to a piece of family property). Other factors, though, would be

---

1. Cf. Volz and Gunkel (mentioned in Sasson, *Ruth*, p. 245).
2. Sasson, *Ruth*, pp. 48-57.

incompatible. These are the different ages cited, the ethnic origin, and the names. Therefore, it is impossible to use only one version—even after bringing into it some elements of the other one—without losing a substantial part of the flavour that marks the second (whatever the choice for the 'basic text' may be). If one wants to preserve the chief features of both stories, they have to be joined in a way that will retain the two heroines, will supply them with a meaningful relationship, and will somehow reconcile (for the sake of credibility) all or most of the conflicting features.

5. The only way to do that is to bind the two women in a simulated mother/daughter relationship which fits both variants—it does not cancel out either Naomi's difficulties or Ruth's troubles. (A true mother/daughter relationship will not do, for then part of the inheritance problem—in the absence of male kin—is solved as a matter of course.) This way most of the main themes common to A and B, or unique to any one of them, can be included in the combined version and the differences minimized, if not disposed of altogether. Thus Naomi, the older woman, is made foster-mother for Ruth's baby.

6. One ought to remember that the Ruth story (Variant B) is an independent story only in the sense that it is one item in a series: the third instalment, so to speak, in a series which begins with Lot's daughters and the birth of Moab and Ammon (Gen. 19.30-38) and continues with Tamar's tale (Genesis 38). All three stories are linked by common themes (foreign women;[1] Moab; the seduction of a male relative for the purpose of giving birth to a male heir; the continuation of the blood line through sexual relations or marriage with a male relative; the author's positive evaluation of the woman's initiative, at least in the cases of Tamar and Ruth),[2] and by the fact that they belong to King

1.   Tamar, too, is considered foreign by some modern commentators.
2.   Even the story of Lot's daughters, if originally an ethnic non-Israelite legend, might have been a heroic tale praising their courage or initiative. Only later, after it had been integrated into the Israelite framework, was the story misinterpreted and used as a crude joke against Israel's neighbours. This is supported by the fact that the author's attitude towards the other two women (Tamar and Ruth) is quite respectful.

David's genealogy. Indeed, the three stories anticipate David's foreign connections and his weakness for women by overtly claiming that these two things were in the king's blood. Thus elements of the Ruth story which relate to King David's heritage could not have been easily dismissed by the author-compiler. On the other hand, the Naomi story contains patriarchal themes (see above) which were probably well known and loved by listeners and authors alike. In short, the author of the combined version (our MT book of Ruth) could neither drop one variant— or parts of it—in favour of the other, nor commit himself or herself by deciding which one was 'truer' or had the greater literary and didactic merit.

7. The final combined version is not without flaws, for the author refuses to part with themes of the original tales even when they become a hindrance rather than an asset. As a result, the book suffers from some unevenness and inconsistencies. The chief difficulties arising from the joining process seem to be: (a) the exchange of roles and dominant positions between Naomi and Ruth at various points of the plot; (b) a tension underlying the motherhood of either Naomi or Ruth, or both; (c) the redemption problem: who is being redeemed—Naomi, Ruth or both?

V

It is widely recognized that in some cases of doubt authors and editors of the Hebrew Bible, especially those of the Torah and the Former Prophets, preferred to combine sources rather than completely to suppress a given source or tradition in favour of another. In so doing they sometimes deleted redundant passages, while at other times leaving parallel materials side by side, contradictions and all. Two such cases from the Pentateuch spring immediately to the mind: the story of the flood (Genesis 7–8); and the story of the town/city (Gen. 11.1-9) which, since Gunkel, has been acknowledged (albeit not unanimously) as a composite narrative in which two similar but originally different tales converge.[1] In both cases the principle and structure of the

1.   H. Gunkel, *Genesis* (HKAT; repr.; Göttingen: Vandenhoeck &

two single tales underlying the final MT versions are quite close, although the contents and means are different. Faced with such a situation, the authors probably preferred to combine two variants rather than to elide one of them. We might suppose that the force of tradition, the author's respect towards both versions and, consequently, this inability to determine which one should be used as an exclusive source were the considerations that informed his decision to create a composite story. I have advanced the hypothesis that a similar process determined the composition of the book of Ruth. As corroborating evidence I shall cite one more example, this time from the Writings—the book of Esther.

The principle of source combination is used in the book of Esther too, but in a different manner. Within this literary composition there is an abundance of—and fondness for—double structures, be they on the lexical-grammatical or the contents-plot level. The examples for each category are too many to be enumerated here, and the interested reader is referred elsewhere.[1] Let me just note the feature which is of the most relevance to the problem under discussion. The author makes use of two chief themes or strands which represent two distinct types of folk-tales, and which are consciously(?) interwoven into one unit. These are the story of the two viziers competing for the king's grace (in this case, Haman and Mordecai), and that of the two women competing for the king's heart and the position of queen (Vashti and Esther).[2] The two strands[3] were modified and

---

Ruprecht, 3rd edn, 1964 [1910]), pp. 92-97; B. Vawter, *On Genesis: A New Reading* (Garden City, NY: Doubleday, 1977), p. 153; H. Gressman, *The Tower of Babel* (New York: 1928).

1. Cf. A. Brenner, 'Esther Through the Looking Glass', *Beth Miqra* 86 (1981–83), pp. 267-78 (in Hebrew).

2. Cf. E. Bickermann, *Four Strange Books of the Bible* (New York: Schocken Books, 1967), pp. 172-73.

3. For another two-strand theory for the book of Esther see H. Cazelles, 'Note sur la composition du rouleau d'Esther', in H. Gross and F. Mussner (eds.), *Lex tua veritas: Festschrift für Hubert Junker* (Trier: Paulinus Verlag, 1961), and also for another viewpoint D.J.A. Clines, *The Esther Scroll: The Story of a Story* (JSOTSup, 30; Sheffield: JSOT Press, 1984).

then worked together so that they would serve the main theme of the book, which is the reversal of fortune—from threatened extinction to victorious revenge—of the Jewish community in Susa and its environs.[1]

To be sure, the combination of two distinct, although similar, sources into one narrative (as in Gen. 7–8 and 11.1-9 and, as I have attempted to show, in Ruth) is not the same as the conscious use of two types of tale in a wider framework. The former technique (incorporation of two traditions/tales with minimum deletion of contents and themes) is simpler and probably earlier.

It is through the repeated literary practice of creating composite tales out of distinct but similarly structured and motivated narratives that the latter technique (use of different tales/tale types within or in the service of a wider framework) could have become acceptable. The flood story, the tower/city narrative and the book of Ruth possibly represent an earlier stage of Hebrew literary development, the book of Esther a later stage, one that could have evolved only through the acceptance, repeated use and diffusion of its predecessor.

VI

So far I have dealt with the process that led to the composition of Ruth. Inasmuch as I have commented upon the relationship between Naomi and Ruth, this was mainly linked to the problems inherent in the narrative and which could have arisen from its (admittedly hypothetical) composite nature and double-barrelled history. I think, however, that a few words regarding the end product (our MT Ruth) as a literary unit complete in itself are in order here.

Naomi and Ruth function harmoniously as a team. Whatever the internal shifts in the balance of power may be, they are in the struggle for survival together and thus cooperate. Naomi is the senior, Ruth the junior partner. Naomi does her duty by her

---

1. Thus the reversal of fortune undergone by individuals—be they (from the author's point of view) the heroes or their adversaries—is secondary, for its function is to highlight and enhance the fate of the community as a whole.

daughter-in-law—she tries to dissuade her from coming to Bethlehem and later propels her towards Boaz. Ruth, however, goes one step further. She is actually motivated not only by duty and obedience, but also by love for her mother-in-law. Her affection and respect are her hallmark. As the neighbours say to Naomi (4.15), Ruth's love makes her more useful than ten male offspring. This emphasis on the emotional commitment of one woman towards another is very special (cf. Boaz's words to Ruth, 3.11-12). A quick glance at the fights and squabbles of women, handmaids and rival sisters in the book of Genesis, for instance, will verify this at once. In that sense Ruth is a unique character, a symbol of unconditional love and loyalty. The impact of this love-motif on the reader is so strong that—in the last analysis—it lends the story depth and credibility, and serves as a focal point which unites the various strands of the plot.

RETURNING HOME:
RUTH 1.8 AND THE GENDERING OF THE BOOK OF RUTH[*]

Carol Meyers

As one of the two biblical books bearing a woman's name, the book of Ruth has attracted considerable attention from feminist biblical scholars and also from women seeking to reclaim their biblical foremothers. Clearly Ruth deserves such attention. Unlike Esther, the other book with a woman's name, Ruth is almost entirely a woman's tale. Esther as heroine shares the limelight to a certain extent with Mordecai; and King Ahasuerus as well as his vizier Haman have prominent roles. Males enjoy no such foregrounding in Ruth. To be sure, Boaz is indispensable to the story; yet he hardly plays a central role.[1] Ruth the

[*] Somewhat different versions of this paper have appeared as '"To Her Mother's House": Considering a Counterpart to the Israelite *bêt 'āb'*, in D. Jobling, P.L. Day and G.T. Sheppard (eds.), *The Bible and the Politics of Exegesis: Essays in Honor of Norman K. Gottwald on his Sixty-Fifth Birthday* (Cleveland: The Pilgrim Press, 1991), pp. 39-51, 304-307; and as 'Behind the Veil of Scriptural Androcentrism: "The Mother's House" in Ancient Israel', in T. Frymer-Kensky (ed.), *Women in Religion and Society* (forthcoming).

1. See A. LaCocque, *The Feminine Unconventional: Four Subversive Figures in Israel's Tradition* (Minneapolis: Fortress Press, 1990), p. 111. LaCocque also points out that Boaz's appearance does not interfere with the central role of the Naomi–Ruth pair; the story follows Ruth and Naomi and not Boaz after the wedding, with Boaz's role as parent of Obed virtually ignored (except in the concluding genealogy, which is possibly an addition to the tale and in any case stands distinct from the narrative). Indeed, the Midrash on Ruth also sees Boaz as secondary—it has him die after only one day of marriage (*Ruth Zuta* 55; *Lekah Tov* [Ruth] 4.17).

Moabitess, great-grandmother of King David, along with her courageous mother-in-law, Naomi of Bethlehem, clearly occupy center stage. From the introduction of 1.1-5, which provides the setting, to the concluding scene in 4.13-17, in which Ruth bears a child and Naomi nurtures him, women dominate both the dialogue and the narrative framework.

The unusual prominence accorded in Ruth to female characters and women's experience has evoked a wide range of interpretive comments and methodological approaches that focus on matters of gender. Thus a burgeoning literature of feminist and womanist biblical criticism can now be added to the plethora of studies concerned with text, date, genre, social and legal features, literary modes and sources, and religious or national purposes.[1] Such traditional works, incredible as it seems, virtually ignore the fact that the dominant androcentricity of Scripture is interrupted by the gynocentricity of Ruth. Even the brief commentary on Ruth by Louise Pettibone Smith, the first woman ever to have an article published in the *Journal of Biblical Literature*, fails to take note of this book's focus on women's lives.[2] Biblical studies have been no different from other disciplines in obscuring or ignoring and thereby devaluing the experience of women as a group.[3] Hence the attention in recent scholarship to the narrative, social and religious roles of women in Ruth is a long overdue corrective to the scholarly perspective

---

For a literary perspective on how the centrality of Naomi, from a perceptual point of view, and of Ruth, from an interest point of view, is achieved, see A. Berlin, *Poetics and Interpretation of Biblical Narrative* (Bible and Literature Series, 9; Sheffield: Almond Press, 1983), pp. 83-86.

1. Manifold examples of traditional studies can be found in the bibliographies of relatively recent commentaries, e.g. J. Sasson, *Ruth: A New Translation with a Philological Commentary and a Formalist-Folklorist Interpretation* (Baltimore: Johns Hopkins University Press, 1979; The Biblical Seminar, 10: Sheffield; JSOT Press, 2nd edn, 1989) and E.F. Campbell, *Ruth* (AB; Garden City, New York: Doubleday, 1975).

2. *The Book of Ruth* (IB, 2; New York: Abingdon Press, 1955); cf. D. Bass, 'Women's Studies and Biblical Studies', *JSOT* 22 (1982), p. 8.

3. See A. Rich, 'Towards a Woman-Centered University', in *On Lies, Secrets, and Silence: Selected Prose, 1966–78* (New York: Norton, 1979), p. 134.

that has been blind to matters of gender in biblical literature and
Israelite history.

As welcome as the new scholarship is that rescues the women
of biblical antiquity from the invisibility of traditional concerns,
the results of that scholarship are somewhat disturbing, for they
are hardly unanimous in their assessment of what they help
make visible to the modern reader of the Bible. The readings of
Ruth exemplify this fact. While they are for the most part positive in heralding a biblical book with female characters of heroic
proportions, there are also critics who claim that, as appealing
as Ruth and Naomi may be, they are little better than pawns in
the literature of patriarchy, exploited for their biological role in
maintaining male lineages.[1]

The former position, a positive assessment of Ruth, was first
staked out in the pioneering work of Phyllis Trible.[2] While not
ignoring the concern for preserving the family patrimony as
determined by male heirs, she highlights the courage, independence and devotion of Ruth and Naomi, who successfully
struggle to survive in what appears to be a man's world. In so
doing, she draws attention to the superb literary artistry at
work in proclaiming the story of these two renowned women.
Others emphasize the fact that, since Naomi and her daughter-
in-law are both childless widows, a marginal category of person
in Israelite society, their success in overcoming that liability
makes Ruth a tale about the divine empowerment of the powerless.[3] And a provocative new perspective suggests that Ruth
(like the stories of Esther, Judith and Susanna) with its
unconventional *figura* (model or type), functions in the postexilic
age as protest literature against the policies of the Jerusalem

1. For a discussion of the 'mixed reviews' of Ruth in feminist schol-
arship, see K.P. Darr, *Far More Precious than Jewels: Perspectives on
Biblical Women* (Gender and the Biblical Tradition; Louisville, KY:
Westminster Press/John Knox, 1991).

2. 'Two Women in a Man's World: A Reading of the Book of Ruth',
Soundings (1976), pp. 251-79. An expanded version of this essay appears
in ch. 6 ('A Human Comedy') of *God and the Rhetoric of Sexuality*
(Philadelphia: Fortress Press, 1978).

3. See A. Laffey, *An Introduction to the Old Testament: A Feminist
Perspective* (Philadelphia: Fortress Press, 1988), pp. 208-209.

establishment.[1] In general, whether they are understood as women who are self-determinative in a man's world or who serve somehow to subvert that world or to circumvent its structures, the women in the book of Ruth can be heralded as exemplars of an impressive range of traits and values worthy of emulation. At the very least, their centrality in the book can hardly be denied.

Such positive perspectives are mitigated by a minority of critical voices claiming that, however courageous and independent Ruth and Naomi may seem, in the final analysis those praiseworthy traits must be seen as serving masculine interests. In seeking to secure the future of their family, they are working in the interests of a man's name and inheritance and are thus the 'paradigmatic upholders of patriarchal ideology'.[2] Indeed, Ruth beguiles a prominent kinsman through her sexuality in an effort to sustain the lineage of Naomi's deceased husband. Such behavior might ordinarily be seen as reprehensible. Yet not only is it tolerated, it is also submerged in an array of otherwise laudatory behaviors precisely because it is motivated by the goal of producing a male heir.[3]

It is not my intention here to enter directly into this discussion of Ruth as a work that either serves or works against female self-interests. Rather, I would like to redirect the question from the issue of female complicity with male values[4] to two other, interrelated, issues. One concerns an appraisal of the book of Ruth as women's literature, and the other concerns the presence of women's literature in ancient Israel as part of a social context in which women were not powerless and subservient.

The first of these issues is related to the matter of authorship. As part of a canon that is almost entirely ascribed to male

1. LaCocque, *The Feminine Unconventional*.

2. E. Fuchs, 'The Status and Role of Female Heroines in the Biblical Narrative', *The Mankind Quarterly* 23 (1982), pp. 149-60.

3. A. Brenner, *The Israelite Woman: Social Role and Literary Type in Biblical Narrative* (The Biblical Seminar, 2; Sheffield: JSOT Press, 1985), pp. 106-108.

4. Cf. how this question is raised, in consideration of the 'other woman' in Proverbs 1–9, by A. Brenner and F. van Dijk-Hemmes, 'On Gendering Biblical Texts' (paper given at the SBL Annual Meeting, 1992).

authorship, Ruth has rarely, even by feminist critics heralding it as a woman's story, been seen as the work of a woman writer. Virtually no one has forcefully maintained that a woman could conceivably have written it. There are exceptions, but these are more in the line of tentative or far-fetched suggestions rather than of confident, well-reasoned claims. Sandmel, for example, explains that the 'delicacy' and gentleness of the narrative, and the fact that this is a rare fictive tale in that it is devoid of conflict, make him wonder 'if its unknown author were perhaps a woman'.[1] And Campbell 'risks' proposing that the story-teller of Ruth can be located either among country Levites, one of whose functions was to teach and edify, among wise women who wove stories to resolve conflict, or among other women who sang of epic events.[2]

Recent scholarship has convincingly reversed the notion that the production of literature in biblical antiquity was almost entirely the result of the compositional activities of men. Once it is recognized that much literature emerges from oral composition and that authorial activity and literacy need not be equated,[3] the possibility of women as authors becomes less improbable. Still, even if the existence of female authors for certain biblical verses, chapters or even books can be accepted, the idea of female authorship seems problematic in light of the fact that the literary context of Scripture, in the redactional and recording stages even if not in all its compositional ones, was that of male scribal activity.

Thus it is perhaps better to focus on the gender perspective of a given passage rather than on the gender identity of its author.[4] Text and author are virtually synonymous in such an

1. *The Enjoyment of Scripture: The Laws, The Prophets, and The Writings* (New York: Oxford University Press, 1972), p. 25.

2. Campbell, *Ruth*, pp. 21-23.

3. See Brenner and van Dijk-Hemmes, 'On Gendering'. Cf. the methodology delineated by R.S. Kraemer, 'Women's Authorship of Jewish and Christian Literature in the Greco-Roman Period' (paper given at a colloquium on Women in Religion and Society; Philadelphia: Annenberg Research Institute, 1991).

4. This is the valuable suggestion of Brenner and van Dijk-Hemmes in 'On Gendering'.

approach. Yet by not specifying a female author as such, the linkage of authorship with the writing down of a work and with the shaping of the final canonical product can be avoided: the text itself should be gendered, viewed as 'signature... as both literary prowess and reflection of human experience'.[1] That is, the text's authority rather than its authorship should be gendered. With this in mind, we can and should seek to identify female texts in the canon, for awareness of the gender origins of a text can and should affect profoundly our reading of it.[2]

To the best of my knowledge, a systematic study of Ruth in terms of the differences between female and male texts has not yet been attempted. Indeed, the identification of determinative features of a text from the perspective of gender, or even whether or not such features exist, is a matter of considerable scholarly debate. Yet we accept the notion that gender is a culturally determined variable that affects literary production and that female experience, even if submerged in predominantly male literature, cannot be obliterated from a literary fabric precisely because women's lives are part of the total social cloth.[3] To use another metaphor, women are 'muted groups'; but their voices can be heard as long as it is recognized that they are not silent and that their self-expression can be discerned even within dominant masculine modes of communication.[4]

1. Brenner and van Dijk-Hemmes, 'On Gendering'.
2. As a recent letter to the New York Times proclaimed, in support of the notion that knowing the authorship 'ineluctably and profoundly shapes the transaction we call reading'. The writer points out how, 'if Shalom Aleichem were somehow proved to have composed *Mein Kampf*, reading that book would suddenly become a very different matter from what it is now'; S.G. Hellman, *Book Review* (January 5, 1992), p. 4.
3. See for example D. Spender, *Man Made Language* (London: Routledge & Kegan Paul, 2nd edn, 1985); E. Abel (ed.), *Writing and Sexual Difference* (Chicago: University of Chicago Press, 1982); E.A. Flynn and P.P. Schweickart (eds.), *Gender and Reading: Essays on Readers, Texts, and Contexts* (Baltimore: Johns Hopkins University Press, 1986); C. Kramarae, *Woman and Man Speaking: Frameworks for Analysis* (Rowley, MA: Newbury House, 1981); and D. Cameron, *Feminism and Linguistic Theory* (New York: Macmillan, 1985).
4. This is the theory set forth by E. Ardener; see the discussion in

Even though the methods of identifying women's texts have hardly been formalized, and because Ruth itself has not been scrutinized fully from such an interpretive perspective, this paper will contribute to both those enterprises by focusing on one phrase in one verse of Ruth. I propose that its uniqueness in certain female contexts in Scripture is inseparable from its location in society. Exploring its cultural context as part of female experience can thus provide reasonable certainty that its literary expression constitutes one instance of the female voice being heard in Scripture and thus one piece of evidence for the female authority of Ruth—for gendering Ruth, or parts thereof, as female.

Ruth 1.8

The text in question is Ruth 1.8, which is part of the first scene of the Ruth and Naomi story. In this opening section of the tale, Naomi finds herself in a strange country, bereft of her husband and her two sons. Hearing that the famine in the land of Judah, which had originally driven her and her family away from home, has subsided, Naomi decides to leave Moab. She starts on the journey to her homeland along with her Moabite daughters-in-law, Orpah and Ruth. Suddenly, she turns to the two younger women and urges them, in an extended and poignant dialogue, not to be part of her return (*šûb*) but rather to effect their own, to their own people and religion (1.15). Naomi initiates this dramatic exchange (which results in Orpah's heeding her plea but in Ruth's rejecting it with her memorable and poignant statement of loyalty, 'Whither thou goest...' [1.16, KJV]) with the exhortation, 'Go, return each of you to her mother's house' (*bêt 'immāh*). Returning home for these young widows involves going to a family setting identified with the mother rather than with the father.

In dealing with this 'surprising'[1] term, scholars typically note that it would be more common to have the widowed women

---

S. Ardener's edited volumes, *Perceiving Women* (New York: Halstead, 1975), and *Defining Females* (London: Croom Helm, 1978).

1. Campbell, *Ruth*, p. 64.

return to their father's house, as Tamar does in Gen. 38.11 ('remain a widow in your father's house') or as is indicated for a priest's widowed daughter in Lev. 22.13.[1] The ancient versions adumbrate this reluctance to accept the existing MT on its own merits: the Alexandrinus LXX reads *patros*; Syriac has 'parents'; and other LXX manuscripts have some variant of 'fathers'.[2] Thus both the ancient and current responses exhibit androcentric bias, basing their consideration of the phrase on male norms. The fact that the phrase 'mother's house' appears here in a brilliant, resoundingly female tale should help us to refocus the investigation of what it signifies so that it may stand on its own as a legitimate social term and as a signifier of a woman's text.

To do so, features of the literary uniqueness of the book of Ruth, as they may generally bespeak a woman's text, can be noted by way of introduction to the uniqueness of the phrase 'mother's house'. But the major goal of my examination of this phrase will be to show how, because of certain similarities of literary genre and social context between Ruth and the few other passages where the term occurs, this verse and perhaps all of Ruth can be heard as Israelite women's language.

Concerning the uniqueness of the work as a whole with respect to gender, the centrality of female characters throughout an entire canonical book has already been noted. Likewise, I have mentioned how the sequential episodes in the lives of Ruth and Naomi, with a dramatic denouement and a happy ending, proceed in the absence of a theme of conflict, which is a characteristic of androcentric literature.

In addition, the role of dialogue in this book may have some relevance to its gender. No other book in the Hebrew Bible has a

---

1. E.g. Sasson, *Ruth*, p. 23. The situations of other unmarried women (in Num. 30.16, Deut. 22.21, and Judg. 19.2-3) also involve a connection to the 'father's house'. Cf. the quaint idea proposed by Smith (*The Book of Ruth*) that 'mother's house' is used, even though Ruth has a father (2.11), because Naomi is thinking of the 'women's quarters', and the whimsical suggestion of P. Joüon (*Ruth: Commentaire philologique et exégétique* [Subsidia Biblica, 9; Rome: Biblical Institute Press, 2nd edn, 1986 (1953)], p. 36) that the use of mother is 'plus délicat, plus féminin' and is appropriate because a woman is speaking.

2. So Campbell, *Ruth*, p. 60.

higher ratio of dialogue to narrative text.[1] Since the story could easily have been told in just a few verses,[2] this expansion of the dialogic mode becomes a salient feature. The characters are made to speak for themselves, rather than have their actions described. Certainly this has the effect of directly delineating character. As Alter has pointed out, the transposition of what is nonverbal or preverbal into quoted speech functions to zero in on the 'essence of things...obtruding their substratum'.[3] Can such a mode of presentation be linked with gender? This question defies, at present, a definitive answer. Yet there is some evidence that frequent change of speakers, a feature of dialogic presentation, is more common in women's speaking than in that of men; dialogic structure may be more cooperative and less hierarchical, and may be more characteristic of female than of male modes of spoken interaction.[4] The fact that it is the archetypal woman Eve, rather than the archetypal man Adam, who is the first human to engage in dialogic speech (Gen. 3.1-5) may be relevant in this regard. If the first humans exhibit features meant to be taken as essential qualities,[5] the priority of Eve as dialogist may encode a cultural feature of female speech.

Finally, the astonishing fact that Naomi never meets Boaz,[6] that none of the dialogues involves the two of them, and that they are never portrayed as interacting directly even though they clearly know about each other (see 2.6, 11, 20; 3.2), may be related to female indirection. The story-teller has intentionally

---

1. Sasson, *Ruth*, p. 227. According to Joüon (*Ruth*, p. 12 n. 1), of the 85 verses in Ruth, 55 verses (i.e. almost two thirds of the whole) are dialogue. Cf. Rashkow's essay in this volume.

2. So Joüon, *Ruth*.

3. R. Alter, *The Art of Biblical Narrative* (New York: Basic Books, 1981), p. 70. See in general his ch. 4, 'Between Narration and Dialogue', pp. 63-87.

4. See E. Aries, 'Interaction Patterns and Themes of Male, Female, and Mixed Groups', *Small Group Behavior* 7 (1976), pp. 7-18.

5. See the discussion of Eve and Adam as archetypes in C. Meyers, *Discovering Eve: Ancient Israelite Women in Context* (New York: Oxford University Press, 1988), pp. 78-81. Cf. B.C. Sproul, *Primal Myths: Creating the World* (San Francisco: Harper & Row, 1979), p. 27.

6. Described by Campbell, *Ruth*, pp. 17-18.

kept them apart. This distancing helps to give Ruth prominence. But it also involves creating a sequence of non-confrontational episodes, whereby Naomi's goals are realized in a way that might not have been the case had she tried to negotiate with Boaz face to face.[1]

Having reviewed some features of the book as a whole that may be indicative of a female text, we turn now to the specific language of 'mother's house' (*bêt 'ēm*) and what it means for the returning home of Naomi's daughters-in-law to be expressed with this phrase rather than with the far more common 'father's house' (*bêt 'āb*). My analysis of 'mother's house', or more accurately 'mother's household', which I take to be some sort of equivalent to 'father's house/household', will involve first an examination of the latter term as a designation of a social unit and then of the other biblical passages featuring the former term.

Relevant Aspects of bêt 'āb

Understanding the *bêt 'āb* as a social unit involves setting it in its context of the overall social structure of ancient Israel. In the formative period of Israelite existence, the so-called period of the Judges, or the several hundred years preceding the rise of the monarchy in the late eleventh century, Israelite society operated on three distinct levels of social organization.[2] The largest of these, according to biblical sources, was the tribe. Although it looms large in Israel's self-conception throughout much of Scripture, that primary level of social orientation was probably not a major factor in the daily life of most Israelites, either in the premonarchic period or (especially) after the restructuring of tribal allotments that was one of the hallmarks

---

1. See C. Camp's discussion (in *Wisdom and the Feminine in the Book of Proverbs* [Bible and Literature Series, 11; Sheffield: JSOT Press, 1985], pp. 124-47) of indirect action as the mode for groups such as women, occupying lower places in social hierarchies, to achieve goals that might otherwise be unattainable.

2. See the detailed socio-literary analysis of N.K. Gottwald, *The Tribes of Yahweh: A Sociology of the Religion of Liberated Israel, 1250–1050* (Maryknoll, NY: Orbis Books, 1979), pp. 237-341.

of Solomon's contribution to the process of state formation.[1]

The secondary level of social organization, the *mišpāḥâ*, or 'protective association of families' (or 'clans', or phratries?) apparently continued as a meaningful unit until the exile if not later. But the tertiary level of Israelite society—the *bayit/bêt 'āb*, or 'extended family', or 'family household'—was the fundamental social unit in the premonarchic period and undoubtedly continued to fulfil that important function in society even after the monarchy was established, at least in non-urban contexts.

This third unit deserves special attention in that it was the arena in which the life activities of all Israelites took place. Any consideration of gender in ancient Israel must thus take into account the dynamics of the *bêt 'āb* as a technical term for the basic element of the community of Israel. At the same time, examination of the *bêt 'āb*, a term found dozens of times in the Hebrew Bible, must not overlook its female-oriented counterpart, *bêt 'ēm*. Yet the scholarly discussion of social terminology has virtually overlooked the fact that in several places in the Hebrew Bible the related term *bêt 'ēm* apparently signifies the same entity as does *bêt 'āb*. In addition to Ruth 1.8, 'mother's house/household' is found in the story of Rebekah in Genesis and in the Song of Songs. In addition, Proverbs contains several references to a household or house in association with a woman. These occurrences of 'mother's house' are striking in view of the overriding importance of 'father's house' in the Hebrew Bible; and the term merits consideration on its own.

The commentaries on the texts containing 'mother's house' for the most part cannot avoid noting this phrase. They treat it in various ways: by considering it an aberration, by seeing it as a reference to a harem or 'women's quarters' in a house, by understanding it to be used if the father is dead or in reference to the female side of the family, by viewing it as a way of saying that a girl is 'running home to mother', or, in some of the early commentaries, by perceiving in it a relic of an original primitive matriarchy. None of these suggestions involves serious attention to the possibility of the term signifying a female text, nor

---

1. G.E. Wright, 'The Provinces of Solomon', *Eretz Israel* 8 (1967), pp. 58-68.

consideration of *bêt 'ēm* as a technical term that may have social equivalence to the far more common *bêt 'āb*.

It is worth noting that the not unexpected failure of biblical scholarship to take seriously the term 'mother's house' is the result of the presence of androcentric bias.[1] That bias exists at several levels: in the ancient texts themselves and also in both the traditional and the contemporary commentaries.[2] Feminist biblical critics readily acknowledge the male bias of the texts, the male authorship of most, if not all, biblical books and also the overriding interest of those books in the public, masculine world of the polity Israel, with its preponderance of male leaders—its kings, prophets, priests, sages and soldiers.[3] The other areas of androcentrism are less prominent but must also be recognized. The ancient translators and tradents injected their own male biases,[4] which tend to be perpetuated in contemporary historical-critical analyses by the unexamined patriarchal assumptions of modern interpreters.[5] Consequently, recovering the remnants of women's deeds and words, which are the clues to the nature of women's lives in the biblical past, must involve an approach that is conscious of the obstacles of androcentrism at all these levels.[6]

The phrase *bêt 'āb*, literally translated 'house of the father', involves both spatial/material and kinship/lineage concerns.

---

1.   A notable exception is Campbell, *Ruth*, pp. 64-65.

2.   Dealing with these biases involves what E. Schüssler Fiorenza calls a hermeneutics of suspicion; see *Bread Not Stone* (Boston: Beacon Press, 1984), p. 16.

3.   See my discussion of this bias in *Discovering Eve*, pp. 11-12.

4.   An excellent example of a study uncovering such bias is J. Barr's 'The Vulgate Genesis and St Jerome's Attitude to Women', *Studia Patristica* 18 (1982), pp. 268-73.

5.   E.g. the fact that Hannah herself offers a sacrifice is explicit in the MT. Yet 4QSam[a] and the LXX deny her the agency of sacrifice; and modern commentators, assuming that women had little or no cultic role, value the versions over the MT. See my forthcoming analysis of this incident in 'The Hannah Narrative in Feminist Perspective', D.W. Young *Festschrift* (Winona Lake, IN: Eisenbrauns).

6.   Schüssler Fiorenza's challenge to discover 'a feminist coin' in a sweep of biblical tradition involves coupling a hermeneutics of remembrance with one of suspicion (*Bread Not Stone*, pp. 14-20).

Despite the apparent simplicity of the term, it is not always possible to identify on the basis of biblical texts exactly what it signifies. The problems in delineating what is meant by *bêt 'ā b* arise from the fact that it is sometimes used in a metaphoric sense for the pseudo-kinship structures that biblical writers have imposed upon their understanding of the people Israel.[1] Hence the phrase can sometimes be found in reference to the primary level of social organization (tribe, *šēbet/mattêh*) and perhaps even to the secondary level (clan, *mišpā hâ/'elep*).

The confusion also exists because of the levels of redaction of the biblical sources representing various chronological periods of Israelite history. The configurations of all of the sub-divisions of Israelite society certainly changed over time. The terminology for the units thus had to be fluid, indicating different understandings of the various sub-units at different times. For example, the experience of exile caused considerable adaptation in the structural organization of both the exiled Judeans and those who remained in Yehud. The traditional language for social units took on new meanings.[2] Since this was a formative epoch for the biblical canon, it was inevitable that sixth-century usages of centuries-old terms should affect the nomenclature of the older texts being collected and edited during and after the exile.

However flexible the term may have been in representing various aspects of family and multi-family lineages, the fundamental grounding of *bêt 'āb* in reference to the smallest unit of Israelite society is what is relevant here. In its core usage as a term for the household unit in ancient Israel, it included both biologically related individuals as well as those with affinal or other ties. It was in effect a living group as much as a kinship group.[3] The 'father's house' achieved its basic configuration in

1. Gottwald, *The Tribes of Yahweh*, pp. 288-90; cf. R. Wilson, 'The Family', *Harper's Bible Dictionary* (San Francisco: Harper & Row, 1985), p. 302.

2. See D.L. Smith, *The Religion of the Landless: The Social Context of the Babylonian Exile* (Bloomington, IN: Meyer Stone, 1989), pp. 93-126.

3. See Meyers, *Discovering Eve*, pp. 128-38, for a discussion of the biblical terminology and of the sociological understanding of what is meant by a 'family household'.

the rural communities in which it functioned at the time of
Israelite beginnings and probably throughout much of the succeeding centuries; and its importance was integrally related to
its role as the basic economic unit, producing virtually all of
what was needed for the subsistence of its members.

Although the term 'extended family' is sometimes used to
refer to the *bêt 'āb*, that designation seems too limiting, in that
bêt 'āb in its economic aspect included structures (buildings),
property (land and equipment) and animals as well as people.[1]
Thus 'family household' is a preferable translation, since it
incorporates the basic kinship orientation of a multi-
generational family while allowing for the various functions of
the household—residency, economic production, social activity,
cultic practices, and so on.[2]

The dynamics of life in the self-sufficient family household
involved a wide variety of agrarian tasks necessary for survival.
Except perhaps for metal tools and implements, individual
households produced all the necessities of daily life—food,
clothing, simple wooden tools and plain, utilitarian vessels.
Providing these essentials involved a carefully orchestrated
division of labor among all family members, male and female,
young and old. Clearly, the survival of the household as a whole
depended upon the contributions of all its members.

Since we are about to examine several passages that, like
Ruth 1.8, link the *bayit* with the mother, it is important to note
that the female's role in the household production system was
no less important than the male's. Women participated in agri-
cultural tasks, were responsible for the processing of crops into
comestibles, made most of the clothing and probably also the
baskets and the ceramic vessels, managed the activities of children and grandchildren (and of servants, hired workers,

1. I.J. Golb, 'Approaches to the Study of Ancient Society', *JAOS* 81
(1967), pp. 1-7.

2. See Meyers, *Discovering Eve*, pp. 142-64, for a summary of various
household functions. The size of the household has been much debated.
As a residential and social unit, the usual estimates have been much too
high. See L.E. Stager, 'The Family in Ancient Israel', *BASOR* 260 (1985),
pp. 17-23, for a more realistic appraisal that takes into account archaeo-
logical and ethnographic data.

sojourners and the like, if present), to say nothing of their role as progenitors. In such situations, households are typically characterized by internal gender balance rather than gender hierarchy.[1]

The word 'internal' is critical here. Whereas outward forms of status and recognition may indicate male privilege, the dynamics within domestic units may be quite different, with women even dominating the multifarious facets of economic life, and also the social and parenting activities, that take place within the family household.[2] Because the public record of ancient Israel, like that of most traditional societies, is so androcentric, aspects of female power within the Israelite household can rarely be seen. Yet the relative invisibility of female power does not mean it did not exist; and occasionally it can be glimpsed even in the male-oriented canon.[3]

Other Biblical Instances of 'Mother's Household'

Genesis 24.28

The longest chapter in the book of Genesis contains the endearing story of how Rebekah became the wife of Isaac. Sometimes called the Wooing of Rebekah, or the Courtship of Rebekah, the

---

1. See E. Boserup, *Women's Role in Economic Development* (London: George Allen & Unwin, 1970), p. 140, and the discussion in Meyers, *Discovering Eve*, pp. 165-73. The complex and time-consuming array of women's tasks is delineated in C. Meyers, 'Everyday Life: Women in the Period of the Hebrew Bible', in C.A. Newsom and S.H. Ringe (eds.), *The Women's Bible Commentary* (Louisville, KY: Westminster Press/John Knox, 1992), pp. 249-53.

2. See Meyers, *Discovering Eve*, pp. 174-81.

3. Schüssler Fiorenza's understanding of the relationship between androcentric texts and historical reality in *In Memory of Her* (New York: Crossroad, 1985) is eloquent and relevant: 'Androcentric texts and linguistic reality constructions must not be mistaken as trustworthy evidence of human culture, history, and religion. The text *may* be the message, but the message is not coterminal with human reality and history' (p. 29); see Part I of her book for a general discussion of the text–reality issue. This analysis is essentially the same as the Ardeners' view of women as muted groups with their own spheres of communication, not readily available to observers of the dominant male expressive forms (see Ardener, *Perceiving Women* and *Defining Females*).

narrative chronicles the journey of the trusted yet unnamed servant of Abraham to the city of Nahor in Mesopotamia, where he
identifies Rebekah as a suitable wife for his master's designated
heir, makes the nuptial arrangements, and accompanies the
bride-to-be back to Palestine, to the Negeb, where Isaac awaits
her arrival. Embedded in this long and vivid account is the well-
known incident of Rebekah at the well, in the course of which
Abraham's emissary asks who the helpful maiden is and
whether he and his entourage of camels might lodge in 'her
father's house', whereupon she hurries home to tell 'her
mother's household' (v. 28) what has happened.

Most commentators relate the appearance of 'mother's
household' to the ambiguity in the Genesis story about whether
Rebekah's father Bethuel was still alive.[1] Although Bethuel is
mentioned in Gen. 24.13, 24, and 50, he plays no role in the story.
Indeed, some suggest that, in v. 50, the appearance of Bethuel
cannot be original.[2] Yet it should be noted that Rebekah does not
respond to the servant's inquiry about room in her 'father's
house' with any remark about his being dead. Either way, *bêt 'āb*
in v. 23 seems to stand as an indicator of her family household,
regardless of who the senior male happens to be. Thus,
'mother's household' in v. 28 must be considered as an
alternative expression for the same societal unit and not as a
function of the particular configuration of Nahor's family.
Ironically, the Syriac of v. 28, with its androcentric bias, assumes
just that in reading 'father's house' for 'mother's house'.

The appearance of *bêt 'ēm* in the Rebekah story must be
considered in light of several relevant features of the Genesis 24
narrative, which have probably not received the attention they
deserve.[3] In its present form, ch. 24 has its own integrity and
stands in relative isolation, despite its context within the

1. E.g. G. von Rad, *Genesis* (OTL; Philadelphia: Westminster Press,
rev. edn, 1972), p. 257; B. Vawter, *On Genesis: A New Reading* (Garden
City, NY: Doubleday, 1977), p. 272; and J. Skinner, *Genesis* (ICC;
Edinburgh: T. & T. Clark, 2nd edn, 1930), p. 344.

2. So E.A. Speiser, *Genesis* (AB, 1; Garden City, NY: Doubleday,
1964), pp. 181-82.

3. So W.M. Roth, 'The Wooing of Rebekah: A Tradition-Critical
Study of Genesis 24', *CBQ* 34 (1972), pp. 177-87.

Abrahamic story and genealogy.[1] Although it depends on the reader's knowledge of the preceding Abraham stories, Genesis 24 has its own complex plot, developed through an intricate series of dialogues and speeches. Because of these features, it can perhaps be classified as a novella,[2] one as compelling as any in Hebrew Scripture.[3]

The story unfolds through the initial agency of Abraham's servant and concludes with Isaac taking Rebekah as his wife. Yet the prominence of the second matriarch in this story, as well as in other passages in Genesis, should not be overlooked. Indeed, because of her role in Genesis 24 as well as the extensive recounting of her collusion with Jacob to secure the birthright for her preferred son, Rebekah emerges as the most fully portrayed matriarch. She is also the only one of the foremothers to whom an oracle is given (Gen. 25.23) directly from Yahweh. Furthermore, in comparison with the delineations of the other matriarchal figures in Genesis, Rebekah appears as a much more active and autonomous individual. The very language of the passages concerning her involves a far more dynamic vocabulary than the language used for her mother-in-law or daughters-in-law. Rebekah 'came out' (24.15), 'went down' (24.16), 'let down her jar' (24.17), 'emptied her jar' (24.20), 'ran' (24.28), 'arose, and rode upon camels' (24.61). A similar vocabulary of activity accompanies the birthright story in Genesis 27.

Not only does Rebekah outshine the other matriarchs, but she is also in a sense equated with the foremost patriarch of all, Abraham. She will leave behind the same 'country', 'kindred' and 'father's house' (Gen. 24.4, 39) as did her father-in-law in the momentous opening of the patriarchal epoch in Gen. 12.1. The Rebekah story echoes the language of the divine call to Abraham. Similarly, Abraham's remarkable departure from his

1. G.W. Coats, *Genesis with an Introduction to Narrative Literature* (FOTL, 1; Grand Rapids: Eerdmans, 1983), p. 167.
2. Coats, *Genesis*, p. 170; Roth, 'The Wooing of Rebekah'.
3. S. Terrien (*Till the Heart Sings: A Biblical Theology of Manhood and Womanhood* [Philadelphia: Fortress Press, 1985], p. 31) notes the great admiration the story has elicited and claims that few novellas can rival or excel the Rebekah story, 'not even that of Ulysses discovering Nausicaa in the Odyssey'.

homeland, signified by the verb הלך ('go', 'go forth'; see Gen. 12.1, 4), is mirrored and intensified by Rebekah's departure. The key verb 'to go' appears seven times in the Rebekah story, thereby emphatically conveying the notion that the shift in her life course is of the same ilk as Abraham's portentous departure from Haran.[1] Finally, Rebekah is blessed, as the future 'mother of thousands of ten thousands' and of the descendants who will 'possess the gate of those who hate them' (24.60), in much the same way that Abraham is repeatedly blessed.[2]

In a way, the prominence of Rebekah in the second generation of Israel's proto-history compensates or substitutes for the relative absence of Isaac stories in Genesis as well as for the relatively weak portrayal of Isaac in the few places he appears. Isaac practically disappears between the extensive biography of Abraham and the many episodes recounted for Jacob.[3] In many ways, Isaac functions more as a symbol, as a passive representative of God's covenantal promise that Abraham will have a child to inherit the land to which he has journeyed, than as a character in his own right.

The several stories involving Rebekah as an active individual thus overshadow the sparse accountings of Isaac. For the transition between the first father Abraham and Jacob (= all Israel), Rebekah's role as mother of nations looms larger than that of her husband as father of nations. Hence Genesis 24 is a woman's story in that it showcases the matriarch who dominates the central generation of the ancestry sequence of Genesis; it is Rebekah who supplies the 'vitality of the line'.[4] Genesis 24 is a strong candidate for being considered a woman's text; or, at least, we can say that Genesis 24 speaks with a double voice, preserving authentic female experience within a male narrative.

---

1. See N.M. Sarna, *Genesis* (The JPS Torah Commentary; Philadelphia: Jewish Publication Society 1989), p. 161.

2. Sarna, *Genesis*; see especially his treatment of Gen. 32.17.

3. Speiser, *Genesis*, p. 103, asserts that Isaac 'can scarcely be described as a memorable personality in his own right' and is important only as a genealogical link.

4. Speiser, *Genesis*, p. 182.

Song of Songs 3.4 and 8.2

The Song of Songs, or Canticles, is surely the most famous collection of love poetry in the Western world. It is also the only biblical book probably spoken more by women than by men. Despite the traditional ascription of authorship to Solomon, which probably occurred at the time of editing because his name is mentioned several times in the work,[1] the author or authors remain anonymous. Yet according to the signification of the speakers in the poem itself, 53 per cent of the text is spoken by females, as opposed to the 34 per cent uttered by males.[2] A female voice begins the collection of love poems and also ends it;[3] the female speaker clearly dominates this extraordinary book.

Not only is a woman's voice heard more directly in the Song of Songs than anywhere else in the Hebrew Bible, but also its major character is a woman, as are many of the supporting cast of characters. References to other females far outnumber mentions of men. Furthermore, female emotions are presented more prominently than male ones. While there is no definitive proof of female authorship, some of the love lyrics that comprise the Song are so fundamentally feminine in texture and tone that the possibility that at least some parts of this book are a woman's composition must be entertained.[4] The question of the author's gender aside, the *treatment* of gender here is virtually unique in the Hebrew Bible. There is little gender stereotyping, with the

1. R.E. Murphy, *Wisdom Literature: Job, Proverbs, Ruth, Canticles, Ecclesiastes, Esther* (FOTL, 13; Grand Rapids: Eerdmans, 1981), pp. 101-102; see also M.H. Pope, *Song of Songs* (AB, 7C; Garden City, NY: Doubleday, 1977), pp. 22-23, 432-33.

2. The other 13 per cent of the text is spoken by choruses or consists of headings or verses of doubtful attribution. For an accounting of the distribution of verses by gender, see A. Brenner, *The Israelite Woman: Social Role and Literary Type in Biblical Narrative* (The Biblical Seminar, 2; Sheffield: JSOT Press, 1985), pp. 47-49.

3. Pointed out by P. Trible (*God and the Rhetoric of Sexuality*, p. 145), who also draws attention to other literary features signalling the prominence of the female.

4. Suggested by Brenner (*The Israelite Woman*, pp. 45-50) among others.

woman being at least as assertive as, if not more so than, the man in the pursuit and celebration of her beloved.

The mutuality of the lovers notwithstanding, the female voice and female characters dominate. Furthermore, in a striking reversal of conventional language, traditional masculine imagery is employed by the poet to portray the female rather than the male. Through the use of military terms and also of certain animal metaphors, the female is repeatedly depicted in figurative language that associates her—and *not* the male— with strength, might, aggression and even danger.[1] The woman more than the man is connected with images of power.

In the context of this series of poems characterized by the prominence and power of females, the use of the term 'mother's house' to signify the female's family household should come as no surprise. This phrase occurs twice in the Song, in 3.4 and in 8.2,[2] when the female expresses how dear her beloved is by speaking of bringing him 'to her mother's household'.[3]

In the first occurrence, the phrase is followed by a parallel reference to the mother's 'chamber' (*ḥeder*). This use of a spatial term need not mean that the preceding *bêt 'ēm* is also spatial. Rather, 'chamber' intensifies, focuses and clarifies the female orientation of its parallel.[4] For it is not simply a bedroom, it is the 'chamber of her that conceived me', an amplification highlighting the mother's procreative role.

1.　For an examination of this reversal of gender-stereotypical language see C. Meyers, 'Gender Imagery in the Song of Songs', *HAR* 10 (1986), pp. 209-23. This article is reprinted in A. Brenner (ed.), *A Feminist Companion to the Song of Songs* (The Feminist Companion to the Bible, 1: Sheffield: Sheffield Academic Press), pp. 197-212.

2.　Note also the recurrent appearance of 'mother', which is found seven (!) times, whereas 'father' is never mentioned; see Trible, *God and the Rhetoric of Sexuality*, p. 158.

3.　My translation, rendering *'el* as 'to' (with Pope, *Song of Songs*; NAB, REB and NEB) rather than 'into' as do the RSV, NRSV, and other translations.

4.　See R. Alter, *The Art of Biblical Poetry* (New York: Basic Books 1985), pp. 62-84, for a discussion of structures of intensification in Hebrew poetry.

The second instance of 'mother's house', in 8.2, involves textual variants that again illustrate the androcentric bias of the ancient translators as well as of modern commentators. This verse, like 3.4, involves a parallel, which reads *t^elamm^edēnî* in the MT. This word could be translated either 'she teaches (or instructs) me' or 'you (m.) teach (or instruct) me'. The translations that understand the former possibility,[1] acknowledging 'mother' to be the referent, are to be preferred, given the female orientation of this verse and of the entire book, and also for other reasons to be discussed below.

The Hebrew word תלמדני, however, takes on other meanings in some of the versions. The LXX, Vulgate and Peshitta all delete it and instead offer translations that would represent an expanded and quite different Hebrew: *w^e'el ḥeder hôrātî* ('to the room of the one who bore/conceived me'). This phrase, clearly influenced by the parallelism of 3.4, has been adopted by a number of influential English translations.[2] Furthermore, as might be expected, many modern critics favor the versions over the MT,[3] if they have not already decided that תלמדני is masculine and that the male lover or even God, and not the mother, must be doing the teaching.[4]

---

1. E.g. the new JPSV, the KJV; cf. M. Falk, *Love Lyrics from the Bible* (Bible and Literature Series, 4; Sheffield: Almond Press, 1982), p. 129. See the NAB for an example of a translation that reads the word as masculine only by also changing the subsequent stich ('there you would teach me to…').

2. E.g. RSV, NRSV, NEB (which reads 'embrace' for 'teach' and also inserts another stich), REB.

3. See R. Gordis, *The Song of Songs and Lamentations* (New York: Ktav; 1974), p. 98, for a rather convoluted conjecture about how the Hebrew may have been corrupted into MT *t^elamm^edēnî* by a scribe confusing the verb הרה ('to conceive'), an original 'she bore me', with the *hiphil* of הרי, the presumed root of *tôrâ*. Others would delete the מ of תלמדני to achieve *tēl^edēnî*, '(who) bore me'. T.J. Meek (*Song of Songs* [IB, 5; New York: Abingdon Press, 1956], p. 140) exemplifies those who assume that maternal instruction 'makes no sense here'. M. Fox (*The Song of Songs and Ancient Egyptian Love Songs* [Madison: University of Wisconsin Press, 1985], pp. 165-66) favors an expansion as an emendation of תלמדני to תלדני.

4. See Pope, *Song of Songs*, p. 659, and the works cited.

All of these suggestions, both modern and ancient, resist the intensification of 'mother's house' in the MT by a word signifying, as does the other reference to *bêt 'ēm* in 3.4, a maternal role, in this case the giving of instruction. The appropriateness of 'mother's house' being associated with the mother as one who teaches can be justified on the basis of anthropological paradigms considered in relation to biblical data, as well as by recognition of the relevance of certain wisdom texts in Proverbs.[1] The readings of ancient and modern biblical scholarship should not be allowed to blur the way in which woman/mother, household and instruction are linked in the MT.

Proverbs
Although the phrase 'mother's house' does not appear in Proverbs, several key passages bring together the figure of a woman and the house/household that is hers. These passages are found in each of the three main sections of Proverbs: in the provocative and enigmatic image of Woman Wisdom in the introductory section (Prov. 1–9), in several related proverbs in the collections that follow, and in the famous acrostic poem (Prov. 31.10-31) that lauds woman and in so doing brings the book of wisdom to an apt conclusion.[2]

In Prov. 9.1, as the culmination of the complex series of passages that personify an abstract wisdom (*ḥokmâ*) as a woman, Woman Wisdom is depicted as having 'built her house', setting it up on the much discussed and debated 'seven pillars of wisdom'.[3] In the succeeding verses, she is depicted as managing

1.   See Meyers, *Discovering Eve*, pp. 149-54, for a discussion of the mother's role in socialization and education in the family household. Cf. the proposal for a genre of 'mother's instruction' in Brenner and van Dijk-Hemmes, 'On Gendering'.

2.   On the structure of the book, see *inter alia* R.B.Y. Scott, *Proverbs, Ecclesiastes* (AB, 18; Garden City, NY: Doubleday, 1965), pp. 14-22, and Murphy, *Wisdom Literature*, pp. 49-50. Scholars divide the various subsections in different ways, but there is general agreement about the discrete nature of Proverbs 1–9, followed by a group of sub-collections and/or appendices, and ending with the poem about the worthy woman (*'ēšet ḥayil*).

3.   The term is variously given architectural, mythological and

her household, serving food and also providing 'insight'.

In two related verses in the collections that follow, woman and wisdom are again associated with the building of a house.[1] The MT of 14.1 reads either 'Wise women (*nāšîm*) build their houses' (although 'house' is singular in Hebrew) or 'The wisdom of women builds her house'. The difficult Hebrew has led most translators, ancient and modern, to delete 'women' from this verse.[2] Yet 'women' surely belongs with the combined themes of wisdom and house. In the case of 24.3, the other passage in the collections mentioning house and wisdom, 'woman' is not actually part of the text. Still, the fact that this verse echoes the house-building language of 9.1 and merges it with the imagery of Wisdom filling treasure-houses with wealth (8.22) indicates that the wisdom by which a house is built is female wisdom.[3]

Finally, the 'worthy woman' poem of 31.10-31 describes a woman skillfully and righteously managing all aspects of a complex household. She directs the members of the household in their various responsibilities. She participates in the actual physical labor involved in a variety of household tasks, especially that of textile production. She is in charge of her household's acquisition of property and in its participation in the market economy of the day. In performing all of these functions, she provides moral leadership for the members of her domain as well as for others who should take notice of her exemplary qualities.

(literary) structural significance; so Scott, *Proverbs*, pp. 76-77, and Murphy, *Wisdom Literature*, p. 52. See also the summary of scholarly perspectives in W. McKane, *Proverbs* (OTL; Philadelphia: Westminster Press, 1970), pp. 362-63.

1. C.R. Fontaine ('Proverbs', in *Harper's Bible Dictionary* [San Francisco: Harper & Row, 1988], pp. 509-10) sees one of these verses (14.1) as part of a midrash on the banquet scene of 9.1-6.

2. The RSV, NAB and the commentaries of Scott (*Proverbs*, p. 96) and McKane (*Proverbs*, p. 231; cf. p. 472) are among those that delete 'women'. Some retain it: NEB, 'The wisest women build their homes'; JPSV, 'Every wise woman buildeth her house'; and NRSV, 'The wise woman builds her house'.

3. Pointed out by C.V. Camp, *Wisdom and the Feminine in the Book of Proverbs* (Bible and Literature Series, 11; Sheffield: Almond Press, 1985), pp. 200-201.

In the process of enumerating the attributes, probably idealized, of an Israelite woman who is clearly a mother (since her children are mentioned in v. 28 and perhaps also v. 15), the poem connects her with 'her household' (*bêtah*) twice in v. 21. Thus 'mother's household' is represented although the phrase as such does not occur. Furthermore, 'wisdom' is an explicit part of the vocabulary of the poem, for instance in v. 26, where the woman is said to speak 'with wisdom'. In v. 26 she is connected with instruction (*tôrâ*), as is the mother of Song 8.2. The phrase 'teaching of kindness' picks up on the association of the mother with instruction—'your mother's teaching'—found in 1.8, 6.20 and 23. Altogether, the maternal instructional role is mentioned four times in Proverbs, once more than is the equivalent paternal teaching role.

The prominence of the interwoven motifs of woman, household and instruction for both the personified Wisdom of chs. 1–9 and the human woman of ch. 31 is noteworthy, particularly since these two sections provide a female-oriented framework for the entire book. Because of the structural and thematic linkage of these two sections, Woman Wisdom may indeed be at least partly modelled after a real, albeit idealized, woman rather than being simply a personification of divine attributes (mythological or Yahwistic).[1]

One could hardly call Proverbs a woman's book, with all its admonitions being directed from father to son. However, despite this male 'axis of communication',[2] the female–wisdom–teaching–house combination does frame and define the book. In addition, the discourse of the long introduction is strikingly concerned with women: 'women's speech occupies an astonishing amount of the text—men, preoccupied with speech, talking about women and women's speech'.[3] It is no wonder, then, that

1. This is the thesis of Camp's book *Wisdom*. See also Fontaine's summary ('Proverbs', pp. 501-503) of the various theories about the origin of the anomalous figure of personified wisdom.

2. See C. Newsom, 'Woman and the Discourse of Patriarchal Wisdom: A Study of Proverbs 1–9', in P.L. Day (ed.), *Gender and Difference in Ancient Israel* (Minneapolis: Fortress Press, 1989), p. 142.

3. Newsom, 'Woman and the Discourse of Patriarchal Wisdom', p. 142.

'mother's house' is found, albeit elliptically, in Proverbs as well as in Ruth, Genesis 24, and the Song of Songs. Proverbs too contains a female voice, a woman's text embedded in a man's book.

Discussion

Each of the parts of the Bible in which the term 'mother's house' is found has its own integrity; each features a unique style, setting, date, and function. Yet, examining the various contexts of *bêt 'ēm* reveals that, distinct and different as they are from each other, they also share certain fundamental characteristics, among which are:

1. *A woman's story is being told*. This is certainly the case for Ruth, feminist objections notwithstanding, as well as for the Song of Songs. The Rebekah story too, despite its location in the patriarchal narratives, showcases the second matriarch, who overshadows her husband. Even Proverbs, where our phrase is only elliptically present, contains more of women's voices than is usually recognized.

2. *A wisdom association is present*. Ruth, like Genesis 24, may exhibit certain features of biblical wisdom,[1] and the Song of Songs is likewise often grouped with wisdom literature.[2] For Proverbs, of course, the wisdom aspect is self-evident.

3. *Women are agents in their own destiny*. Although it is often assumed that gender hierarchies in ancient Israel precluded female autonomy, all the women in Ruth and in these other passages assume active roles. To a greater or lesser extent, they initiate or decide on actions that affect the course of their lives.

4. *The agency of women affects others*. Ruth and Naomi

---

1. So Roth, 'Wooing of Rebekah', p. 180. Roth draws on the analysis of R.M. Hals (*The Theology of the Book of Ruth* [Biblical Series, 23; Philadelphia: Fortress Press, 1969]), who discovers a similarity between the Ruth and Rebekah novellas.

2. As in Murphy's *Wisdom Literature*. Murphy is careful to note that 'wisdom literature' is not itself a genre and so can be an inclusive designation. The Song surely has many wisdom interests and connections—Solomon, nature, the individual, no direct divine involvement; cf. Terrien, *Till the Heart Sings*, pp. 45-46.

become progenitors of the house of David.[1] Rebekah's participation in the decision to leave her household is the prelude to
her prominence, more than Isaac's, as parent of all Israel. In
Proverbs, Woman Wisdom is close to Yahweh in status—present
at creation, existing everywhere, source of instruction (*tôrâ*);
and the worthy women is solely responsible for the well-being of
her own household and also that of others in need. The woman
in the Song of Songs does not have such broad influence, but the
lyrically drawn emotional power she has over her beloved
represents in its own way the enormous strength, and also the
essence, of female power in its effect on others.

5. *The setting is domestic*. While this may seem obvious, since
the word בית is part of the phrase being considered, this is a point
to be emphasized. No matter how broad the ramifications of the
women's deeds, the women are related to the household's
activities. Even Woman Wisdom's cosmic role is couched in the
metaphor of the house she builds and the table over which she
presides.

6. *Marriage is involved*. Arranging a marriage is implicit in
Ruth[2] and the Song of Songs; it is explicit in the Rebekah story.
Proverbs offers a somewhat different perspective: the worthy
woman is obviously married, and Woman Wisdom functions
somewhat as a divine consort.[3]

The significance of these features can be summarized by
emphasizing that all involve a female perspective on issues
which elsewhere in the Hebrew Bible are viewed from the male
perspective that dominates Scripture. The term 'mother's house'

---

1.   Boaz is the father, and the Moabite Ruth is the mother; but Ruth
4.17 announces that, 'A son is born to Naomi'! Thus both Ruth and
Naomi are ancestors of the royal house and the messianic line.

2.   Immediately after Naomi instructs her daughters-in-law to return
home to their mother's household, she invokes Yahweh's blessing on
them. This blessing includes the assumption that, upon returning
home, they would be remarried in their own homeland; that is, marriage would be the result of their re-entry to the mother's household.

3.   The theories linking *ḥokmâ* with mythological goddess figures (as
reviewed by Camp [*Wisdom and the Feminine*, pp. 23-68]) retain some
validity even if a human model for female Wisdom is accepted; after all,
goddesses too were shaped by the data of the human realm.

has drawn us into the internal or household setting which circumscribed the life activities of virtually all Israelite women (and probably also of most Israelite men). Within that setting, women's voices were heard, their presence was valuable and valued, and their deeds had a profound influence on others.[1]

However, despite the domestic setting of their daily activities, the influence of women went beyond the family household. The validity of this statement comes first from considering the configuration of Israelite households. It is difficult in analyzing family structure and household function to resist imposing contemporary models on an ancient society. One of the most troubling and misleading examples of the way current scholarship makes assumptions about past households that may not be applicable is in the assumption of a private–public dichotomy. That is, family and household are often considered 'private', and the sphere of supra-household activities, be they cultic, political or economic, is viewed as 'public'. In this dichotomy, gender becomes aligned in predictable ways: women = private, men = public. Women's sphere of influence is thereby conceived of as limited to private, domestic-centered or household activities.

It is now clear that this model has serious limitations in analyzing gender roles in contemporary life; and it is inappropriate for considering the dynamics of gender behavior in archaic societies dominated by household production, in which the household and the workplace are virtually identical.[2] The

1. The leadership of women viewed internally, in terms of their household roles, may be reflected in the use of the term g^eberet for Sarah, in reference to her relationship with Hagar (Gen. 16.4, 9). The usual translation, 'mistress', is too coy and sexist, since the male equivalent, in terms of external leadership, involves a man's power over others (see Gen. 27.29, 37; cf. Josh. 7.17).

2. The classic formulations of the dichotomizing model are reviewed and explored by, e.g., E.C. Dubois *et al.*, *Feminist Scholarship: Kindling in the Groves of Academia* (Urbana: University of Illinois Press, 1985), pp. 113-25; M.Z. Rosaldo, 'The Use and Abuse of Anthropology: Reflections on Feminism and Cross-Cultural Understanding', *SIGNS* 5 (1980), pp. 396-401, 407-409; and C. Bose, 'Dual Spheres', in *Analyzing Gender: A Handbook of Social Science Research*

family is a cultural construction; while there are inevitable cross-cultural connections and continuities, using data or models familiar to us from Western industrial life brings the risk of obfuscating and misunderstanding radically different structures and processes.[1] The critique of the private–public dichotomy means, for the case of ancient Israel, a rejection of the notion that family life was distinct from the general social relations involved in economic, political and religious life.[2] Female power in household life had implications that transcended the immediate spatial or relational configurations of the household. Or, to put it another way, the boundaries of 'household' were far more fluid in relationship to the general culture of ancient Israel than is normally thought.

Having made these points about 'household', whether it be named by a male ('father's household') or female ('mother's household') voice in Scripture, it now becomes possible to consider what is involved in at least one feature of household life revealed in Ruth 1.8 and the other texts examined above. The marriage aspect of the passages considered is salient in this regard. Israelite women apparently had a role equal to if not greater than their husbands in arranging the marriages of their children, although this is not always easy to discern under the androcentric layering of the texts. Naomi hopes to send Ruth and Orpah home in order that, in their mother's households, they will secure new marriage liaisons; and, unsuccessful in having

(Minneapolis: University of Minnesota Press, 1988).

1. See J. Casey, *The History of the Family* (Oxford: Basil Blackwell, 1989), p. 166. Even 'family' and 'household' are elusive terms; see the discussions of Meyers, *Discovering Eve*, pp. 140-42; R.R. Wilk and R.M. Netting, 'Households: Changing Forms and Functions', in R.M. Netting, R.R. Wilk and E.J. Arnould (eds.), *Households: Comparative and Historic Studies of the Domestic Group* (Berkeley: University of California Press, 1984), pp. 1-28; and P. Laslett and R. Wall (eds.), *Household and Family in Past Time* (London: Cambridge University Press, 1972).

2. Cf. a similar rejection, in understanding Palestinian families of the Roman period, by M. Peskowitz, '"Set Your Eyes on Family": Thinking about Families in Tannaitic Judaism and Roman Galilean Culture' (paper presented at the Society of Biblical Literature Annual Meeting, Kansas City, 1991).

Ruth return home, Naomi instigates Ruth's conjugal pairing. Rebekah's mother clearly plays such a role, as, later, does Rebekah herself. The woman of the Song of Songs, in bringing her beloved to the 'mother's house', the place of her own birth and of her mother's 'teaching', is no doubt involving her mother in her love arrangements. It cannot be assumed, in texts where fathers are said to secure marital liaisons, that they are acting on their own; rather, it is likely that the male voice reporting the liaison is overpowering the female voice that in fact participates in securing mates for a couple's offspring.

In forming marriages, alliances are formed between one *bêt 'āb* and another, or between *mišpā ḥot*, or even between tribes. Marriages, while intensely personal, private and domestic, also have a critical supra-household dimension and are thus public arrangements[1] with economic if not political implications. The woman's role in effecting nuptial agreements demanded perspicacity and diplomacy,[2] features of wisdom exemplified on a national level by Solomon and his affairs of state, and thus was not a trivial function affecting only the lives of the individuals involved.

To consider once more our term 'mother's house', we may say that its appearance may be startling in an androcentric document such as the Bible, but its existence as a meaningful term in Israelite society should not be unexpected. It may be rare and surprising in the male-dominated written word, but would not have been so in life as lived at the time. As anthropologists have discovered, the male-oriented, formal record of a society does not map accurately onto 'informal reality', in which women are also powerful actors in daily affairs and in family decisions on matters ranging from the mundane to the momentous. The biblical angle of vision rarely lets us view the female role or hear the female voice. Yet in some instances, as in the survival of 'mother's house' as a counterpart to the usual term for family household as the fundamental unit of society, the wisdom and

1. See the discussion in Meyers, *Discovering Eve*, pp. 154-55.
2. Camp's examination (*Wisdom and the Feminine*, p. 139) of the link between indirection (through speech) and wisdom is particularly relevant to this point.

power of women in ancient Israel become fleetingly visible. When Naomi exhorts her daughters-in-law to return home to their mother's household, she allows us to hear the language of female experience. Ruth 1.8 surely constitutes powerful evidence for the presence of a female text.

Part II
GENDERED AUTHORSHIP?

FEMALE COMPANIONSHIPS:
IF THE BOOK OF RUTH WERE WRITTEN BY A WOMAN...

Adrien J. Bledstein

If women wrote portions of the Hebrew Bible and their writings were incorporated as part of the sacred literature, what, then, would this mean for how a text is read?

Ancient Israelite women, constrained by what was indeed a patriarchal culture, are known to use satire (bold or subtle use of incongruities, parody and irony) to prod powerful men to re-evaluate their behavior. This is evident in women's songs, stories and dramatizations of events. The judge and prophetess Deborah in her song of victory over the tyrant Sisera taunts Israelite warriors of tribes who stayed at home:

> Among the clans of Reuben
> Were great decisions of heart.
> Why then did you stay among the sheepfolds
> And listen as they pipe for the flocks? (Judg. 5.15-16).

She satirizes privileged Canaanite women imagining the allotment of captured 'wombs' while awaiting Sisera's triumphant return (5.30). Later, King David is persuaded with fabrication by the woman of Tekoa to bring his son Absalom home from exile. Women's voices are both heard and effective (2 Sam. 14).

Besides recorded oral participation, women also wrote. As the Bible says, both Jezebel and Esther wrote (*wattiktōb*: 1 Kgs 21.8; Est. 9.29). From surrounding cultures are extant copies of prayers and letters by the hand of the daughter of Sargon of Akkad, princess-priestess-poetess Enheduanna (c. 2300 BCE). In wall paintings, women in Egypt are depicted as scribes, so we can expect that some Hebrew women as well as men were literate. Geniza scholar and folklorist S.D. Goitein proposed as early as 1957 that the book of Ruth was composed by a 'wise, old woman'.[1] Reading Ruth through the filter of imagining the book as written by a wise woman with a sense of humor and irony changes what we see.

The background of Ruth is the period of Judges, a time when powerful men lost perspective regarding their place in relation to Yahweh, the deity of Israel. Concomitant with the men's haughtiness comes use or abuse of women as a motif underlying nearly every episode in the book of Judges. Caleb offers his daughter as a trophy (Judg. 1.11-15). Sisera (chs. 4–5) and Abimelech (9.50-54) suffer—in the heroic scheme of values—the most humiliating defeat: each is killed by a woman. Jephthah is an outcast hooligan because his mother was a whore and his brothers disavow any connection with him—until they need him (11.1-11). Later he blames his victim daughter for the rash vow of his ambition (11.35). Samson the mighty is seduced by his own simplicity, appetite and the mercenary woman he is attracted to (ch. 16). The tribe of Benjamin exceeds the Sodomites in their behavior, aroused by violent sex, intent on humiliating men and contemptuous of women in every way (ch. 19). A Levite hacks up the body of his ravaged wife to rally the troops for vengeance (19.29–20.10). Israelite men condone wiping out a whole settlement and abducting maidens at a festival of Yahweh to supply surviving men of Benjamin with wives (chs. 20–21).

Typical of this period of Israelite madness, another Levite officiates at a sanctuary with idols, some devoted to Yahweh, and sells his services to the most powerful, highest bidder (chs. 17–18). Reading the book in this way, I suspect that one voice in Judges, possibly a woman's, intends to satirize men who in their behavior emulate the gods and demi-gods their muddled beliefs embrace.

Nevertheless, during this same pre-monarchic period, individuals are singled out as not being caught up in the cultural schizophrenia—when 'every man did what was right in his own eyes' (Judg. 17.6; 21.25). In the first book of Samuel Hannah,

---

1. S.D. Goitein, 'Women as Creators of Biblical Genres', *Prooftexts* 8.1 (1988). Originally published in Hebrew (Tel Aviv: Yavneh, 1957).

wife of Elkanah, worships Yahweh at Shiloh (1 Sam. 1). And in the book of Ruth, Naomi's commitment to Yahweh allows her the freedom to complain bitterly to the deity she worshipped even in exile. Ruth from Moab chooses Yahweh over the gods and goddesses of her people, and Boaz well understands the limits of human power.

Female companions Naomi and Ruth embrace Boaz, and all three characters embody the spirit of the covenant with Yahweh. Their relationships call upon a reader to rethink three Hebrew terms: *ʾēšet ḥayil* ('woman of valor'), *ʾîš gibbôr ḥayil* ('valiant warrior', and see below) and *ḥesed* ('loving kindness'). In the context of the book of Ruth, each term has unusual connotations which offer a view of humans who worship Yahweh and transcend the patriarchal abuses rampant in those days of Israelite dementia.

The book of Ruth stands alone against the period of Judges as a humane tale of death, grieving, friendship, healing, rejuvenation and continuation of life in a community. Often lost in interpretations of the three central figures are the qualities of earthiness, shrewdness and practicality combined with an urge toward life in a covenant community. Too often Ruth is characterized as self-effacing,[1] doing what she is told by a pushy mother-in-law and entrusting her fate to a businessman. However, a grammatical observation by Cyrus Gordon[2] alters the translation of a crucial passage and, as we shall see later, this new translation supports a very different reading of the characters, the law, and what may be a woman storyteller's purpose. In my treatment of Ruth I shall primarily use the 1979 translation by Jack Sasson[3] and shall indicate where on occasion I differ from this.

The tale begins traditionally, with the setting of the time,

1. See e.g. A. LaCocque, *The Feminine Unconventional: Four Subversive Figures in Israel's Tradition* (Minneapolis: Fortress Press, 1990), pp. 96, 99, 100.

2. C. Gordon, *Forgotten Texts* (New York: Basic Books, 1982), pp. 170-71.

3. J.M. Sasson, *Ruth: A New Translation with a Philological Commentary and a Formalist-Folklorist Interpretation* (Baltimore: Johns Hopkins University Press, 1979).

during the Judges; the problem, a famine in Judah; and the action of a man, Elimelech. Accompanied by his wife, Naomi, and two sons, Mahlon and Chilion, he crosses the Jordan and settles in Moab. Promptly Elimelech is dead, the sons marry Moabite women, Orpah and Ruth; then the sons die. Narration is concise and moves swiftly to the essence of the problems facing the widows, an underclass in the patriarchal world established by the time of the expulsion of the first human pair from Eden.

As reflected in the opening and closing of the book, the social circumstances are androcentric. A man determines the movement of the family in the first instance, and the line of male genealogy from Perez to King David concludes the book. Within the story men hold wealth and power, and the laws are meant to protect male inheritance. However, the thrust of the story's message is at odds with the social circumstances. Untraditionally for a patriarchal story, attention shifts from the men who do not survive to the women who act in order to make survival possible. (Such a shift of focus from men to women is common also in the J narratives of Genesis.)

Bereaved of her husband, then of her sons, Naomi is cut off from both protection and continuation of life through any descendants because her sons' wives have no children. Though grieving, Naomi attends to the welfare of her daughters-in-law.

The drama opens with the three women in a moment of transition, on the road between Moab and Judah where food is again available. Emerging from her own agony, Naomi interrupts the journey to insist that Orpah and Ruth go back to their homes, kin and families in Moab. She knows well the hardships of being an alien. They both refuse, and she urges them with arguments which reveal Israelite law, her values, her character, and an understanding of her circumstances.

Three values are stressed through her words to them: first, the importance of the mother's house;[1] secondly, Yahweh's *ḥesed* (loving kindness), which is likened to theirs; and thirdly, security in a new marriage (romantic love plays no role here).

---

1. Cf. Meyers' article in this volume.

Among Israelites, the levirate law requires that a brother marry the widow of his brother in order to rear a son for the deceased; Deut. 25.5-6 says,

> When brothers dwell together and one of them dies and leaves no son, the wife of the deceased shall not be married to a stranger, outside the family. Her husband's brother shall unite with her: take her as his wife and perform the levir's duty. The first son that she bears shall be accounted to the dead brother, that his name may not be blotted out in Israel.

For example, in Genesis 38 Onan son of Judah marries his brother's widow but avoids providing an heir by coitus interruptus, and is killed by Yahweh.

After telling the young women to turn back, Naomi asks rhetorically, 'Are there still more sons in my womb to be your future husbands?' (1.11). These alien women have no further obligation to her. She cannot provide sons for them to marry. Even if she could, would they really want to wait until the sons were grown? Her questions prod them to regard their own futures, which are not bound to hers. Then she ends on the note that her bitter situation is an act of Yahweh, the divinity she worships. Who wants to be with someone shunned by her deity?

Orpah reluctantly turns back, but Ruth firmly rejects Naomi's insistence that she go home:

> Do not press me to desert you, to resist following you; for wherever you go, I too will go; whatever your shelter, I will share it; your people will become mine, and your Divine Being will be my own. Wherever you die, I will die, and be buried alongside. May Yahweh strike me at any time with afflictions, if anything but death parts us (1.16-17).

Sasson's translation captures the unsentimental intensity of Ruth's determination. In no uncertain terms (contrast with the familiar, poetic 'Entreat me not to leave thee'), Ruth declares that she will stick with Naomi.

Ruth has found a human being whose values and concerns afffirm what is most important to Ruth herself as a childless young woman who has also suffered loss. Naomi's harsh realism, spelling out their circumstances, is both irascible and combined with concern for each of her former daughters-in-law.

Ruth's situation with Naomi is one of soulbinding companionship comparable to that between Jonathan and David. The
narrator underscores Ruth's resolution: 'when Naomi realized
how determined she was to accompany her, she ceased arguing
with her' (1.18). Naomi knows there is nothing more to say.

Arriving in Bethlehem, they are greeted by old acquaintances
in Naomi's community. Surrounded by those who knew her
when her life was full with husband and sons, she unleashes her
grief, expressing bitterness and rage at the emptiness of her
present circumstances (1.21). She complains to Yahweh as
Shaddai, the title of Yahweh as the Nurturing One, invoked
when fertility is an issue. Often translated 'the Almighty',
'Shaddai' is more likely to mean 'the Nurturer', arising from the
root word denoting 'breast'.[1]

The narrator concludes with a summary statement for the first
third of the book: 'This, then, was how Naomi returned, with
her daughter-in-law, Ruth of Moab, accompanying her from
Moabite territory' (1.22). 'This, then' emphasizes the narrator's
previous elaboration of the specific circumstances surrounding
Naomi's return, probably known to the audience only in the
more concise form of the introduction. Using three such summary, transitional, statements in this brief tale, the narrator
draws attention to the essence of the events as she recounts
them. Awareness of this stylistic tool becomes important later.

The introduction of Boaz is remarkable. He is a *gō'ēl*,
redeeming kinsman to Elimelech, and called an *'îš gibbôr ḥayil*,
usually translated 'a mighty man of valor', that is, a hero in
war. *gibbôr* arises from 'be strong' which, in Arabic, signifies
'one who magnifies himself, behaves proudly, a tyrant who is
bold, audacious'.[2] This is the meaning employed by the J
narrator in Gen. 6.4, which satirizes the 'heroes of old' whom,
ironically, Yahweh wipes out in the flood. However, Boaz is
nowhere presented as a warrior. Other Hebrew meanings of
the combination *'îš gibbôr ḥayil* are: a man of substance,
magnanimity, consideration, ability, strength or efficiency. As
we will see, Boaz is all of these.

1.   Sasson, *Ruth*, p. 34.
2.   BDB, p. 150.

Sasson's translation of Ruth's question in 2.2, '[shall] I go to the fields and glean among the ears of grain, in the hope of pleasing him?' reveals initiative on her part and suggests that the women have talked about Boaz's character. She intends both to provide food for the two of them and to open a possibility of hope for a future. That Ruth 'happened'—by luck, as implied in the Hebrew—to find herself on the field of Boaz is playfully ironic given her intention. It also may suggest a divine hand in her good fortune if, as Sasson remarks in his notes, one field is nearly indistinguishable from another.

Boaz is a singularly hearty character. In 2.4 he warmly greets his workers with a blessing, and they respond in kind. He is not an absentee, nor a sullen, boss who snoops around, prodding slackers. Not only supportive but alert, he immediately notices a stranger who is not distinguished as a beauty.

I owe much to Sasson's insights. He adds dimensions to the characters of Ruth and Boaz through a careful reading of the series of subtle communications implied in the Hebrew. Sasson suggests that Ruth's request to glean required no permission, as it was the law that anyone might do so. But to gather grain among the bundled stalks needed the owner's permission; so this request was her way of assuring an introduction to the chief.

Boaz not only gives her permission but, in his generous way, he also provides protection and water. With dramatic flourish, she flings herself on the ground before him and exclaims, 'Why is it that I please you enough to notice me? I am but a foreigner!' (2.10). This elicits from him high praise for what he has heard about her. He admires her for her care of her mother-in-law, for leaving her native land and joining a new people. Then he calls for Yahweh's blessing on her: 'May your full reward come from Yahweh, Protector of Israel, under whose wings you seek shelter' (2.12).

In turn Ruth is grateful for his attention, yet she points out that there is no change in her status. Her choice of word for 'handmaid' is šiphâ, related to mišpâhâ, 'family' or 'clan'. Sasson suggests that she is pressing to be considered as one of the people, if only on the lowest rung, in this patriarchal setting. Boaz considers her request until mealtime, then his inclusion of her in the meal raises her status. Again he is generous, providing more food than she can eat.

When Ruth presents the 29 pounds (Hebrew *'êpâ*; 2.17) of barley she has gleaned, shares the leftovers and reports to Naomi all that she 'has accomplished', she teasingly leaves the name of her benefactor for dessert. Her friend is impressed.

In Naomi's response, 'Blessed be he to Yahweh, who has not withheld his kindness from the living or the dead' (2.20), there is a deliberate ambiguity. Does *ḥesed*, 'kindness' or 'consideration', refer to Yahweh, to Boaz, or to both? Perhaps this ambiguity is meant to indicate that, after Ruth's successful initiative, the bereft Naomi has an inkling of hope that Yahweh may bless the two of them through this decent man.

'So she kept close to Boaz's girls, gleaning until the end of the barley and wheat harvests. Meanwhile she lived with her mother-in-law' (2.23). Thus the second part of the story is summarized.

From one harvest to the next, two or three months later, Ruth and Boaz have had considerable time for exposure to one another. Naomi then reveals her plan for securing Ruth a future with Boaz, and perhaps also a future for herself: Ruth is to bathe (the ritual cleansing before marriage?), perfume herself, and dress up, then go to the threshing floor under the cover of night. Hiding until Boaz is cheerful from food and drink and lies down to sleep, Ruth is to approach him in the dark, 'bare his "legs"' (many commentators have remarked that 'legs' is a euphemism for genitals; cf. Rashkow's article in this volume), and cuddle up to him. Naomi assures her that he will tell her what to do next (3.1-4).

Ruth responds, 'I will do as you say' (3.5). Does Ruth 'obey' Naomi? Or, is she so invigorated by Naomi's idea as to willingly risk the fine reputation she has acquired? Interpretations of the following passages leave two issues inadequately addressed. One issue is the question of Ruth's enthusiastic response. This entails appreciation of the daring, consideration, intelligence and flair of each of the two women. The second issue is the legal complexity of the situation which drives Ruth to a secret tryst, in the time of Judges when men held power over women.

Ruth does not hesitate. As we will see, she enacts the plan

with inspiration in her choice of images and, we might imagine, in her manner as well. There is nothing passive nor merely obedient in the character of Ruth.

When Boaz awakens, startled by a presence, he demands to know who is there. She responds, 'Ruth, your handmaid'. This time *'âmâ*, meaning a 'marriageable woman', is the term she chooses. Furthermore, she pointedly recalls his blessing of her, 'may Yahweh spread his wings over you' (2.12)[1] by telling him to spread his 'wing/robe' over her, indicating marriage (3.9). Without pausing in her audacious proposal, she pushes even further, emphasizing that he is a *gō'ēl*, 'redeemer', thus drawing his attention not only to marriage with her but also to his assuming an obligation as a kinsman of Elimelech to rear an heir, and to purchase the land in order to provide for Naomi.

Ruth's dual aim, her marriage and Naomi's security, accounts for Boaz's reaction:

> May you be blessed by Yahweh, daughter. You have acted with more kindness (*ḥesed*) in the last instance than in the first, without going after young men, poor or rich (3.10).

The 'first instance' is her proposal, perhaps spoken with some affectionate irony, as he refers to her daring in baring his 'legs' and cuddling up to him. The last instance is her regard for Naomi, an exclamation of admiration for her consideration of Naomi's future. (The 'first instance' is usually thought to be Ruth's accompanying Naomi and choosing to worship Yahweh.)

His recognition of these two points becomes clear with his words and actions. He agrees to all she asks of him because of her reputation as an *'ēšet ḥayil* which, I suggest, in this story means a woman of sound judgment, wholesome values, and energetic pursuit of what is important. He then takes it upon himself, without speaking with Naomi, to offer the land to the closest redeemer.

Whereas Naomi's chief stated concern is a contented marriage for Ruth, we may surmise from her plan that her unstated hope is an heir for herself. Ruth's concern for herself includes

---

1. See P. Trible, *God and the Rhetoric of Sexuality* (Philadelphia: Fortress Press, 1978), p. 184.

Naomi's security for old age and posterity. The friendship of these wilful women is inclusive, a combination of self-interest and consideration for others. In those days, Boaz was the rare man who appreciated the nature of their companionship and was pleased to be included.

Through his early generosity, Boaz has surely conveyed his appreciation of Ruth as a woman and his care for Naomi as a widow in need. Though he does not initiate marriage nor seek further responsibilities, when they are thrust upon him Boaz grasps the matter and carries on with verve. He responds spontaneously, delighted to be chosen by Ruth over younger men (cf. Bal's article in this volume). Had he projected onto these women cynical, purely self-interested motives and been fearful of the seductive power of woman—as Gilgamesh justly felt threatened by Ishtar in the *Epic of Gilgamesh*—he would not have appreciated this particular woman. He could have treated her as a whore and sent her away, as Prince Amnon did after raping his sister Tamar in 2 Samuel 13.

Clearly, Boaz is an honorable man who wants Ruth as his wife. He immediately discerns how he can get around the redeemer, who legally precedes him as kinsman with both the right and obligation to purchase the land left by Elimelech. As the widow of a man with no living brother, Ruth may marry any man. However, if she marries a redeemer, she may provide for Elimelech, Naomi and Mahlon an heir to the land, which was understood to be allotted by Yahweh to that family in perpetuity.

Boaz tells her to stay the night so that, I suggest, they may consummate their marriage. This is a lawful act committed secretly, a necessary measure in order to assure that Ruth will not be bound to an unworthy man who, like Onan son of Judah, might take her as a wife but spill his seed so as not to rear a son for the deceased (Gen. 38.8-9).

One form of marriage in the Bible is simply that the two eligible, consenting parties have intercourse (for example, Isaac takes Rebekah into his tent in Gen. 24.67). Translators and interpreters have assumed that buying the land allotted to Elimelech and marrying the widow are inextricably linked. However, the narrative indicates that when a brother is not

living, redeeming the land and marrying the widow may be separate, thus giving the widow latitude in choosing a husband. If,
however, she wants to rear an heir for her deceased spouse, she
must marry a 'redeemer', a relative in the larger family. Boaz
knows he is next after another. Thus he acquires Ruth as his
wife through intercourse. With no little irony he tells her to stay
the night, then to let the redeemer 'choose' whether or not to
buy the land (3.13). Boaz knows that if Ruth is blessed with a
child by him, the redeemer will be obligated to pass the land on
to the heir of Elimelech.

Boaz sends her away before anyone can witness so that the
redeemer may have no prior knowledge of their union. Again,
he is generous with grain, at least thirty pounds ('six measures
of barley', 3.15).

When Naomi hears Ruth return in the dark, she asks not
'Who's there?' or 'Is it you, dear', or even 'How did you fare, my
daughter?' (RSV) but, literally and archly, 'Who are you, my
daughter?' Naomi expects a new identity, and Ruth tells her 'all
that the man had done to her' (3.16; literal translation). Naomi
knows that Ruth's welfare is assured. At stake now is her own
future, whether or not Ruth bears a child.

Then the young woman gives Naomi the grain, saying Boaz
bade her 'not to return empty-handed to [her] mother-in-law'.
We do not hear Boaz say this, though his behavior surely indicates his consideration. I would suggest that Ruth's invention of
Boaz's words is her deliberate way of assuring Naomi that she
is no longer 'empty', as when she returned to Bethlehem.

'Sit still, my daughter, until you know how the matter falls.'
Naomi's own fate is still in the balance. But knowing Boaz's
resolute character, Naomi is certain that the time will not be
long, for 'he will not rest until the matter is settled that day'
(3.18).

Boaz handles the legal transaction masterfully and efficiently.
First he gets the redeemer, called 'So-and-So',[1] who just
happens to come by (divine intervention again?), and ten elders
as witnesses. Secondly, he sells Naomi's land, which the

---

1. See E.F. Campbell, Jr, *Ruth* (Garden City, NY: Doubleday, 1973),
p. 141.

redeemer is happy to acquire, as there are no apparent strings attached. Thirdly, Boaz announces his own marriage to Ruth, with the express purpose of rearing an heir for Mahlon (4.1-5).

Sasson translates the confusing Hebrew in this critical passage differently: 'Know that on that very day you are purchasing the field from Naomi, *I am acquiring* Ruth of Moab, wife of the deceased, in order to perpetuate the memory of the deceased upon his estate' (4.5; my emphasis). Echoing the sense of all previous translations, RSV reads, 'the day you buy the field from the hand of Naomi, then Ruth the Moabite, widow of the dead, *you buy* to restore the name of the dead to his inheritance'.[1] If these translations were correct in assuming that Boaz and Ruth are not at this point already married, then the women's subterfuge and the episode at the threshing floor would have been just for sexual titillation.

I believe the woman narrator, and at least her female listeners, knew from experience that the unsavory character called So-and-So could demand the unmarried widow along with the land, pull an Onan-style trick, and disregard Naomi altogether. Vulnerable to men who play God, the women and Boaz use subterfuge.

The problematic Hebrew has ומאת, which Gordon, drawing upon Ugaritic precedents, translates 'but'.[2] *qānîtî*, rendered 'I am acquiring Ruth' or 'you...buy Ruth', literally signifies 'I have acquired'. This Hebrew verb, which appears twice in the same form (vv. 4.5 and 4.10), has been tagged as an error because the enclitic 'but' has not been recognized by anyone before Gordon. I suggest, following his work, that Boaz simply and pointedly says,

> on this day you acquire the field from the hand of Naomi, *but* I have acquired Ruth of Moab, the wife of the deceased, to raise the name of the deceased on his estate (4.5; my emphasis).

1. Sasson's rendering is based on the *kethib*, the consonantal (קניתי) text of the crucial Hebrew verb translated; the RSV follows the *qere*, the Masoretic instruction to read the verb according to the pointing, giving the reading 'you acquire' (קָנִיתָ).

2. Gordon, *Forgotten Texts*, pp. 170-71.

No wonder So-and-So responds, 'In that case, I cannot redeem in my behalf, lest I damage the future of my own estate' (4.6); and he urges Boaz to go ahead and buy the land as well.

The 'redeemer' promptly gives up his right to the land because, if Ruth and Boaz have a child who is a redeemer, the land will go to that child. The land was a good buy if there was no possibility of someone's inheriting it! This is precisely what Boaz anticipates. He plays his own game with So-and-So in order to make it possible that Boaz could redeem the land now for Naomi's benefit. Whether or not there is a child is now up to Yahweh.

The men then go through the sandal ceremony for transfer of property. This is different from *ḥᵃlîṣâ*, when the woman removes the brother's sandal and spits in his face, humiliating the man who will not build up his brother's house.[1] The latter is not necessary because neither Ruth, the Moabitess, nor So-and-So, the kinsman, are obligated to perform the levirate ceremony. Ruth and Boaz choose to fulfil the law for the welfare of Naomi, whose only insurance in old age is the generosity of Boaz or a grandson willing to support her.

The whole community catches on and is delighted with the turn of events. All the people at the gate are witnesses and call a blessing on Ruth, that she should be like Rachel and Leah in building the house of Israel. They also invoke the house of Perez, 'whom Tamar bore unto Judah' (4.12). The link of the book of Ruth to the episode of Judah and Tamar in Genesis 38 is now explicit. Ruth, like Tamar, seduces the man she chooses to provide an heir for. Unlike Tamar, Ruth is a free agent. So long as Shelah lives and does not perform *ḥᵃlîṣâ*, Tamar is restricted to

---

1. Deut. 25.7-9: 'But if the man does not want to marry his brother's widow, his brother's widow shall appear before the elders in the gate and declare, "My husband's brother refuses to establish a name in Israel for his brother; he will not perform the duty of a levir." The elders of his town shall then summon him and talk to him. If he insists, saying, "I do not want to marry her", his brother's widow shall go up to him in the presence of the elders, pull the sandal off his foot, spit in his face, and make this declaration: "Thus shall be done to the man who will not build up his brother's house!" And he shall go in Israel by the name of the family of the unsandaled one' (NJV).

the family of Judah, so she acts in order to become a mother. What these women have in common is that they both turn patriarchal restraints to their own purposes, and they are ancestresses of the dynasty of David. Their subversive originality in dealing with a survival situation is both respected by Yahweh-fearing men and blessed by Yahweh (each bears sons).

Other important links are with Rachel who, like Ruth, was barren for a long while, and with Leah, who was fertile. Each matriarch offers her handmaid as a concubine for Jacob and adopts the children. Naomi is 'built up' through Ruth, as Rachel and Leah are through Bilhah and Zilpah. Note that Sarah is left out, perhaps because her relationship with Hagar is filled with mutual hostility and adoption does not occur.

> This, then, was how Boaz took Ruth, she became his wife, he had relations with her, and Yahweh allowed her to conceive (4.13).

With this third summary statement of preceding action the narrator underscores the extraordinary behavior which resulted in blessings for all three characters. For possibly ten years Ruth was married to Mahlon in Moab and not blessed with a child. Three months in Judah, a few nights with Boaz, and she is pregnant! Can one doubt that the Nurturer (שׁדי, 1.21) has a hand in this, providing a grandson for Naomi?

ḥesed, 'consideration', includes shrewdness in getting around a So-and-So who happens to have power in the androcentric culture which resulted from humans wanting to be like gods in Eden.[1] Inventiveness, flair, consideration, sensitive understanding of another's need and trustworthiness are among the characteristics of Ruth, Naomi and Boaz (and Tamar, from whom Boaz is descended), founders of the royal dynasties of Judah and Israel. How very different from the actual household of David, as described by the Court Narrator. Amnon embodies the Arabic meaning of *gibbôr*, 'one who magnifies himself, behaves proudly, a tyrant who is bold, audacious', as he rapes

1.   See A.J. Bledstein, 'The Genesis of Humans: The Garden of Eden Revisited', *Judaism* 26.2 (1977), pp. 187-200.

his sister Tamar. In Israel, she says, he is one of the base fellows. In the book of Ruth, Amnon's great-great-grandfather is presented as the opposite, as an ideal for an *'îš gibbôr ḥayil*.

The women of Bethlehem, rejoicing with Naomi on the birth of the grandson, make explicit the narrator's primary concerns:

> Blessed be Yahweh who, on this very day, did not cause to cease for you a redeemer. May his name be proclaimed in Israel. He shall become a life-restorer for you, and is to sustain you in your old age; for he was born to a daughter-in-law who loves you and is dearer to you than seven sons (4.14-15).

Naomi's complaint in 1.20-21, that 'Yahweh has brought me back empty', is now resolved with the birth of the 'life-restorer'.[1] In the ancient world it was believed that seven sons secured a man's well-being in the underworld. With no little irony, these women give the ultimate in praise to one daughter (in-law).

With a litany of male genealogy, the story ends traditionally just as it began. As if gently mocking a too masculine cultural bias, the account of these women survivors and their man of choice is bracketed by the expected opening and closing of a tale recorded in ancient Israel.

Let us imagine, for a moment, that a man wrote a version of David's ancestors, recording a threat to the family heritage. The Bible has many inscriptions by priestly scribes, such as we read in Chronicles. On that model, the story might read something like this:

> During the time of the Judges, a famine occurred in the land, so Elimelech of Bethlehem in Judah migrated to Moabite territory together with his wife and two sons. Upon the death of Elimelech, his wife was left alone with her two sons who married Moabite women. After living there for about ten years, the two sons died also. So the woman returned, with a daughter-in-law accompanying her from Moabite territory. Boaz, a redeeming kinsman of Elimelech, took the Moabite woman in order to rear an heir and begot a son called Obed, he being the father of Jesse, who was the father of David. This is the genealogy of Perez: Perez begot Hezron; Hezron, Ram; Ram, Amminadab; Amminadab, Nahshon; Nahshon, Salmah; Salmah, Boaz; Boaz, Obed; Obed, Jesse; and Jesse begot David.

1. See Campbell, *Ruth*, p. 164.

If the received tradition was something like this bare outline, typical of priestly scribes who tended to omit women's names, this might explain how each name of people and places in the received book of Ruth has significance in relation to their function in a story elaborated by a woman. The mother-in-law who inspires devotion is Naomi ('pleasantness'; in 1.20 she asks the woman to call her *mārâ*), meaning 'bitterness'). Ruth, 'companionship' or 'water to saturation',[1] may be likened to a fountain of living waters which refreshes and replenishes. The daughter-in-law who turns her back is Orpah ('nape of the neck'). Elimelech ('my divinity rules') may, in the days of the Judges, imply ironic meaning—who was Elimelech's deity? The two sons who die in exile are Mahlon ('sickness') and Chilion ('destruction'), probably not the original names.

The man chosen by the women to redeem them is Boaz ('in him is strength'), an admirable nickname for a new kind of hero. The name of the child who serves to connect them with the future, Obed ('servant'), may be the actual given name. Coincidentally, the town Elimelech left and to which Naomi returns is Bethlehem ('house of bread'), representing sustenance, and the clan territory around Bethlehem is Ephrathah ('fertility', named for Ephrat, the wife of Caleb[2]). The tribe which Ruth joins is Judah ('praise YH', short for Yahweh, the Protector of Israel[3]).

Such deliberation in choice of names suggests that the title of the scroll, *Ruth*, focuses attention on companionship and replenishment. Three people embrace to the fullest what the Bible calls *ḥesed*, 'consideration'. Divine *ḥesed* is expressed through their actions. Thus the narrator more fully defines both *'îš gibbôr ḥayil* and *'ēšet ḥayil* as embracing *ḥesed*. The man, in his magnanimity and sensitive appreciation of these women, does not fear women nor experience the need to dominate them. He is able and willing to participate wholeheartedly in nurturing and caring relationships, which, in this case, requires that he

1. See LaCocque, *The Feminine Unconventional*, p. 115.
2. See F.M. Cross, Jr, *Canaanite Myth and Hebrew Epic* (Cambridge, MA: Harvard University Press, 1973), p. 95.
3. Cf. Bal's and Bronner's articles in this volume.

rear a child for another man and provide, at his expense, continuity for another man's family on the land Yahweh has provided.

The woman of valor can recognize a man of good character, and dares to risk her reputation in order to initiate a relationship which may result in securing continuity of life for her mother-in-law and her deceased husband, as well as security for herself. Each character fully understands both the patriarchal restraints of the society and the possibilities of trusting others to cooperate in fulfilling the spirit of faith in Yahweh.

The date of the author is most commonly considered to be fifth century BCE, primarily because it was in that time that Israelite men were required to divorce their foreign wives. The book of Ruth is seen as a response to that edict. However, the language is classic to the monarchic period.[1] The features of the book of Ruth to which I have called attention in this essay—characterizations, themes, irony and a healing sense of humor—mark the narrator as J, the Yahwist and 'master' storyteller of the Bible.

I suggest we think of this narrator as Tamar, the daughter of David, who could have written during the latter part of David's and the early years of Solomon's reigns. She was the great-great-granddaughter of Ruth, Naomi and Boaz, and descended from the earlier Tamar of Genesis. Her depiction of Boaz introduces a radical definition of *'îš gibbôr hayil* in that heroic age of Judah and Israel, an ideal opposed to devastating realities involving *gibbôrîm*, 'heroes'.

Tamar's tragicomic vision and insight as a writer, I suggest, arise from her having experienced tragedies which might befall even a royal woman in a patriarchal culture. According to 2 Samuel 13, her half-brother Amnon raped her and threw her out. By leaving Amnon unpunished, David abandoned his devastated daughter; and his inaction precipitated further disaster. Her brother Absalom assassinated Amnon, avenging his own honor tarnished by the humiliation of his sister. Later, his attempt to unseat David in civil war resulted in Absalom's own violent death. Experiencing and living beyond these griefs,

1. See G.A. Rendsburg, *The Redaction of Genesis* (Winona Lake, IN: Eisenbrauns, 1986), pp. 107-20.

Tamar might be motivated to imagine and redefine the nature of an *'îš gibbōr ḥayil* at the same time she draws attention to the survival tactics of female companions.

I imagine her as both the 'master' storyteller of the Bible and as the Court Narrator who gives us the history of David's family. In her latter years this prolific, gifted writer could be the mature woman who wrote the book of Ruth, an ironic–idealistic woman's view of living with the Covenant. She anticipated, through narration, Jeremiah's later vision: 'Yahweh has created a new thing on earth: female surrounds a mighty man' (Jer. 31.22).

RUTH: A PRODUCT OF WOMEN'S CULTURE?

Fokkelien van Dijk-Hemmes

Together with the books of Esther and Judith, the book of Ruth is one of the few biblical books in which women play a major role. Like them, it even bears a woman's name. Could this indicate that the author of this particular book is not, as is usually the case, self-evidently male? Should it perhaps be seen as an indication of female authorship?

In his illuminating article 'Women as Creators of Biblical Genres', in which he investigates the literary traditions of women in the Bible, S.D. Goitein correctly states that 'there is no proof that books *about* women were written *by* women'.[1] To Goitein, in fact, the reverse seems plausible, since 'it is natural that the praise of woman generally be found on the lips of man' (see Prov. 31.28). Notwithstanding his observation that there is nothing in Ruth (nor in Esther or Judith) 'to distinguish [it] in any way so as to suggest that a woman wrote [it]', and despite the fact that there are no indications in the Bible which point to a women's narrative tradition, Goitein does not exclude the possibility that the book of Ruth 'was the fruit of the spirit of an elderly prophetess-"wise woman"'. His argument in support of this conjecture is that the 'narrator's interest, and even more so her inner knowledge, are concentrated around Naomi'.[2]

Searching for more convincing arguments in favour of a possible female author of the book of Ruth, I would like to rephrase my initial question as follows: are there indications that the book

---

1. S.D. Goitein, 'Women as Creators of Biblical Genres', *Prooftexts* 8.1 (1988), p. 4.
2. Goitein, 'Women', p. 31.

of Ruth might stem from a women's culture? In recent years the hypothesis of a women's culture has been set up (in various forms) by anthropologists, sociologists and socio-historians in order to connect with the primary cultural experiences of women as expressed by women (despite the prevailing andro-centricity of interpretive theories and frameworks). With the aid of the concept of women's culture a distinction can be made between the roles, activities, preferences and rules of behaviour prescribed for women and those activities, preferences and functions which arise from the lives of women themselves. The literary critic Elaine Showalter has adopted the concept of 'women's culture' for her research into women-authored liter-ature. The most fruitful and enlightening elaboration of the idea of 'women's culture' is, according to Showalter, that developed by the anthropologists Shirley and Edwin Ardener. According to the latter women form 'a *muted group*, the boundaries of whose culture and reality overlap, but are not wholly contained by, the *dominant male group*'.[1] This means on the one hand that women are 'muted' in the sense that their voices are not heard or may not be heard at the authoritative 'speech-making' level of society. On the other hand it implies that women's culture should not be seen as a separate world, cut off from the dominant culture, but should rather be seen as forming an invisible background to the dominant culture. Within this subter-ranean women's culture women redefine 'reality' from their own perspective. However, since they are also part of the dominant culture that marginalizes them, the language that they speak, or write, is often 'double-voiced, containing a domi-nant and a muted story'.[2]

Inspired by Showalter's application of the concept of women's culture, I derive the following criteria from it for plausibly attri-buting female authorship to a text, in this case the book of Ruth;

1. E. Ardener, 'Belief and the Problem of Woman', in S. Ardener (ed.), *Perceiving Women* (New York: Halsted Press, 1978). Cf. Meyers's article in this volume.

2. E. Showalter (ed.), *The New Feminist Criticism: Essays on Women, Literature and Theory* (London: Virago, 1986), p. 266.

or, rather, for recognizing the voice speaking in a text as an F (female/feminine) voice:[1]

1.   the text should contain traces of an intent which is less than normally androcentric;
2.   there should be talk in it of a (re)definition of reality from the female perspective, so that
3.   the narrative contains defineable differences between the view of the male and the female figures.

As for the first criterion, Brenner[2] has pointed out that the story about Naomi and Ruth offers a marked contrast to the stereotypic biblical image of women as rivals, as seen in the cases of Sarah and Hagar, Rachel and Leah, and Hannah and Peninna. Since Naomi and Ruth also form a pair, they have the potential to act in binary opposition; however, they are a model of cooperation and mutual respect. They support each other instead of competing and, in this way, they reveal in an exemplary fashion how fruitful (in both a metaphorical and a literal sense) the cooperation between women can become. The relation between them is so close that it is described with the verb רבק, 'cling together' (cf. Gen 2.24). The book of Ruth thus contains, in sharp contrast to the prevailing androcentric depictions of relationships between women in the Bible, a celebration of the cooperation between them. We might see this as indicating the presence of an F voice.

The second and third criteria are also satisfied. At the beginning of the book of Ruth Naomi, in her extensive address to her daughters-in-law (Ruth 1.8-13), defines reality expressly from the perspective of a woman. Her daughters-in-law have to return to the 'house of their mother', in order to subsequently find peace in the 'house of their husband'. The expression 'house

1.   For the concept of an 'F voice' see A. Brenner and F. van Dijk-Hemmes, *On Gendering Texts: Female and Male Voices in the Hebrew Bible* (Leiden: Brill, 1993).
2.   A. Brenner, 'Female Social Behaviour: Two Descriptive Patterns within the "Birth of the Hero" Paradigm', *VT* 36 (1986), pp. 257-73; reprinted in A. Brenner (ed.), *A Feminist Companion to Genesis* (The Feminist Companion to the Bible, 2; Sheffield: Sheffield Academic Press, 1993).

of the mother', as used by Naomi, is quite exceptional in the Hebrew Bible. Besides Ruth it appears only in the Song of Songs (3.4; 8.2) and in Rebekah's story (Gen. 24.28). 'In the light of the importance of the concept of "father's house" in Israelite society', Carol Meyers considers it quite significant that in a female-orientated text like the Song of Songs the term 'father's house' is replaced by 'mother's house' (see her chapter in this volume). According to her this is an indication that the Song of Songs was a product of popular culture; or, as I have stated elsewhere, of women's culture.[1] If this is correct, then the same obtains for the book of Ruth.

Another example of redefining reality from a woman's perspective is to be found in Naomi's speech to Ruth in ch. 1. In this speech the bearing of sons is not related to the interest of the 'house of the father' but is seen instead as life insurance for women.[2] And again, at the end of the book of Ruth, a similar vision is tersely pronounced by the 'neighbouring women'. They redefine the reality wished for Boaz by the men of Bethlehem—the creation of a noble line of descent (Ruth 4.11-12)—by proclaiming that a son has been born to *Naomi* (4.17). The meaning that the women assign to the birth of this son is formulated completely in terms of its significance for the grandmother (instead of for the father). The new-born son is her 'redeemer', who returns her vitality to her, and who will look after her in her old age (4.14-15). The language used in the Naomi and Ruth story can thus be characterized as double-voiced. The dominant M (male/masculine) view is strongly countered, though of course not muted, by the story told by the women.

In addition to these arguments regarding content, formal arguments can be added in support of my proposal to see the Naomi and Ruth story as a product of women's culture and more specifically, with Goitein, as a creation of an old prophetess or wise woman. It has the characteristics of a popular story[3] that—in view of its 'elevated prose style'[4]—

1.   Brenner and van Dijk-Hemmes, *On Gendering Texts*.
2.   See also P. Trible, *God and the Rhetoric of Sexuality* (Philadelphia: Fortress Press, 1978), pp. 166-99.
3.   See J.M. Sasson, 'Ruth', in R. Alter and F. Kermode (eds.), *The*

probably came into being and was transmitted within circles of professional narrators. Following Gunkel[1] and inspired by the studies of Parry and Lord,[2] Campbell suggests that in ancient Israel there existed a 'guild' of professional storytellers. These were itinerant Levites whose task it was to educate the people, but also wise women. In the village square, or at the well, they would recite their stories at fixed times to the assembled public, and these stories were handed down within the 'guild' from generation to generation. If this suggestion is valid, then it is quite possible that the Ruth and Naomi story belonged to the repertory of a female professional storyteller, a woman old and wise like one of the heroines of her story, Naomi.

With regard to another characteristic of style, the *inclusios* that surround the various episodes in Ruth, Campbell risks the assumption that 'the audience participated in crafting these delightful *inclusios* during the period of the oral transmission of the story'.[3] This rightly draws attention to the fact that oral transmission always happens in an interplay between narrator and public. In the Song of Songs this phenomenon is clearly visible in the form of the dialogues between the I persona and the 'daughters of Jerusalem'. It demonstrates that orally transmitted songs or stories are always, though in varying degrees, the products of a collective process.[4] Even if, as in the case of Ruth, the interplay between narrator and public can only

Literary Guide to the Bible (Cambridge, MA: Harvard University Press, 1987), pp. 320-28, and Ruth: A New Translation with a Philogical Commentary and a Formalist-Folklorist Interpretation (Baltimore: Johns Hopkins University Press, 1979).

4.   E.F. Campbell, Ruth (AB, 7; Garden City, NY: Doubleday, 1975), p. 19.

1.   H. Gunkel, Genesis (Göttingen: Vandenhoeck & Ruprecht, 1910), p. xxxi.

2.   A. Parry (ed.), The Making of Homeric Verse: The Collected Papers of Milman Parry (Oxford: Oxford University Press, 1971); A.B. Lord, The Singer of Tales (Cambridge, MA: Harvard University Press, 1960).

3.   Campbell, Ruth, p. 14.

4.   See for instance M. Bal, Murder and Difference: Gender, Genre and Scholarship on Sisera's Death (Bloomington: University of Indiana Press, 1988), pp. 66-73.

be advanced as a hypothesis it is nevertheless highly plausible that this story is indeed a collective creation of women's culture, a story shaped by the cooperation between (a tradition of) wise women narrators and their actively engaged (predominantly F) audience.

NAOMI AND RUTH: FURTHER REFLECTIONS

Athalya Brenner

My essay on 'Naomi and Ruth' was written in 1981 and published two years later. At that time I was agitating to label the book of Ruth 'women's literature', in the sense that it was conceived for women and—perhaps—by a woman or women; but I did not know how to approach the issue of reading biblical passages from the (quite problematic) perspective of a womanly reader, let alone on the premise of female authorship. Recently, with the help of other readers, I have become a trifle more confident about raising this issue.

By itself, the centrality of a female figure (or two, as is the case in the Ruth scroll; but see Bal's essay in this volume) does not automatically imply that a female voice controls the textual proceedings. Nonetheless, if other textual elements uphold the central position of female interests, even though those elements comply with androcentric views,[1] probabilities swing in favour of a dominant textual position of female focalization and a female *voice*.

Is the child born, the sought-for true 'redeemer', Boaz's son? Of course he is. But, as van Dijk-Hemmes writes in this volume, within the narrative framework of Ruth—excluding the genealogical list, 4.18-22—the emphasis is on the child as Ruth's biological son and Naomi's adopted son. The end of ch. 4 signifies that Naomi benefits the most from the child's birth. This birth, rather than Boaz's unquestionable paternity, is certainly the

---

1. P. Trible, *God and the Rhetoric of Sexuality* (Philadelphia: Fortress Press, 1978); Y. Zakovitch, *Ruth: A Commentary* (Hebrew; Miqra LeYisrael; Tel Aviv: Am Oved; Jerusalem: Magnes, 1990).

foremost issue of the story—especially as the narrative itself is concluded before the genealogy. The focalization, then, is—surprisingly enough—a women's rather than a man's although, to be sure, a traditional social hierarchy of family politics is observed (and the genealogy is patrilineal).

At the end of the narrative (prior to the genealogy), both Ruth and Boaz lose their subjectivity; Naomi and Obed retain theirs. Obed is the true 'redeemer' but in terms of the text a baby, a voiceless minor. Naomi, who puts the baby in her lap, performs the last act. The neighbouring women are given the last word, including the naming speech. Women's culture[1] exists within men's culture and is, in many respects, subordinate to the latter. Still, in this text it is ultimately allowed precedence and concluding power over the male culture within which it is usually submerged and hardly recognizable.[2] The female joy expressed here, the celebration of a successful quest, finally appear to have less to do with patriarchal values than at first meets the eye.

Not only women's joy but also women's desires are widely acknowledged alongside the more conventional, socially encouraged female virtues. Ruth is a diligent worker, kind and seemingly obedient. Her sexuality, however, is denied neither by Naomi, nor by herself, nor by the narrator. It hardly matters whether the nocturnal scene at the threshing floor is that of *unrealized* erotic tension (as suggested by Zakovitch[3]) or else of sexual consummation (as suggested by Bledstein in this volume). One can leave this important and interesting issue undecided, provided the foregrounding of Ruth's sexuality *per se* is recognized. This is the means chosen by Naomi, and followed by Ruth, for stirring Boaz toward the required decision; it would seem that a juridical approach, which is Boaz's choice, would not have supplied the sought-for solution by itself.

A comparison of the preparations undergone by Ruth in ch. 3 to the preparations undergone by females in the Esther scroll

1. A. Brenner and F. van Dijk-Hemmes, *On Gendering Texts: Female and Male Voices in the Hebrew Bible* (Leiden: Brill, 1993).
2. Cf. Trible, *The Rhetoric of Sexuality*, and the paper by van Dijk-Hemmes in this volume.
3. Zakovitch, *Ruth*.

(Esther 2) might be instructive when considering the proposal that a male voice informs the proceedings. At any event, it is obvious that female sexuality and female initiative are far from censured in both texts (Ruth and Esther). Is this so only because it is imagined by readers, even before reading ch. 4, that Ruth's sexual initiative is motivated by the wish to acquire a male child (or, in the Esther scroll, by the wish to save the Jews)? Such an assumption is not corroborated by the beginning of ch. 3 (or by Naomi's phrases to her daughters-in-law in ch. 1), although it is seen later to have some validity. To begin with, Naomi declares that a solution must be found for Ruth as a patronless individual (3.1), not as a childless woman: whether the two are one and the same in the ancient cultural milieu is a moot point. Ruth herself, to begin with, acts as a provider rather than looking for one.[1]

Did women in antiquity realize themselves exclusively or chiefly as mothers, or is this another example of tendentious (textual) propaganda designated to further social (male) ideology? Or is the assumption of the indispensability of children, especially sons, for ancient Hebrew women another case of biased reading? Somehow we all agree that the lack of sons, the physical risks that giving birth entailed notwithstanding, was mourned by biblical women and men alike; we largely attribute women's practise of birth control and legitimized escape from childbirth to another age, another religious ideology. At any rate, Ruth's desire for a mate and male protection for its own sake seems overtly acknowledged in ch. 3. There is no reason to include the security of having a son in the initial plan—for Ruth it is a bonus, not the initial goal. Likewise, for Naomi, it is a bonus initially (ch. 1) unhoped for.

The motivation for reading the son's birth as the ultimate goal of the two women stems from Naomi's lack of and desire for sons. Significantly, when Ruth gets what Naomi wants for her, the husband Naomi assumes she desires or needs, she retires backstage. Naomi is the one who is 'redeemed' by the child, a turn which corresponds to her continuing role in the story as a mother figure. Thus a distinction is made between two possible female desires: a desire for a mate, and a desire for a child.

---

1.   Trible, *The Rhetoric of Sexuality*, pp. 180, 184-85.

These two types of desire are illustrated by means of two related though distinct personae. In short, the female voices in the scroll are not stereotyped: they are related yet differentiated. They might be read as reflections of joyous female release from existential hardships, be the problem the lack of a mate, the lack of a child, or both.

Although there is no way of 'proving' that the scroll was authored by a female, there is also no reason to privilege its supposed authorship by a male. Furthermore, the issue should not be restricted to, and formulated in terms of, the question of *authorship*, which is to some extent extrinsic to the text itself; rather, it must be shifted to definitions of *authority* and *voice*, which are intrinsic to it. From the perspective of authority, the dominant voices reconstructed in the text appear to be F (female/feminine). In that sense, the scroll is an expression of women's culture and women's concerns.

My original reconstruction of the scroll's literary history constitutes a speculation which assigns much force to oral traditions. At the time I did not relate orality specifically to the concept of *female* traditions. I feel safer in doing so now, drawing on the work of—among others—Goitein and van Dijk-Hemmes.[1] I therefore wish to specify now that, in my reconstruction, the 'family traditions' referred to might be women's traditions. With hindsight, I still see my proposed reconstruction of the scroll's textual history as a plausible inter-pretation which, obviously, does not exclude others. But I have come to realize that no interpretation should ignore the femi-nization of social concern and personal ambition which occupies centre stage in the scroll.

Once a recognition of the scroll's feminized universe is enter-tained, it highlights other features of narrative and characteriz-ation. The narrative is, first and foremost, a story of individual (physical and social) survival. Whose survival story? Not the survival of Elimelech and his sons—they die quickly within the exposition. Not Boaz's, since his primary survival is assured by his social station and economic circumstances. The survival

1. S.D. Goitein, 'Women as creators of Biblical Genres', *Prooftexts* 8.1 (1988), in Brenner and van Dijk-Hemmes, *On Gendering Texts*.

theme belongs primarily to two women. We have to reach the middle of ch. 4 in order to understand that community interests mainly coincide with, and reflect, the interests of the female figures. Who might be interested in a presentation of female interests as community interests rather than the other way round? A possible answer to this query is women, eager to hang on to any exemplum that might grant them some empowerment in similar situations of defencelessness, isolation and bereavement. Or perhaps men, eager—for some reason—to adopt a women's viewpoint.

I have previously attempted to show that, on the psychological as well as the textual level, Ruth and Naomi are two facets of a single personality, dramatically split. Each of the two is motivated by a particular desire; together they present a synthesized figure of 'full', ideal(ized) femininity, sexual as well as matronly. Together, Naomi and Ruth are the one whole. The fact that they are split in the story, in accordance with two separated role models, brings us back to the initial question of authority and voice. Is the splitting off of female functions a reflection of stereotypical male views of female nature? Is the device of finally uniting the split halves—for at the end of ch. 4 Naomi and Ruth coalesce and merge into the mother function—a reflex of male views of women?[1] Or does the voice in the narrative sound like a woman's voice, a woman well trained and socialized into a male world (Goitein, Campbell, van Dijk-Hemmes?)[2] The critical choice each reader makes is a matter of gendered reading inasmuch as it will affect interpretation through the recognition of gendered text authority.

---

1. Cf. Bal's article in this volume.
2. Goitein, 'Women'; E.F. Campbell, *Ruth* (AB; Garden City, New York: Doubleday, 1975), in Brenner and van Dijk-Hemmes, *On Gendering Texts*, and in this volume.

Part III
ON SOME ANCIENT COMMENTS

A THEMATIC APPROACH TO RUTH IN RABBINIC LITERATURE

Leila Leah Bronner

Introduction: Acting for Love

The book of Ruth presents the sages of the Midrash and Talmud with a unique social and religious problem. In the figure of Ruth they are faced with a Moabite woman, a descendant of a people that the Pentateuch emphatically proscribes from entering the congregation of the Lord (Deut. 23.1). In the biblical verses she is depicted from the start as an exemplary woman—a heroine by the merit of her own actions—before she enters the Israelite fold. The problem of when the story was actually put into written form remains unresolved and bears on our concerns here, but what matters more for this discussion is the fact that the Talmudic sages generally accept the traditional claim that it was written by Samuel (*B. Bat.* 14a). Yet they place Ruth not after Judges in the biblical canon but among the Writings, indicating that they too are unsure of its date. Faced with the cognitively dissonant exemplary character of this foreign woman, who will also become the ancestress of the Davidic line, the rabbis of the Talmud feel that they have to halakhically legitimize Ruth's conversion. Then, having accomplished her acceptance into the fold, they wish to underscore her merit and extraordinary kindness and valor, which make her a suitable figure to stand at the beginning of the Davidic (messianic) line.

They study the book closely and take any good characteristic of Ruth, enlarging and embellishing it to portray her as a very special woman, a paragon of piety and virtue. Ruth is the only 'convert' to have a biblical book named after her—a profound and unparalleled honor. Moreover she is, with Esther, one of only two women to have this distinction. I shall examine several themes in the Midrash related to the life and character of Ruth, which will reveal a Ruth possessing the feminine virtues the rabbis want to hold up for emulation. In her introduction to the section on Ruth in the *Interpreter's Bible*, Louise Pettibone Smith remarks that 'Ruth acts always for love and trust of Naomi, "doing all that she bade her"'.[1] I would expand that to say that Ruth, in both the original biblical narrative and in the midrashic retellings, is seen to act out of love for Naomi, but also out of a more general love and generosity, embodying the quality known in Hebrew as *ḥesed*, a term generally rendered in English as 'loving kindness' and discussed further below.

The Theme of *ḥesed*

The theme of kindness is central to the book of Ruth. Rabbi Ze'ira stresses this characteristic of the narrative: 'This scroll [of Ruth] tells nothing either of cleanliness or of uncleanliness, neither of prohibition or permission. For what purpose then was it written: To teach how great is the reward of those who do deeds of kindness' (*Ruth R.* 2.13). *ḥesed* is indeed one of the key words controlling the text. The word occurs three time: at the beginning, in the middle, and at the end of the story (Ruth 1.8, 2.20, 3.10). The scroll commences with the *ḥesed* Ruth does for Naomi—from gleaning in the fields to bringing food—and the *ḥesed* she does in honoring the memory of the dead in Naomi's family (which becomes, by marriage, her own). 'And Naomi said to her daughter-in-law, "blessed be he of the Lord, who has not left off his kindness [*ḥesed*] from the living and from the dead"' (Ruth 2.20). Boaz says to Ruth, 'Your last act of *ḥesed* is better than your first that you did not go after the young men whether rich or poor'. He promises to look after her needs.[2]

Every character acting in this brief story—from Naomi to Ruth to Boaz to the minor characters—behaves in a manner that demonstrates this heroic concept of some form of *ḥesed*. The main actors of the story all act in the spirit of *ḥesed*; some

1. L.P. Smith, *The Interpreter's Bible*, II (New York: Abingdon Press, 1954).
2. Ruth 3.10; see Y. Zakovitch, *Ruth: A Commentary* (Hebrew; Miqra LeYisrael; Tel Aviv: Am Oved; Jerusalem: Magnes, 1990).

perform ordinary ḥesed, and some—especially Ruth—extra-ordinary ḥesed. Their exemplary behavior is somewhat reminiscent of that of the patriarchs and matriarchs. The Ruth narrative resembles the older narratives in language, content, and style (Ruth 3.3-9; cf. Gen. 24.12-14). Ruth, like Abraham—the founder of the nation, the first of the proselytes—leaves the house of her father and mother and goes to join a people who, as far as she knows, will not accept her because of her foreign origins (*Gen. R.* 59.9; *Suk.* 49b). Yet she will not be dissuaded and joins the Israelite nation, with no thought of reward for this act of affiliation, and in this lies her great ḥesed. The rabbinic sources emphasize the superabundancy of ḥesed, its 'more-than-enoughness'. As Maimonides puts it, the concept of ḥesed

> includes two notions, one of them consisting in the exercise of beneficence toward one who deserves it, but in a greater measure than he deserves it. In most cases the prophetic books use the word ḥesed in the sense of practising beneficence toward one who has no right at all to claim this from you.[1]

Ruth's mode is the second, to practice benevolence toward people who have no claim on her for it.

The Righteous Proselyte

Both the Midrash and the Talmud place great importance on the story of Ruth's conversion, at times emphasizing similar aspects of the event, at other times focusing on different aspects. Having recognized Ruth as a צדקת, 'righteous person' (*Ruth R.* 2.12), the sages find themselves needing to 'justify' her affiliation with the Jewish people; hence they seek to make her conversion 'kosher' by rationalizing it halakhically. Ruth's initial Moabite-ness is a problem: the Pentateuch forbids Moabites from entering the congregation of the Lord because they have violated the principle of hospitality, having denied the Israelites water and bread during their desert wanderings and, further, having hired Balaam to curse them.[2] The rabbis interpret this Pentateuchal

---

1. Maimonides, *The Guide to the Perplexed*.
2. Deut. 23.4ff.; the Ammonites are also included in the prohibition,

prohibition to mean that *male* Moabites are forbidden to come into the congregation of the Lord, basing this interpretation on the use of the male singular form in the biblical text. It is the Moabite *men*, not the Moabite women, who have violated the laws of hospitality by denying assistance to the Israelites. This ingenuity of interpretation enables the sages to sanction Ruth's acceptability (*Yeb.* 76b).

The Talmud and the Midrash describe in detail Ruth's conversion, which is placed within the framework of the famous scene in which Naomi begs her two daughters-in-law to return to their own parents and people (1.7-18). Naomi tries to reason with them and dissuade them from remaining with her—a course that holds out no hope and no future for them. Orpah heeds her advice and goes home to Moab. Ruth, by contrast, utters the famous speech, 'Entreat me not to leave thee, and return from following after thee' (Ruth 1.16). The midrashic exegesis begins its minute description of Ruth's conversion by commenting on this verse. Ruth first tells Naomi that she has fully resolved to become converted to Naomi's God under any circumstances, but it is better that it should be at Naomi's hands than at those of another. Naomi responds by relating the laws of conversion, because she realizes how sincere Ruth is in her resolve. (The Jewish attitude toward conversion is quite different from that of actively proselytizing religions such as Christianity; converts are not solicited, and when prospective converts present themselves they are discouraged at first, and must prove their sincerity and conviction. It is also prohibited to dissuade a proselyte too much, and here, since Naomi is now convinced of Ruth's determination, she sets out the rules. This is a talmudic law which the sages in Yebamot derived from the Ruth and Naomi episode [*Yeb.* 47a]; it is discussed further later.)

According to the *Midrash Ruth Rabbah*, Naomi says to Ruth, 'My daughter, it is not the custom of daughters of Israel to frequent Gentile theatres and circuses', to which she replies, 'Whither thou goest, I will go' (*Ruth R.* 2.22). 'Gentile' is the translator's choice; the Hebrew '*obdê kôkābîm*, literally

---

which was to apply for ten generations; seven nations can never intermarry with Israelites, and must be destroyed.

'worshippers of the stars and constellations', would be better rendered as 'pagans' or 'idolators'; moreover, the mention of theaters and circuses betrays the times when the Midrash was composed, and is anachronistic in the context of when the story of Ruth is set. The daughters of Israel, Naomi continues in the Midrash, dwell in homes that have a *mᵉzûzâ*—a scroll bearing certain biblical verses which is attached to the doorpost in obedience to Deuteronomic law (Deut. 6.9). Ruth indicates her acceptance of this precept, and declares that she will lodge only where Naomi will lodge. The biblical phrase, 'thy people shall be my people' is taken in the Midrash to indicate her acceptance of all the penalties and admonitions of the Torah. Her acceptance of all the remaining commandments, according to the rabbis' interpretation, is expressed by the rest of the sentence, 'Thy God [shall be] my God'.

The midrashic sources, as we have seen, place great importance on Ruth's conversion. The talmudic sources likewise harp on this theme, at times emphasizing similar aspects of the event and at other times new and different aspects. The Talmud takes Naomi's behavior toward Ruth as the paradigm to teach that one must not over-dissuade a proselyte. The talmudic sages cite the verse, 'And when she [Naomi] saw that she [Ruth] was steadfastly minded to go with her, she left off speaking unto her' (Ruth 1.18) as scriptural justification for the principle that one should not dissuade a would-be convert too much.[1] In the talmudic reading, Naomi begins the conversion ritual by teaching the importance of the Sabbath observance. She tells her that Jews are prohibited to go beyond the set Sabbath boundaries (*tᵉḥûm šabbāt*) on the day of rest. Ruth replies, 'Whither thou goest I will go'. Naomi then turns to sexual matters between men and women. Private meetings (*yiḥûd*) between men and women (besides husband and wife and family members) are forbidden. Ruth replies, 'Wherever you lodge, I will lodge'. Naomi tells her that the Jews have been commanded to observe 613 commandments. Ruth replies, 'thy people shall be my people' (Ruth 1.16). According to the *gematria* (the talmudic

---

1. *Yeb.* 47a; *Ruth R.* 1.14; *Ruth Zuta* 49.44; D. Hartman, *Das Buch Ruth in der Midrasch-Litteratur* (Leipzig, 1901), p. 98.

tradition of numerology, in which each letter is given a numerical value), the name Ruth adds up to 606. The sages speak of the seven precepts of the laws that all descendants of the Noahides[1] had to obey. Thus the sages claim that even Ruth's name indicates her acceptance of all the 613 commandments of the Torah: her name equals 606 and, with the addition of the seven Noahite precepts she already observes, it totals 613, the number of commandments of the Torah.[2] The passage in *Yebamot* continues to interpolate discussions of Jewish law within the dialogue of Naomi and Ruth.

The selections from rabbinic sources describing Ruth's conversion present an image of a steadfast and determined person, firm in her decision to join the Israelites. The image is in keeping with all the other depictions of her in the biblical sources and in the rabbinic retellings. Once she decides to cast her lot with her mother-in-law's people, she displays no questioning or doubts about what is expected of her as a member of her adopted people. She accepts all the duties and requirements with no complaint, and expresses her willingness to comply with all that is required of her.

The process of Ruth's conversion, as described in the biblical verses, is far from the conversion process developed in later, codified Jewish practice. The rabbis try to interpolate features of the 'official' process into their retelling of her story, but prominent features of what became part of the halakhic process once it was codified (for instance immersion) are generally absent from the rabbinic accounts; in fact, one Midrash actually has Ruth immersing herself, which is based on the verse in which Naomi says to her, 'go wash thyself'.[3] All this interpretive labor

---

1. The seven Noahite laws are considered in rabbinic tradition as the minimal moral duties enjoined by the Bible on all people: *Sanh.* 56-60; *Yad, Melakhim* 8.10, 10.12. Jews are obligated to observe the whole Torah, while every non-Jew is a son of the covenant of Noah (Genesis 9).

2. P. Melzer, *Ruth* (The Five Scrolls; Jerusalem: Mosad Harav Kuk, 1973), p. 21.

3. Ruth 3.3; in *Ruth R.* 5.12, the Midrash explains as follows: 'wash yourself, clean yourself from your idolatry by ritual immersion'; see M. Zlotowitz and N. Scherman, *The Book of Ruth* (Art Scroll Tanach

has several motives: first, to show what constitutes a proper conversion in the Jewish tradition (the convert had to be sincere and determined, and willing to accept the intense duties and obligations of Jewish law); secondly, to show a paragon of docile, loyal, compliant female behavior; and thirdly, to legitimize Ruth's conversion, in order to bolster the legitimacy of the Davidic line.

The rabbinic sources emphasize the need for a convert to assent to the host of ritual requirements of Jewish law. They do not expend much attention on the desirability of conversion itself. Their focus on making certain that a conversion is sincere and valid contrasts sharply with the attitude evident in the books of Ezra and Nehemiah. Both Ezra and Nehemiah call for the foreign wives of the returning Israelite exiles to be sent back to their own people. Why do they insist on this? No adequate answer has been given, though several explanations have been advanced. I would suggest that the concept of conversion had not been formulated by the time of Ezra and Nehemiah.[1] Moreover, as others have suggested, it may have seemed risky to Ezra and Nehemiah during their historical period for a small, newly established, unstable province like Judah under the Persians to allow its members to intermarry with their neighbors. This might erode the identity of the people and undermine the relative independence and autonomy of the province. To a great extent, such concerns centered on questions of identity, especially in relation to maintaining their unique religion. The Judeans were divided between those who had remained in the land and those who returned from Babylonian exile. To allow too many foreign women to marry into the nation, some feared, would further threaten its unity.

Another explanation has recently been proposed, suggesting that the reason behind the expulsion of the foreign wives was economic. The laws of inheritance extant among the foreign peoples who had married Judeans gave women some rights to inherit land, which, if exercised, might cause lands belonging

Series; New York: Mesorah Publications, 1976), p. 109.

1. S. Safrai, *The Jewish People in the Days of the Second Temple* (Hebrew; Tel Aviv: Am Oved, 1970), pp. 32ff.

originally to Judean men to fall into the hands of foreigners in the event of the husband's death.[1] Until recently, many scholars have seen the book of Ruth as having been written—against Ezra and Nehemiah—for the polemical purpose of permitting foreigners into the 'congregation of the Lord'. The book of Ruth has been regarded as representing a universalistic trend among the Jews, in a vein similar to that of the exilic prophecy of Deutero-Isaiah; whereas the books of Ezra and Nehemiah represent a narrow nationalistic trend, oriented toward protecting the identity of the community from dilution by inter-marriage. According to this view, 'Ruth was a protest paper by the universalists against the stringency of Ezra–Nehemiah nationalism, based on a subtle reminder that David's grand-mother was a Moabitess'.[2]

More recently, this view has generally been rejected, scholars adducing to support their view the book's mild tone, which would bely a harsh polemical intent. The difficulty in dating the composition of Ruth compounds the difficulties we have in assessing its purpose and motive. A very wide range of datings have been offered for its composition, ranging from pre-exilic times to a late postexilic date, and a definitive date would be very helpful in settling these questions. I have already men-tioned that the rabbinic sources, which are our concern here, take the book as having been written by the prophet Samuel, and place it in the canon among the Writings, indicating some uncertainty about the date, but still placing it squarely in pre-exilic times.

The Resonance of Names

The thematics of the Ruth narrative—the theme of *ḥesed* in particular—are evident from the names of the characters in the story, and are brought out by the rabbis' attentive interest in the subject. The ancient peoples of the Middle East and the

---

1. T.C. Eskenazi, 'Out from the Shadows: Woman in the Postexilic Period', *JSOT* 54 (1992), pp. 25-43.
2. E.F. Campbell, Jr, *Ruth* (AB, 7; New York: Doubleday, 1975), pp. 26-27.

Mediterranean world believed in the potency of names, and closely identified the name with the person to which it referred. The sages considered names to be of special import in the book of Ruth; the names of all the actors in the Ruth story are discussed in *Midrash Ruth Rabbah* and in other rabbinic texts, and the rabbis offer one or more explanations of the significance of each.

The character Elimelech bears a name that means 'to me belongs royalty'. Elimelech is eager for the status of royalty; he seeks position and honor for himself, but does not seem particularly eager to give of himself on behalf of the people. He never demonstrates courage or *ḥesed*, and is denigrated by the sages for leaving Judah and evading his responsibilities as a leader in time of crisis. His behavior fails to live up to what his name would require of him—he claims the right of royalty but not its obligations. He serves in the narrative as the antithesis of the quality embodied in its heroines and heroes, *ḥesed* both ordinary and extraordinary (*B. Bat.* 9a, *Ruth R.* 1.2). Elimelech has two sons, Mahlon (meaning 'the sickly') and Chilion ('the one who came to an early end'); both die young, fulfilling the meaning of their names.

Naomi, the wife of Elimelech, whose name means 'sweetness, pleasantness', personifies everything pleasant (*Ruth R.* 2.5). She demonstrates *ḥesed* in her behavior, and—after some trying, bitter experiences—eventually enjoys an agreeable and sweet life. In the biblical narrative, Naomi herself notes that during the sad and difficult part of her life her name seemed inapposite:

> Call me not Naomi, call me *mārâ* [that is, 'bitter']; for the Almighty hath dealt very bitterly with me. I went out full, and the Lord hath brought me back home empty; why call ye me Naomi, seeing the Lord hath testified against me and the Almighty hath afflicted me (Ruth 1.11).

Boaz has a name that is easily glossed: *bôʿaz* means 'in him is strength'.[1] And Boaz is a man of substance and strength. Gallant in his actions, he sets *ḥesed* and justice on its correct course by redeeming his kinsman's inheritance, and goes beyond duty by

---

1. A.J. Rosenberg, *The Five Megillot* (London: Soncino Press, rev. edn, 1984), p. 121.

marrying a widow—an outsider, a woman alone. In the first sentence in which he is introduced in the biblical narrative, Boaz is called a *gibbôr ḥayil* (a mighty man of valor), the masculine equivalent of *'ēšet ḥayil* (woman of valor),[1] a term of praise applied to Ruth in the scroll and by the rabbis.

The rabbis find the figure of Orpah difficult to characterize and explain, and this leads them to treat her in ways that reveal much about the midrashic process in general. They are not sure what to make of Orpah as she is presented in the original biblical narrative—she is loyal (when her loyalties conflict, she agrees with Naomi's suggestion to return to her own people), and this loyal behavior (and the docile, obedient quality shown by her willingness to follow her mother-in-law's counsel) is good. But it is not *as* good as Ruth is in her decision to disregard Naomi's advice and remain with her adopted people. Orpah's name, according to the Midrash, comes from *'orep*, which is the Hebrew for the nape of the neck; her name is said by the sages to refer to her turning her nape to Naomi when she agrees to return to Moab. That the sages point to this moment in her history as the one signified by her name indicates that they consider this the most important part of her story. Whether her action and motives here are to be judged good—and exactly how good—is a difficult judgment for the commentators to make. The difficulty Orpah poses for the sages is answered by energetic midrashic invention: to explain and interpret the story given in the biblical account, they embroider further stories—a basic procedure in the midrashic mode of interpretation. The rabbis who want to emphasize Orpah's goodness proffer stories that support such a view; those who see her as more bad than good offer stories that show her in a negative light. For example, midrashic tradition holds that Orpah is the mother of Goliath, an enemy of Israel, and the rabbis seem to find this fitting. For some midrashic commentators Orpah is not only not completely good, she is downright infamous. According to some midrashim, her son Goliath was derided as 'the son of a hundred fathers', which implies a serious slur on his mother's

1. L. Ginsberg, *Legends of the Jews* (7 vols.; Philadelphia: Jewish Publication Society of America, 1946), V, p. 258 n. 271.

character (*Ruth R.* 2.20, *Soṭ* 42b). Both kinds of stories, those that malign Orpah and those that extol her, are invented out of whole cloth as needed by the sages to prove their case. The final result is that the figure that emerges in the midrashim about her is as ambiguous as in the original biblical story.

Let us return to the significance of Orpah's name, which, the sages hold, speaks of her action in turning the nape of her neck to her mother-in-law when she agrees to Naomi's own suggestion that she and Ruth return to their own people. Orpah, facing conflicting loyalties, behaves well, in that she follows Naomi's counsel and also returns to her original familial loyalty, but she does not demonstrate the extraordinary *hesed* shown by Ruth, who makes a sort of leap of loyalty in electing to stay with her husband's people, whom she has come to feel are her own. We have seen that some sages regard Orpah quite positively, but rank her considerably lower than Ruth. Their midrashic exegesis embroiders her story by holding that she is the mother of Goliath, who would be an enemy of Israel—a move that seriously derogates her, and which is intensified by certain further haggadic elaborations (for instance the imputation of promiscuity). Some of this exaggeration of Orpah's failings may be the result of a process by which Ruth's goodness is constructed and presented in both Scripture and Midrash, the establishment of binary oppositions being a widespread strategy in narrative construction, and one much in evidence in the materials being considered in this study.

There are a variety of interpretations given in the Midrash for Ruth's name. Rabbi Johanan suggests a derivation from *rāwâ* ('to saturate'): 'Because she was privileged to be the ancestress of David, who saturated the Holy One, Blessed be He, with songs and hymns' (*Ber.* 7b). The name Ruth is also thought to be derived from the root *ra'ah* ('to see'), for Ruth 'sees' or considers her mother-in-law's words (*Ruth R.* 2.9). Non-midrashic sources such as the *Syriac Targum*, as well as modern scholars working from etymological evidence, consider it to derive from the root *rĕ'ût*, 'friendship' or 'female companion'.[1] I find this the most persuasive derivation and also the most

---

1.   BDB, p. 946.

appealing, as it keeps its focus on Ruth's own character (unlike the midrashic explanations, which advance other agendas, including bolstering the legitimacy of the Davidic line).

In making their case for Ruth's specialness and her fitness to stand as foremother of David, the sages describe Ruth's departure from the land of Moab into the land of Israel in language virtually identical to that used in describing the departure of the patriarch Jacob from the land of Canaan. They say that a righteous person's departure from a place leaves a void. The saintly person is the 'shining light', 'brilliance', 'distinction' and glory' of a place (*Ruth R.* 2.12). Ruth's departure is said by the rabbis to have depleted Moab of a great and saintly person; this is high praise, and the like is said of no other woman in midrashic literature. Ruth is shown throughout the biblical narrative as consistently giving and kind. As the main character of the book, Ruth continuously exhibits the spirit of *ḥesed*, the dominant theme of the text. Some maintain that Naomi also exudes this quality, as does Boaz. But what is remarkable in the narrative and the commentary is that a foreigner/convert is allowed to take the lead as the epitome of *ḥesed*—indeed, her case is unique in all of Scripture—and that such an exemplary character is female is also extremely rare.

Modesty: The Mark of Feminine Virtue

The sages crown the deserving with many and varied laurels. Ruth's modesty is pointed out by the sages and given great emphasis, as this is a quality they consider very important, especially in a woman. The prophet Micah says 'walk humbly [modestly] with God' (Mic. 6.8). Modesty is in midrashic thought a highly prized, beautiful quality, which should be cultivated by both men and women—in different ways appropriate to their gender. Women are commanded to develop this quality to a higher degree of perfection than is expected of men. 'The king's daughter is all glorious within' (Ps. 45.14; cf. *Num. R.* 1.3) is often quoted when proper female behavior is being set forth. The prescribed behavior entails keeping out of public space for reasons of modesty. Women's lives were meant to be highly private;[1] as the rabbis tend to put it, this is an intrinsic part of women's nature. This set of expectations is connected to the laws of $\c{s}^e ni\acute{u}t$ (modesty), which literally means 'being hidden'. These laws are designed to keep women from mingling with men or being in their presence, except in very circumscribed situations (they must not be alone with any men besides their own husbands or immediate family members; that is, their behavior must be governed by the laws of *yihud*—see above on Naomi instructing Ruth for her conversion).

Women are seen by the rabbis as seductive, and their behavior and demeanor must be regulated so as to preclude the eventuality of situations in which men will be tempted by their irresistible charms. Men are not expected to be able to control themselves unless women keep out of their presence and cover themselves and their hair (considered a powerful *'erwâ,* 'sexual incitement' [see *Ket.* 72a])—they are even forbidden to sing in the presence of men outside their family (*Ber.* 24a). From this concept of modesty a code of dress and manners for women developed in talmudic and midrashic sources. Women were expected to observe this code of behavior, and men were expected to respect it. There are stories in the Talmud in which men remove the headcovering of women in the street and are fined for such violations (see *Ber.* 20b). The rabbis say that the mother of Rabbi Kimhit deserved the blessing of having seven sons because of her meritorious practice of keeping her hair covered continuously, so that 'not even the beams of her house have seen the plaits of her hair' (*Yom.* 47a). So great was her merit that all seven sons became high priests (*Yom.* 47a, *y. Meg.* 72a, *Num. R.* end of ch. 2). The trepidation before the power of feminine allure, exhibited to some extent in the biblical sources and heightened in rabbinic exegesis, results in this extreme praise of female modesty. It also leads to highly complicated attitudes toward beauty, as will be shown later.

---

1.   But see Meyers' assessment (in her article in this volume) of gender roles in ancient Israel. According to her, the dichotomy between the 'private' and 'public' domains is a modern projection.

According to the rabbinic sources, Ruth is richly endowed with the quality of modesty. The sages say that what attracted Boaz to her was her modest walk and behavior. Whereas all the other women bend down to gather the ears of corn, Ruth sits while she gathers; all the other women hitch up their skirts, while Ruth keeps hers down; all the other women jest with the reapers, while Ruth is reserved (*Ruth R.* 4.6, Šab. 113b). According to the rabbinic retelling of her story, Ruth displays several exemplary qualities when reaping in Boaz's field: not only her modesty is in evidence but also her lack of greed, as she takes care not to take more than she was permitted according to the law of gleaning (indicating not only a lack of greed, but that she had knowledge of these laws and observed them [*Pe'ah* 6.5]). A reader of the book of Ruth might gather the impression that in ancient Israel the laws of alms for the poor (cf. Lev. 19.9-10, 23-24), especially for strangers, orphans and widows (cf. Deut. 24.19-21), as outlined in the Pentateuch, were observed; and the sages suggest that when Ruth had chosen to stay with Naomi and to adopt the Israelite laws, she learned these laws and obeyed them.

From their initial meeting in the field, Ruth and Boaz both demonstrate exemplary behavior and, moreover, mutually recognize one another's goodness. Boaz is magnanimous toward the strange woman gleaning in his field, and Ruth is careful not to exploit his kindness and his hospitality. Boaz is so impressed by the Moabite maiden that he encourages her to stay and glean in his field, admonishing his workers not to touch or reprimand her in any way (ch. 2). Something symbolic seems to be afoot in this scene in the field, when Ruth meets her future husband. The relationship begins because of her virtuous actions and because of Boaz's capacity to recognize them as such. His appreciation for Ruth's fine qualities comes to fruition during their subsequent meeting—the encounter at the threshing floor, engineered by Naomi (ch. 3). Their meeting and marriage has such an air of aptness—despite (or perhaps because of) all the elements of chance that entered into their meeting—that the sages see the gracious hand of Providence guiding them toward one another.[1]

---

1. The Soncino Bible, *Ruth*, p. 123.

The book of Ruth is, as Alter says, a 'betrothal narrative',[1] full of symbols of fallowness and fertility. Ruth is fallow but, as Boaz will offer her food and water that physically sustains her, when he becomes her husband he will make her fruitful—and both will thereby become progenitors of the Davidic dynasty.

Ruth's modesty remains intact when, at Naomi's instruction, she goes to Boaz at night at the threshing floor. Modern readers are likely to see this scene as fraught with eroticism. Ruth's bold action might easily be misconstrued by Boaz and by anyone who might have observed her. Yet Naomi dares to send her; and the sages, knowing the dangers of such a potentially brazen act, turn the scene into a heroic moment in which Ruth's modesty is proved once again, as is Boaz's continence and virtue. According to the Midrash, Boaz is one of the three most chaste men in the Bible, the others being Joseph and Palti (*Lev. R.* 23.11, *Gen. R.* 15.16, *Ruth R.* 3.13).

Naomi instructs Ruth thus when she sends her to the threshing floor to lie at Boaz's feet: 'Wash thyself, therefore, and anoint thee, and put thy raiment upon thee, and go down to the threshing floor' (Ruth 3.3). The Talmud says that Ruth reverses the order of Naomi's instructions, because she fears she might meet a man on the way, and her beauty will excite him, or he might take her for a harlot (*Šab.* 113b)—again, conduct that can be taken as evidence of her concern to behave so as to preserve her modesty. Yet even in the paragon of female virtue thus depicted the sages find and note a flaw: Ruth reports earlier that Boaz has told her to 'stay with the young men' (Ruth 2.21) whereas he has actually said to stay with the young women (Ruth 2.8). What might have been passed over as no more than a slip of the tongue is taken by the sages as an indication of impure thoughts on Ruth's part, a lapse they attribute to her heathen or Moabite background, from which, they say, she has not entirely freed herself (*Ruth R.* 5.11). This criticism is, however, short-lived, and the rabbis return to acclaiming Ruth's virtue, holding up for particular praise her prodigious modesty.

1. R. Alter, *The Art of Biblical Narrative* (New York: Basic Books, 1981), p. 58.

Ruth—Beautiful?

Nowhere in the biblical text is Ruth said to be beautiful. Despite
this some sages ascribe physical beauty to her—a common
ascription in their commentaries on exemplary female biblical
figures. Why do they add beauty to her already long list of well-
established admirable qualities? The sages praise beauty, and
point it out in male figures as well as female characters. They
say, for example, not only that Adam is beautiful, but that he is
even more beautiful than Eve (*B. Bat.* 58a); and even more
beautiful still is the *š*kinâ (one of the names for God in talmudic
literature, meaning 'Divine Presence' [*B. Bat.* 58a, *Pes. K.* 181]).
Neither the attractiveness of Adam nor of Eve is spoken of in
Scripture; these are midrashic traditions. Not only biblical
figures but also rabbis, for example Rabbi Johanan (*Ber.* 20a)
and many others (*B. Bat.* 58a), are said in talmudic writings to be
beautiful. Although there are some dissenting views and
counter-attitudes evident in the Midrash (some holding that
beauty is or can be vain and deceptive, as in *Mishnah Ta'anit*
[*Ta'an.* 4.8; see also *Bar.*]), the rabbis generally consider physical
beauty as a good thing, something to be appreciated, celebrated
and enjoyed—a gift from God. Beauty is bestowed by the rabbis
on Ruth as part of the midrashic process whereby she is
idealized even more than in the biblical tale, so as to make her
worthy of engendering the Davidic dynasty. This is in keeping
with the rabbis' marked propensity to bestow beauty on
important female characters in Scripture—underscoring the
comeliness of characters actually said to be beautiful in the text
and, as with Ruth, endowing with beauty characters the Bible
had neglected to favor in this manner.

When discussing the exemplary women of the Bible, rather
than the women of their own day, the rabbis generally treat
beauty as a desirable and admirable quality. The beauty of these
characters is taken as something that shows them to be perfect
creations of a perfect creator. When it comes to women of
their own day, the picture becomes more complicated. The
rabbis rarely mention individual women in the Talmud, and
the physical appearance of the few that they do name is not

discussed. This seems to reflect the rabbis' concern for sexual propriety. The beauty of the actual women around them is a dangerous matter, for it is fraught with the possibility of exciting uncontrollable and impure passions. The female characters of the Bible are evidently remote enough, so there is no problem where they are concerned.

There are patterned ways whereby the rabbis discover the beauty of biblical women in the scriptural materials relating to them. One midrashic trope is to say that a woman looks far younger than her years. This convention is applied in closely parallel midrashic traditions about Ruth and Sarah. Sarah's speech, 'After I have waxed old, I have had youth' (Gen. 18.12) is glossed by Rabbi Ḥisda as meaning, 'After the flesh was worn and the wrinkles multiplied, Sarah was rejuvenated and returned to her original beauty' (*B. Meṣ.* 87a). The rabbis further embroider Sarah's story by saying that she was as beautiful when she died—at the age, given in the Bible, of 127 (Gen. 23.1)—as she had been as a girl of twenty (*Gen. R.* 40.4, *Sanh.* 69b). Similarly, the rabbis say that Boaz took notice of Ruth because, at forty, she looked like a girl of fourteen (*Ruth R.* 4.4). In Scripture Sarah, after many years of barrenness, finally bears a child at the remarkable age of ninety (Gen. 18.17). Although Ruth's age is not specified in the biblical text, as one who has been widowed after ten years of marriage she is certainly a mature woman when she meets and marries Boaz. The rabbis give her age as forty, although the biblical narrative would be at least as plausible if she were a good ten years younger. This not only makes the youthfulness of her appearance the more striking, it also makes her bearing a child somewhat remarkable, in a way that is reminiscent of Sarah's prodigiously late maternity. The Midrash also claims that Ruth was lacking the main portion of the womb, but the holy one shaped a womb for her 'And gave her pregnancy' (*Ruth R.* 7.14 on 4.13). It is reported that Boaz, who is eighty when he marries Ruth, dies on the wedding night, after his son is conceived.[1]

---

1. *Ruth R.* 2.55; *Lekah Ruth* 4.17. This rabbinic story conjures up the image of Abraham, who begot his first child, Ishmael, when he was 86 years old and was 100 years old when he begot Isaac (Gen. 16.16; 21.5).

These midrashic nuances suggest that the marriage between Boaz and Ruth was hampered by many obstacles that had to be overcome to engender the birth of an important figure. For now, it is sufficient to note the thematic connection of female beauty, rejuvenation, and maternity following protracted barrenness.

The way in which the rabbis go about establishing Ruth's beauty is worth some attention. They resort to a fairly strenuous bit of textual interpretation, taking the fact that the Hebrew word *miqrêh* could be translated as 'hap' ('happening') or 'chance', or 'occurrence'. The word *miqrêh* is also connected by Rabbi Johanan with the word *q^erî*, a word from the same root, used in a stock fashion in rabbinic literature to refer to a nocturnal emission. In the portion of the narrative where Naomi sends Ruth to glean in the field, there is a verse that runs, 'and her hap was to light on the portion of the field' (Ruth 2.4). Although in the context of the narrative this sense would seem to modern readers rather remote, one midrashic reading seizes on the word 'hap' here, and takes the passage to indicate that Ruth was beautiful—so beautiful that any man who glimpsed her would have a sexual reaction (a 'pollution', as the rabbis would phrase it).[1] The rabbis also seize on the narrative threads that indicate that Ruth behaves with scrupulous modesty to avoid situations where her comeliness might be dangerously seductive, as we have seen in the section on modesty.

Royal Origins

Midrashic lore gives Ruth royal origins (*Ruth R.* 1.4; 2.9). According to the sages, not only Ruth but also her 'sister' Orpah (who will later, also according to Midrash, give birth to Goliath) is the daughter of King Eglon. The sages bestow royal origins on several foreign women mentioned in the Bible. For example, there is a midrashic tradition that holds that Hagar was the daughter of Pharaoh (*Gen. R.* 45.1). Hagar in the biblical narrative is the mother of an enemy of Israel (Ishmael).

---

1. *Ruth R.* 4.6; cf. *Meg.* 15a, where the sages discuss biblical beautiful women and suggest that Rahab by her beauty causes men to experience night pollution. Scripture nowhere describes her as beautiful.

Midrashic tradition maintains the same of Orpah, saying that she is the mother of Goliath (see above).

The sages relay a similar story about the biblical figure Timna, who appears in Genesis (Gen. 36.12) as the concubine of Eliphaz, one of the sons of Esau, and the mother of Amalek. Her story echoes those of Ruth, Orpah and Hagar. Midrashic lore holds that she 'asked to be received into the faith of Abraham, but they all, Abraham, Isaac and Jacob, had rejected her', whereupon she declares, 'Rather will I be a maidservant unto the dregs of this nation, than mistress of another nation'.[1] ('And so', according to the Midrash and talmudic tales as retold by Ginsberg, 'she was willing to be concubine to Eliphaz'.) The Midrash thus comes up with an explanation of why her son is an enemy—and, it is interesting to note, at the same time takes a positive attitude toward accepting would-be converts: 'To punish the Patriarchs for the affront they had offered her, she [Timna] was made the mother of Amalek, who inflicted great injury on Israel' (Gen. 20.3ff., *Gen. R.* 45.1). The Midrash on Pharaoh and Hagar includes similar language. After having been smitten by the beautiful Sarah and then immediately falling ill and therefore letting her go (Gen. 12), Pharaoh is impressed by the God of Israel for saving her in this way, as well as being impressed by the character of both Sarah and her husband. He later decides to give his daughter Hagar to Sarah, because he feels it better for her to be a maid in the House of Abraham than a princess in his own land.

The question of Ruth's royal origins is attended to at length in the midrashic sources. According to the rabbis Ruth's father was Eglon, king of Moab. They portray Eglon as a person of high ethical standards and, though a heathen, a righteous man (*Sanh.* 60a). The judge Ehud goes to Eglon in a ruse to kill him, saying, 'I have a message for you from the lord, the God of Israel'. When Eglon rises to honor God's name, Ehud kills him (Judg. 3). The rabbis claim that the reward for Eglon's piety was to have sired Ruth, from whom the messianic line would descend. Thus the line of David is royal on both sides, the father's and the mother's (*Ruth R.* 1.4; 2.9; *Sanh.* 105b).

---

1. *Sanh.* 99b; Ginsberg, *Legends of the Jews*, I, pp. 422ff.

Marriage, Birth, Redemption

There are some important themes in the closing chapter of the book that greatly affect our comprehension of the story. The entire Ruth narrative, though only four chapters long, moves consistently toward a climactic ending that results in the marriage of Ruth and Boaz, followed by the birth of Ruth's child from whom David—and the redemption of the Israelites—will eventually spring. As described above, several problems have to be faced by the two widows before Ruth takes courage, goes to the threshing floor and says to Boaz, 'spread thy wing over thy handmaid as thou art the redeemer' (Ruth 3.9)—that is, as he is the near kinsman of her husband's family, he should assist her and her mother-in-law in their plight by redeeming the land and marrying her.

Ancient and modern scholars alike disagree over whether certain passages in the book of Ruth deal with the custom of levirate marriage (Deut. 25.5-10), or with the law of the redemption of the land.[1] Some scholars, following the view of Josephus (*Ant.* 5.10, 4), express the opinion that the events concerning Ruth and Boaz (ch. 4) do describe a levirate marriage, but that is incidental to the primary matter of the redemption of the land. That is, the duty of the *gô'ēl* ('kinsman', from the biblical verb *gā'al*, 'to restore an object to its primal condition') to marry Ruth was incidental to the duties stemming from the laws concerning the redemption of property of a descendent; hence the narrative's departure in a number of details from the prescribed levirate marriage laws. The matter of the property—where it is situated, the nature of its disposition under the laws and customs governing inheritance rights where women are involved, and related issues—is very complicated and many of its aspects are obscure. For our purpose it is is sufficient to note that talmudic and midrashic discussions of these matters in the book of Ruth tend to focus on the redemption of the property, as in a passage from *Baba*

---

1. Lev. 25.25; see also Ibn Ezra. Deut. 25.5; Nahmanides, Gen. 38.8; Malbim, Ruth 4.5ff.

Meṣiʿa commenting on this verse from Ruth: 'Now this was the manner in former times in Israel concerning redeeming and concerning changing, for to confirm all things; a man drew off his shoe, and gave it to his neighbor' (Ruth 4.7). *Baba Meṣiʿa* notes that it is not clear in the biblical text whether Boaz gives the shoe to the kinsman or the kinsman to Boaz, and the question is not settled (*B. Meṣ.* 47a). What matters for the present discussion is that, despite what some commentators have argued, the transference of the shoe in Ruth 4.7 has nothing to do with the *ḥᵃlîṣâ*, the ritual of the taking off of the shoe in a levirate marriage described in Deuteronomy. Rather, in the Ruth story the shoe transfer formalizes a property exchange—the one other kind of transaction in which the shoe ritual was practiced (*y. Kid.* 160c, *Ruth R.* 1.11).

Edward F. Campbell holds that the book of Ruth bears witness to a pre-Deuteronomic form of levirate marriage, whereas Jack Sasson agrees with M.Z. Segal and Robert Gordis that what is described in Ruth has nothing at all to do with the levirate customs.[1] Under the laws of *gᵉʾûlâh* (the laws of redemption of property codified in Lev. 25) the kinsman must redeem Naomi's land. Segal suggests that the Ruth story implies the practise of laws of inheritance not included in the Pentateuch, whereby a woman could inherit property from her husband.[2] The Talmud and Midrash never treat Ruth as a woman who needs to get *yibbûm* (the fulfilment of the levir's duties toward her). Naomi clearly tells her daughters-in-law to return to their mothers' home as she has no more sons to give them (Ruth 1.11ff.)—when Naomi's sons died, there were no surviving brothers to fulfil the levirate laws. The widows are free to act as

---

1.   Campbell, *Ruth*, p. 133; J.M. Sasson, *Ruth: A New Translation with a Philological Commentary and a Formalist-Folklorist Interpretation* (Baltimore: Johns Hopkins University Press, 1979), pp. 137ff.; R. Gordis, 'Love, Marriage and Business in the Book of Ruth: A Chapter in Hebrew Customary Law', in H.N. Bream, R.D. Heim and C.A. Moore (eds.), *Light Unto My Path: Old Testament Studies in Honor of Jacob M. Myers* (Philadelphia: Temple University Press, 1974), pp. 248ff.; M.Z. Segal, *Introduction to the Bible*. III. *Ruth* (Hebrew; Jerusalem: Kiryat Sefer, 1955), p. 691; cf. Num. 27.8-11.

2.   *Ruth*, p. 691.

they wish. In Deut. 25.5-10 the rite has become obligatory: the woman *must* marry the levir, and only he can release her from the legal requirement either by marrying her (*yibbûm*) or by granting release (*ḥᵃlîṣâ*). There is a ritual that must be performed when a levir grants *ḥᵃlîṣâ*, and the woman takes part in it. In the Ruth narrative, Ruth is not present during the episode in which the shoe is exchanged, and this bolsters the argument that the shoe-removal ceremony described in Ruth is not a levirate rite. It is, rather, a legal procedure to redeem the land and transfer ownership from kinsman to redeemer.

The guiding theme of the book of Ruth, *ḥesed*—the kindness beyond the call of duty exemplified by Ruth, Boaz, Naomi and other characters—continues to operate in the final phases of narrative. Ruth is not obligated to marry Boaz but does, though he is old. He notes the *ḥesed* this entails, saying, 'thou hast shown more kindness in the end than at the beginning, in as much as thou didst not follow the young men, whether poor or rich' (Ruth 3.10). Had she been a *yᵉbāmâ* (one obliged to submit to levirate law), she would have been obliged to act in accordance with the requirements satisfied with *yibbûm*, and there would be no *ḥesed* in fulfilling the legal requirements. Likewise, Boaz is not one who simply fulfils the legal requirements of levirate marriage—he too acts out of kindness beyond duty. Moreover, Boaz is not an ordinary levir—he is not, in fact, the brother of the deceased husband and has no legal obligation to marry Ruth under the levirate rule. Rather, he is but a kinsman willing to redeem the land when a nearer kinsman refuses. In marrying Ruth he also 'raises up a name to the dead'. The willingness of this exemplary couple to accept obligations not incumbent upon them by law or custom makes them paragons of righteousness, living embodiments of *ḥesed*.

The theme of the redemption of the land is given in elaborate detail in the biblical narrative, and has also evoked lengthy and complicated midrashic exegesis. We have seen that the midrashic project regarding Ruth is greatly concerned with legitimizing her as the ancestress of David, the line from which the redeemer of Israel will spring. The theme of the redemption of the land can perhaps be seen as foretelling the theme of the messianic redemption of Israel.

Concluding Reflections

The Ruth narrative is the story of a foreign woman who chooses to cast her lot with her husband's people when she finds herself a childless widow. She demonstrates loyalty and steadfastness in her resolve to remain with her late husband's people, accepting their religion and customs and behaving in a fashion in keeping with the values of the Israelite community, as learned from her mother-in-law Naomi. As her story unfolds, she finds—with the help of Naomi and under the laws of her people—a worthy new husband, and produces a child. Although the Bible never explicitly says that she had been barren during her first marriage, the fact that she had no children during this ten-year union leads us to infer that she was effectively barren during the prime of her life. The path to her second marriage has to circumvent obstacles and difficulties, giving its positive outcome—especially the child born late in his mother's life—a miraculous quality.

I have argued that the sages emphasize certain aspects of Ruth's story and embellish it in ways that bolster her fitness as an ancestress of David and also as an ideal of feminine behavior. Thus to the loyalty, steadfastness, *hesed* and obedience she displays in the biblical text they add beauty, royal lineage and highly exaggerated modesty. Ruth may be regarded as the paragon of all the virtues the sages believe a woman ought to embody. Ruth's role is to be a faithful, modest daughter-in-law and, by remarrying and bearing a male child, to continue the male line of her deceased husband.

It is in marriage and motherhood that Ruth fulfils her role; and, by her dedication to these, the feminine functions and values respected and venerated by the sages, she wins their approval and esteem. They compare her to the matriarchs who built the house of Israel, whose merit derives almost wholly from their fulfilment of the maternal role. The sages accord great respect to the exemplary women of the Bible, more than they ever show toward any actual women of their own day. Ruth is afforded especially high honor. She is, however, praised to a great extent for qualities the sages themselves ascribe to her, in particular for sexual modesty and for committing herself to the wifely and maternal role. An embodiment of *ḥesed*, a loyal and obedient wife, a righteous proselyte—she is a fitting ancestress of the line of David.

The qualities Ruth displays in the biblical narrative itself and, even more, her qualities as developed in rabbinic interpretation—modesty, obedience, devotion to wifely and maternal duties—are not the qualities sought by feminists. As attractive as her character is, Ruth is not independent, autonomous and free of male control; on the contrary, she is docile and submissive, and this is why the sages laud and honor her. Other female characters in the Bible—for example Debora and Hulda—do embody forceful, independent qualities; and I intend to explore such biblical women in future studies.

Ruth according to Ephrem the Syrian

Jane Richardson Jensen

Before turning to Ephrem's images of Ruth, I shall give some information on Syriac Christianity and Ephrem; in particular, points which pertain to the subject of images of women. Syriac Christianity has several distinctive features: its language, its expression of theology and, in the early period, its interest in celibacy. As the name implies, the Syriac Churches use Syriac as the language of worship. Syriac is the Eastern or Christian dialect of Aramaic and differs significantly from the languages of the Western religious heritage (Latin and Greek). One significant linguistic feature of Syriac is that there is no neuter gender. Forms which can be determined grammatically are either masculine or feminine.

Unlike Western theology, which is based on definitions, Syriac theology is expressed in symbolism. The very word for symbol (*rāzā*) also means 'mystery'. Poetry is a particularly suitable vehicle for dealing with symbols or mysteries, as is evident in the writings of Ephrem.

All branches of early Syriac-speaking Christianity are known for their asceticism.[1] Scholars disagree about the place marriage and children were accorded in the Syriac Church; although Ephrem himself embraced the celibate life, he seems to have accepted marriage and children for others. Despite his church's preference for celibacy, he shows pastoral sensitivity to women who are unable to conceive.

---

1. R. Murray, *Symbols of Church and Kingdom: A Study in Early Syriac Tradition* (Cambridge: Cambridge University Press, 1975), pp. 11-18, 154-58, reviews the scholarship on the origins of Syriac asceticism.

Ephrem seems to have been born in Nisibis in 306 CE and to have ministered as a deacon there until the area was ceded to the Persians in 363. Then he moved to Edessa, the centre of northern Mesopotamia, where he wrote copiously until his death in 373. Nisibis (modern-day Nusaybin) and Edessa (or Urfa) are now in the southeastern part of Turkey, near the border with Syria. Nisibis is close to the Tigris River, while Edessa is near the Euphrates.

Ephrem is commemorated as a saint in the Syriac Churches (the Church of the East, the Syrian Orthodox, the Maronite, the Chaldean and the Syrian Catholic Churches), in the Roman Catholic Church and in the Scottish Episcopal Church among others. Pope Benedict XV declared him to be a Doctor of the Church in 1920.

Although Ephrem wrote commentaries, prose and verse homilies, he is best known for his metrical poetry or hymns. I wish to present Ephrem's commentary on Ruth in the general context of his use of female imagery.[1] He freely personifies abstract ideas, such as baptism, the Church and Sheol, as female. For example in *Hymns of Virginity* 7.8 he portrays baptism as a mother and the priest at the baptism as a midwife bringing the spiritual baby to second birth. Ephrem also applies female imagery to males, particularly himself and the bishops of the Church of Nisibis (see *Hymns of Nisibis* 6.13-15). He even depicts God as the Father and the Son as Mothers (*Hymns of Resurrection* 1.7, *Hymns of Nativity* 4.149-154). Ephrem's portrayals of women indicate that misogyny is not a factor in his avoidance of female imagery for the Holy Spirit. Yet he believes in a hierarchically ordered Holy Trinity with the Father first, the Son second and the Spirit third. To maintain the proper order of the Trinity, the Holy Spirit needs to be distinguished from the Syrian Goddess who is powerful and independent of her consort.

Ephrem discusses a number of biblical women. Yet in all of his vast literary corpus, there are only two passages about Ruth.

---

1. For more detail, see J.E. Richardson, 'Feminine Imagery of the Holy Spirit in the Hymns of St. Ephrem the Syrian' (PhD dissertation, University of Edinburgh, 1991).

Both of these are in the cycle called *Hymns of Nativity*. Both refer to Ruth's lying down with Boaz (Ruth 3), and so there is some overlap in the comments. The first excerpt is the thirteenth strophe of the first hymn:[1]

> Ruth lay down with Boaz because she saw the medicine of life hidden in him.
> Today her vow is fulfilled because the giver of all life arose from her seed (*H. Nat.* 1.13).

In this hymn Ephrem sees the fulfillment of various biblical prophecies in Jesus' life. He also considers the actions of certain biblical characters, such as Ruth or Tamar, and phenomena from the natural world, like the worm who gives birth asexually, the virgin earth and the staff of Aaron, as witnesses to Jesus' messiahship. To Ephrem there are a host of people (of both sexes) who foreshadow the messiah in their lives or deaths or perceive him and act on their perceptions. Along with the words of Isaiah, the psalmist (i.e. David), Micah, Balaam, Zechariah, Jacob and Solomon, Ephrem accepts Ruth's lying down with Boaz as corroborating evidence that Jesus is the messiah.

In strophe 13 Ephrem credits Ruth with two actions: lying down with Boaz and making a vow. He seems to realize that Ruth lay down beside Boaz rather than at his feet as suggested by the English translations of Ruth 3.4, 7, 8. This is indicated by his referring to Ruth's seed in the next line. Since the genealogies in the Bible are normally traced from the fathers and the mothers are usually omitted, it is significant that Ephrem claims that the giver of life arises from Ruth's seed, not Boaz's. Nevertheless it seems as if Jesus' whole (human) essence comes from Boaz because Ruth sees the messiah hidden in Boaz. Ephrem does not say whether she also sees the messiah hidden in herself. This omission is probably based on the ancient notion of the woman as a vessel into which the man plants the seed which grows into a baby. It is paradoxical that in strophe 13

---

1.   The excerpts given are my translations. The Syriac with German translations of the *Hymns of Nativity* are in CSCO 186. For an English translation of all of the *Hymns of Nativity*, see K.E. McVey, *Ephrem the Syrian: Hymns* (New York: Paulist Press, 1989).

Boaz seems more like a vessel, and Ruth is the one taking the seed. When Ruth looks at Boaz, she sees not only the future messiah hidden in him, but the medicine of life. The medicine of life is one of Ephrem's many titles for Jesus,[1] and indicates his outlook on life—the world is ill and needs a doctor.

Ruth's vow is probably at the end of her entreaty to Naomi in Ruth 1.16-17. After claiming Naomi's lodging, her people, her God, and her burial place, Ruth vows, 'May the Lord do so to me and more also if even death parts me from you'. In Moab Ruth has suffered the humiliation of not being able to conceive in ten years of marriage and then the death of her husband. But Ruth's loyalty to Naomi (and to her society's patriarchal system) is quickly rewarded; she gives birth to a son and the giver of life arises from one of her descendants.

H. Nat. 1.13 is one of the three instances where Ephrem seems to laud engaging in pre-marital sex. However, in *H. Nat.* 1.13 he overlooks Ruth's courage in doing what she does; he suppresses the sexual aspect of Ruth's lying down with Boaz by providing spiritual justification for her action. Ephrem also supplants sexuality with spirituality in *H. Nat.* 9.7, 12, 14-16. At first he seems to be extolling two virtuous women for being sexually aggressive before they are married. However, there are exceptional circumstances: Ruth and Tamar do what they do to bring about Jesus' birth. It would seem that the end justifies the means. The following strophes from *H. Nat.* concentrate on Ruth:

> 7. Chaste women were chasing after men because of you: Tamar desired a man who was widowed, and Ruth loved a man who was old. Also that Rahab who captivated men was captivated by you.
> 12. Ruth is proclaimed who sought your riches instead of Moab. Tamar rejoiced that her lord, who proclaimed her name instead of the son of her bitterness, came. Even her name was calling you to come to her.
> 14. Ruth fell down in the threshing floor for a man for your sake. Her love made her bold for your sake who teaches

1. S. Brock (*The Luminous Eye: The Spiritual World Vision of St. Ephrem* [Rome: CIIS, 1985]), surveys the different types of imagery that Ephrem uses. The medicine of life is discussed on pp. 77-91.

persistence to all penitents. Her ears despised all the voices for
the sake of your voice.

15. The throbbing coal went up and fell down in Boaz's bed.
She saw the high priest who was hidden in his loins: [she was]
fire for his incense. She ran and was a heifer for Boaz. She
would bring forth you, the fatted calf.

16. She went begging for her love of you. She gathered straw.
You paid her quickly the reward of her wretchedness. [She
reaped] the roots of kings instead of ears [of corn] and the sheaf
of life which descended from her instead of straw.

Ephrem lauds chaste women for chasing after men (strophe 7).
He includes Rahab, a former prostitute, in a strophe with Tamar
and Ruth. Whereas Tamar and Ruth pursue a man to bring
about Jesus' birth, Rahab, who has been catching men for her
livelihood, is caught by Jesus.

In strophe 12 Ephrem proclaims Ruth for choosing to leave
her home so that she will be in a position to bring about Jesus'
birth. This line about Ruth is inserted into a strophe about
Tamar because proclamation is the theme of strophe 12. The
chaste women of strophe 7 are rewarded in strophe 12 for
sacrificing their chastity. Jesus will share his wealth with Ruth,
and he proclaims Tamar's name, not her son's. Tamar's name
itself calls out to Jesus.[1]

Ephrem dramatizes Ruth's and Tamar's degradation even
more in strophe 13. It concentrates on Tamar, but Ephrem
includes Ruth when he says, 'Honourable women became con-
temptible for you'.

Ephrem describes a rather erotic scene in strophe 14. Ruth
falls down in the threshing floor for a man; that is to say, she
boldly lies down beside Boaz.[2] Ephrem acknowledges that she is

---

1. Ephrem seems to be combining the masculine singular impera-
tive *pe'al* of the verb 'to come' (*ta*) with 'lord' (*mar*) so that Tamar's
name can be understood as 'come! Lord'.

2. English translations of Ruth 3.4, 7, 8 have Ruth lying at Boaz's
feet. The Hebrew רגליו refers to the whole leg from the hip down to the
feet. Naomi's instructions to Ruth (Ruth 3.4) indicate that Ruth is going
to the threshing floor to arouse Boaz. 'He will tell you what to do' means
sexually as well as legally. Boaz does not want Ruth to be found on the
threshing floor with him, to protect her honour (v. 14). W. Burkert
(*Greek Religion: Archaic and Classical* [trans. J. Raffan; Oxford: Basil

going to the threshing floor to seduce Boaz by saying 'her ears despised all the voices'. No one but Naomi knows her plan. So the voices she hears are those of social conscience. Ruth is able to do what she does because of her love for Jesus who teaches persistence to all penitents—those who turn to him. Ephrem affirms Ruth's persistence and in no way condemns her actions.

At first Ephrem seems to advance the sexual nature of Ruth's actions (strophe 15). He calls her a throbbing coal who lies down *in* Boaz's bed—not at its foot, she actually looks at Boaz's genitals, she is sexually aroused (fire), she is a heifer eager to become pregnant. However, Ephrem modifies the sexual element by spiritualizing it. Boaz's genitals are arousing because they contain the seed of the high priest. Ruth's sexual excitement becomes fire for the high priest's incense. The language Ephrem uses changes a seduction on the threshing floor into a religious event worthy of a temple.

Strophe 15 describes a woman lying in a man's bed hoping to become pregnant. Ephrem skips from the seduction to Ruth's reward (strophe 16) without mentioning the redemption procedure and marriage. She goes 'begging' and gathers straw (Ruth 2.2ff.) because she loves Jesus. He indirectly repays her efforts when she becomes pregnant with Obed, David's grandfather, Jesus' famous ancestor. She has gathered straw to keep herself and Naomi alive, and as a result the sheaf of life descends from her.

The images of Ruth in these two passages are ambivalent. From one perspective Ruth is portrayed as an active, perceptive, persistent, hard-working woman. She violates social conventions, risking her life, for God's purpose. Neither the Bible nor Ephrem intimates that God suggests the actions to her. Rather she perceives the future messiah in Boaz and takes action to bring about what is to come. But from the other perspective the messiah is hidden in Boaz, not, apparently, in Ruth. The sexual

Blackwell, 1985], p. 159) relates the story of Demeter's conceiving Plutos ('Wealth') from copulating on the threshing floor at harvest. Even though Ephrem was probably unaware of the practices of Demeter's worshippers, seduction on the threshing floor would not have been unheard of.

nature of Ruth's action is overlaid with its spiritual justification. So Ruth the risk-taker becomes metaphorically Ruth the heifer who gives birth to the fatted calf.

Ephrem's hymns are gathered into collections entitled by later editors. It seems plausible for Ephrem to omit Ruth from, for instance, *Hymns of Nisibis*, of *Virginity*, *Easter*, *Fasting*, *Heresies*. However it is surprising that she is not mentioned somewhere in the *Hymns of Faith*. Since the hymns in a given collection do not all concern the subject of the title, but sometimes digress to other subjects, Ephrem could have included Ruth anywhere. It may be that Ephrem is prepared to acknowledge Ruth's role in bringing about Jesus' birth in hymns generally concerned with the nativity because Ruth is Jesus' foremother. Since he spiritualizes the sexual aspects of Ruth's experience, her sexual aggression may be problematic to him, a celibate deacon in a church which esteemed celibacy.

Part IV
COMMENTS IN ART

RUTH AND THE WOMEN OF BETHLEHEM

Zefira Gitay

Leonard Baskin, in his illustration of the Ruth scroll, chooses to portray the women neighbors as if they were watching the event through the windows of their houses (fig. 1).[1] It is only the female figures who are depicted in the illustration. They are inserted within the framework of the letters that create the Hebrew word השכנות (neighbors). Baskin's illustration is vivid and suggestive. It brings to life the question of the role of the women within the story of the book of Ruth.

The story of the book of Ruth focuses on the image of a woman whose actions and emotions have been exalted by the biblical narrator. It is a story of a woman who has lost every- thing she had had—her family and also her possessions. She is a woman of worth nonetheless, and her merciful actions are designed to be rewarded. But who is Ruth? What is her role in the scroll? And why is she depicted as the heroine who bears the title of the book?

Ruth marries a foreigner. Her husband, the son of a family from Bethlehem of Judah, came with his parents and his brothers to Moab, due to a famine in their own country (Ruth 1.1). Now Ruth is a Moabite, and the text seems to stress her origin (e.g. 2.2, 21) even though the discourse does not require this recurrent emphasis.[2] Why? The emphasis on Moab implies the intent to call attention to this unique phenomenon. The scroll

1. The illustration appears in A.H. Friedlander (ed. and trans.), *The Five Scrolls* (New York: CCAR Press, 1984), p. 242.
2. See D. Harvey, *The Book of Ruth* (IDB, 4; New York: Abingdon Press), p. 133.

alludes to various biblical episodes, thus inviting comparisons and implications. The relationship between Moab and Israel reflects an animosity that was created in the past. The overstressed reference to Moab may allude to the historical, hated enemy. The tradition regarding the exodus emphasizes the destructive role of Balak, the king of Moab, who refused to assist the people of Israel (Num. 22.2ff.). Moreover, when the people of Israel were staying at the outskirts of Moab in Shitim, 'the people began to have sexual relations with the women of Moab' (Num. 25.1). Another reference to this complex relationship between the Israelites and the Moabites is based upon the Deuteronomic law that specifically restricts the Israelites from marrying Moabites:

> No Ammonite or Moabite shall be admitted to the assembly of the Lord. Even to the tenth generation, none of their descendants shall be admitted to the assembly of the Lord because they did not meet you with food and water on your journey out of Egypt... You shall never promote their welfare or their prosperity as long as you live (Deut. 23.3-6).

And then there is Ezra's call for divorcing the foreign wives, namely the Moabites (Ezra 9.1-2; Neh. 13.1). Thus, there is a question as to how it happens that Mahlon, Ruth's husband, comes to Moab, and even more intriguing is the question of Mahlon's decision to marry Ruth, the native Moabite.

It seems that, in biblical Israel, migration from the land was not a unique occurrence. The natural phenomenon of famine was a recurring problem, as Gen. 12.12-20 illustrates. Abraham goes to seek food in Egypt. However, because of this move Abraham finds himself involved in an unfortunate situation, where he designates Sarah, his wife, as his sister (vv. 10-14). Do we find there a hint, condemning Elimelech's migration as well? Will that explain the tragedy of his death in Moab, together with his two sons who marry Moabites?

Attention should be drawn to the involvement of the Judean men with the Moabite women. As a rule, the Bible does not welcome mixed marriages.[1] The phenomenon of mixed

---

1. See for instance Samson's parents' reservations concerning his intention to marry a Philistine woman (Judg. 14.3).

marriages is rejected by Ezra (Ezra 9.1-2; Neh. 13.1) and by the Deuteronomist, especially in regard to the Ammonites and the Moabites (Deut. 23.2). The idea of marrying women of a nation that represents perversion and prostitution is illustrated by the Aramaic translation, the *Targum*, which singles out the marriage of Naomi's sons to the Moabite women as the cause for their death.[1] The Midrash elaborates the subject, claiming that the father would not allow his sons, during his lifetime, to marry local women of Moab.[2] Furthermore, Naomi states regarding her suffering: 'No, my daughters, it has been far more bitter for me than for you, because the hand of the Lord has turned against me' (1.13); and further, 'I went away full, but the Lord has brought me back empty; why call me Naomi when the Lord has dealt harshly with me, and the Almighty has brought calamity upon me?' (1.21).[3] We may read these statements, which point at God as the cause of Naomi's tragedy, as the Divine's reaction to her family's intimate relations with Moab and the Moabite women.

Nonetheless, as for the Moabites' approach to this sort of intermarriage, it seems that Ruth the Moabite has little concern with regard to marrying a Judean man. One does not hear in the text any reference to questions that might have been raised by her. Besides, at the time when Ruth marries her husband, Orpah, another Moabite woman, marries Ruth's brother-in-law Chilion.

Whatever causes the death of the men of Elimelech's family, the outcome is that the three women, Naomi and her two daughters-in-law, are now widowed. Naomi has spent ten years in a foreign land (1.4), and what can she do now? She is left with two daughters-in-law, no grandchildren, and no land

1. See E. Levine, *The Aramaic Version of Ruth* (AnBib; Rome: Pontifical Biblical Institute, 1973), p. 20.

2. *Midrash Lekah Tov* for Ruth, cited in Y. Zakovitch, *Ruth: A Commentary* (Miqra LeYisrael; Tel Aviv: Am Oved; Jerusalem: Magnes, 1990), p. 49.

3. For the meaning of '*nh* see J.M. Sasson, *Ruth: A New Translation with a Philological Commentary and a Formalist-Folklorist Interpretation* (The Biblical Seminar, 10; Sheffield: JSOT Press, 2nd edn, 1989 [1979]), p. 35.

or relatives who can redeem her. The storyteller points out that, on the death of both Naomi's sons, Naomi and Elimelech have no more living sons who can take care of the widows.[1] Ruth and Orpah, the Moabite women, might have produced a simpler solution, that is, to return to their source families which, supposedly, have to support them—as indeed Naomi advises her daughters-in-law to do: 'Go back each of you to your mother's house' (1.8). This custom of returning to the family's house was quite common—as we hear in another case, where a woman in Judah is widowed and her father-in-law suggests that she should return to her family's house: 'Then Judah said to his daughter-in-law Tamar, "Remain a widow in your father's house"' (Gen. 38.11).

Thus, what is Naomi supposed to do? She is a foreigner in Moab. Her relatives have stayed in Bethlehem of Judah. Naturally, she follows the same pattern suggested by her to the daughters-in-law, and she too goes to her family (in Judah): 'Now Naomi had a kinsman on her husband's side, a prominent rich man, of the family of Elimelech, whose name was Boaz' (2.1). This would mean that Naomi, who is returning back to her homeland where she still owns some property, 'has come back from the country of Moab, [and] is selling the parcel of land that belonged to our kinsman Elimelech' (4.3). The audience who is participating in the story knows that, for Naomi, it will be an ordeal to return to Bethlehem, since she has left her homeland together with her family, but now she returns alone: 'I went away full but the Lord has brought me back empty. Why call me Naomi when the Lord has dealt harshly with me, and the Almighty has brought calamity upon me?' (1.21). Therefore, one might not be surprised that Naomi is hesitant and afraid of the reception that awaits her at home. Furthermore, perhaps she also fears the consequences of the *foreignness* of her Moabite daughter-in-law who joins her; which may explain the refusal of the first redeemer, 'Mr So and So', to marry Ruth (4.6). Thus Naomi does not encourage her daughters-in-law to join her in her journey. She does not invite the Moabite women to follow

---

1. See A. LaCocque, *The Feminine Unconventional* (Minneapolis: Fortress Press, 1990), p. 94.

her back to Bethlehem; she lacks the means to provide for their needs and, she may suspect, the nationality of her daughters-in-law will cause her problems regarding her $g^e'\hat{u}l\hat{a}$—a fear which is exacerbated by their subsistence at a near-starvation level. In short, Naomi is a widow, and there is no hope for her to have sons who will be able to 'redeem' and feed her and her daughters-in-law (1.12-13).

The scene describing the women's return journey is illuminating. They do not speak (1.18); a tense atmosphere has been created. Their feeling of hesitation and skepticism is captured by the Dutch painter Willem Drost (1652–1680). The artist portrays Naomi as an old lady whose attitude is undecided. She raises her hand to the younger woman Ruth, but it is questionable whether her gesture is a rejection or a blessing (fig. 2). We may ask whether this attitude reflects Naomi's frustration and irritation regarding her Moabite daughter-in-law who, in joining her, might jeopardize her future.[1] Orpah, however, may understand the situation, as she returns back to her family in Moab. The text nevertheless implies that Ruth realizes the consequences of her migration to Judah. She does not expect a great fortune in her new life in Bethlehem; she portrays her future life in simple words, and assures Naomi that she has no special needs: 'Do not press me to leave you or to turn back from following you! Where you go I will go; where you lodge, I will lodge' (1.16).

The reception of the women of Bethlehem is striking. Ruth is ignored, perhaps even condemned, by the local people. Ten years have passed since Naomi had been in Bethlehem and she might imagine that possibly no-one will recognize her. Further, if they do recognize Naomi, they might not be delighted to see Ruth. And indeed, the welcoming reception of the entire town expresses its opinion: 'When they [Naomi and Ruth] came to Bethlehem, the whole town was stirred because of them; and the women said: "Is this Naomi?"' (1.20). The women of Bethlehem

---

1. See P. Trible, *God and the Rhetoric of Sexuality* (Philadelphia: Fortress Press, 1978), pp. 172-73; also D.N. Fewell and D.M. Gunn, *Compromising Redemption: Relating Characters in the Book of Ruth* (Louisville, KY: Westminster Press, 1990), p. 74.

ignore the Moabite woman, addressing Naomi alone.

The question now will be, who are the town people whom Naomi must deal with? In this regard the text refers specifically to only one group of people—the women of the town (1.19-20). Thus the question is, why does Naomi address only the women and why does she avoid talking with the men?

We may suggest that Naomi, who knows her people, is worried about the social status of herself and of her daughter-in-law who has joined her on the journey home. When they enter the city Naomi tries to forestall any harsh words her people might utter against them: thus, immediately upon her arrival, she addresses the women and explains to them:

> Call me no longer Naomi, call me Mara, for the Almighty has dealt bitterly with me. I went away full, but the Lord has brought me back empty. Why call me Naomi when the Lord has dealt harshly with me, and the Almighty has brought calamity upon me? (1.20-21).

Naomi needs sympathy: she calls for comfort, and seeks the support of her fellow people. It seems that the only ones who might understand her are the women. Why? Because of their natural empathy and mutual understanding as women but also for another reason, as implied in the scroll. Ruth is a threat; she is a Moabite and, by joining Naomi, will have to be redeemed by a Judahite man. Naomi cannot approach the men of the town directly. But the women will be the ones to embrace her, and they have the power to restore her social status. Then the men will have to follow their example and fulfil their own duty, as prescribed in the law. Naomi probably knows that she can resort to the legal authorities. According to the law, the kinsman has to take care of her (Gen. 38.8), but the women do not *have* to associate with her. Therefore, her discourse is addressed to the women. Boaz also understands the important role that the women have to undertake in regard to resolving the situation. When Ruth is found in his field, he suggests to her to seek the company of the young women (2.8). In his painting, the French artist Jean François Millet (1814–1875) depicts the scene in the field where Boaz asks Ruth to join his reapers for lunch. Boaz points his hand in the direction of the women who sit near him, expecting them to take care of Ruth, who stands next to him and whom he directs towards the group (fig. 3).

Hence the writer, who is aware of the complexity of the situation in which Ruth and Naomi find themselves, specifies the female gender of both groups, town women and reapers. Upon reflection, therefore, it may as well be suggested that the entire scroll was written by a woman who was sensitive to women's points of view and their predicament: a tragic dependency on men. This might also explain the repeated application of the feminine form to the verbs.[1] An example of women who might have been story-tellers is that of the 'wise women', mentioned on several occasions in the Bible.[2] Besides, feminine plural forms are used not only by Naomi—who *addresses* the women of Bethlehem (1.1)—but also repeated by the narrator who *speaks about* the women, those who name the baby born to Ruth (4.14). It is not by chance that the feminine plural is used here also: the women, albeit a secluded group, have a crucial role in the overall design. They are not a passive audience; they are active participants. Arthur Szyk, in his illustration to the book of Ruth,[3] depicts the involvement and attitudes of the people of the town—especially the women, who are curious and inquisitive about the two women who enter the town after a long journey. They show some concern and hospitality but, at the same time, mock the new arrivals. For their part, Naomi and Ruth are reserved and hesitant in regard to the audience (fig. 4). The women of Bethlehem are the ones who will restore Naomi's place in local society (4.14-15). Ruth's respectability largely depends upon their goodwill for, ultimately, they will be the ones to declare the newborn son, the great-grandfather of the monarchic house of David, a 'redeemer' (4.17). And they will bestow upon Naomi the honor of raising the child of Ruth and Boaz: 'Then Naomi took the child and laid him in her bosom,

---

1. See S. Sandmel, *The Enjoyment of Scripture: The Laws, the Prophets and the Writings* (London: Oxford University Press, 1972), p. 25.

2. See 2 Sam. 14.1-20, 20.14-22, and the discussion on the role of 'wise women' in E.F. Campbell, *Ruth* (AB; Garden City, New York: Doubleday, 1975), pp. 22-23.

3. New York; Heritage Press, 1947, p. 19.

and became his nurse. The women of the neighborhood gave him a name, saying, "a son has been born to Naomi"'(4.16-17).

The women of Bethlehem play a crucial role in the development of the story. As such, their role is comparable to that of the elders of the city, whose important legal task is the restoring of Naomi's status through levirate marriage.[1] On the one hand, they do not rush to accept Naomi and her daughter-in-law on their return from Moab (1.19); but, when Ruth's actions prove her sincerity, the women are the ones to praise her: 'for your daughter-in-law who loves you, who is more to you than seven sons' (4.15). They are the ones who can comprehend the greatness of Ruth's deeds. They see her as a woman who has lost all she ever had: land, God and husband. She struggles to restore her status by clinging to her foreign mother-in-law Naomi. We note that Ruth is nowhere defined by the women, or by the narrator, as a beautiful person. This is in opposition to the description of other matriarchs, like Sarah, Rebekah and Rachel (cf. Gen. 12.11; 24.16; 29.17). Neither is Ruth specifically characterized as a 'wise woman'; she is an ordinary Moabite woman who is an alien in Bethlehem. Nonetheless, Ruth is obedient: she listens to Naomi, and does what her mother-in-law asks her to do (3.5) even when her obedience might destroy her reputation (3.4).

Because of her deeds Ruth is blessed and rewarded. Her husband Boaz designates her a 'worthy woman' (3.11), the same praise employed in the 'worthy woman' poem of Prov. 31.10-31 ('*ēšet ḥayil*).[2] The people at the gate of Bethlehem and the elders bless her house: 'May the Lord make the woman who is coming to your house like Rachel and Leah, who together built the house of Israel' (4.11). And the women of Bethlehem see Ruth as a worthy woman who is worth more to her mother-in-law than seven sons (4.15).

---

1. A reference to Trible's comment (*The Rhetoric of Sexuality*, p. 94) is in order here: 'Repeatedly, these women stand as opposites to the elders'.

2. In the Petersburg Manuscript the book of Ruth is placed immediately after the book of Proverbs, which is concluded by the 'worthy woman' poem (as cited in Zakovitch, *Ruth*, pp. 14-15).

Thus, it seems that the story of Ruth is not only a story of a woman who follows her husband's family and comes to a foreign land, but also the tale of the women of Bethlehem who are confronted with a foreign woman, a Moabite devoted to her Judahite mother-in-law. Ruth restores not her own rights but, rather, her late husband's rights for his land; and becomes a heroine although her figure is almost avoided towards the end, when Naomi becomes the active figure and nurses the son that is born to Ruth and Boaz (4.16).

In view of Naomi's central role in the story, a question cannot be avoided: why is the book not named after her? Is it because, in the eyes of whoever named the book, Naomi does not forgive Ruth for marrying her son? Or because Ruth insists on following Naomi to Bethlehem of her own initiative? Is Naomi not delighted with the company of her daughter-in-law? In terms of the story, it seems that Ruth does not succeed in winning Naomi's favor easily. We recall Naomi's tense attitude toward Ruth on their way back to Bethlehem. And, throughout the entire story, Naomi does not say to Ruth even once that her deeds are, in her view, gracious, or that she considers her a 'worthy woman'. The entire dialogue between Naomi and Ruth revolves around practical matters: Naomi's interests are her property and her restored status. All the while Ruth is just an instrument in Naomi's hands. Thus Ruth is the righteous one who comes to be, thanks to her obedience, the real heroine of the story. That is to say, Ruth is indeed a Moabite, yet she is portrayed as an exceptional example of female devotion, and she appears in most of the episodes of the story, more than any other figure of the scroll.[1] Ruth is the figure to whom the story attributes the term *hesed* (3.10), a term which designates loyalty and love beyond the mere call of duty and law.[2] Whoever named the scroll after Ruth read it carefully; and the naming choice implies a criticism of Naomi.

1.   Zakovitch, *Ruth*, p. 5.
2.   See LaCocque, *Feminine Unconventional*, p. 87.

Figure 1. Leonard Baskin, *There is a Son born to Naomi*

Figure 2. Willem Drost, *Ruth and Naomi*

Figure 3. Jean François Millet, *Harvesters Resting (Ruth and Boaz)*

Figure 4. Arthur Szyk, *Naomi comes to Bethlehem*

Ruth*

Cynthia Ozick

For
Muriel Dance, in New York;
Lee Gleichmann, in Stockholm;
Sarah Halevi, in Jerusalem; and
Inger Mirsky, in New York

1. *Flowers*

There were only two pictures on the walls of the house I grew up in. One was large, and hung from the molding on a golden cord with a full golden tassel. It was a painting taken from a photograph—all dark, a kind of grayish-brown; it was of my grandfather Hirshl, my father's father. My grandfather's coat had big foreign-looking buttons, and he wore a tall stiff square yarmulke that descended almost to the middle of his forehead. His eyes were severe, pale, concentrated. There was no way to escape those eyes; they came after you wherever you were. I had never known this grandfather: he died in Russia long ago. My father, a taciturn man, spoke of him only once, when I was already grown: as a boy, my father said, he had gone with his father on a teaching expedition to Kiev; he remembered how the mud was deep in the roads. From my mother I learned a little more. Zeyde Hirshl was frail. His wife, Bobe Sore-Libe, was the opposite: quick, energetic, hearty, a skilled *zogerke*—a women's prayer leader in the synagogue—a whirlwind who kept a dry goods store and had baby after baby, all on her own, while Zeyde Hirshl spent his days in the study-house. Sometimes he fainted on his way there. He was pale, he was mild, he was

---

* This article is taken from C. Ozick, *Metaphor and Memory* (New York: Knopf, 1989).

delicate, unworldly; a student, a *melamed*, a fainter. Why, then those unforgiving stern eyes that would not let you go?

My grandfather's portrait had its permanent place over the secondhand piano. To the right, farther down the wall, hung the other picture. It was framed modestly in a thin black wooden rectangle, and was, in those spare days, all I knew of 'art'. Was it torn from a magazine, cut from a calendar? A barefoot young woman, her hair bound in a kerchief, grasping a sickle, stands alone and erect in a field. Behind her a red sun is half-swallowed by the horizon. She wears a loose white peasant's blouse and a long dark skirt, deeply blue; her head and shoulders are isolated against a limitless sky. Her head is held poised: she gazes past my gaze into some infinity of loneliness stiller than the sky.

Below the picture was its title: *The Song of the Lark*. There was no lark. It did not come to me that the young woman, with her lifted face, was straining after the note of a bird who might be in a place invisible to the painter. What I saw and heard was something else: a scene older than this French countryside, a woman lonelier even than the woman alone in the calendar meadow. It was, my mother said, Ruth: Ruth gleaning in the fields of Boaz.

For many years afterward—long after *The Song of the Lark* had disappeared from the living room wall—I had the idea that this landscape (a 1930s fixture, it emerged, in scores of American households and Sunday-school classrooms) was the work of Jean-François Millet, the French painter of farm life. 'I try not to have things look as if chance had brought them together,' Millet wrote, 'but as if they had a necessary bond between them. I want the people I represent to look as if they really belonged to their station, so that imagination cannot conceive of their ever being anything else.'

Here is my grandfather. Imagination cannot conceive of his ever being anything else: a *melamed* who once ventured with his young son (my blue-eyed father) as far as Kiev, but mainly stayed at home in his own town, sometimes fainting on the way to the study-house. The study-house was his 'station'. In his portrait he looks as if he really belonged there; and he did. It was how he lived.

And here is Ruth, on the far side of the piano, in Boaz's field, gleaning. Her mouth is remote: it seems somehow damaged; there is a blur behind her eyes. All the sadness of the earth is in her tender neck, all the blur of loss, all the damage of rupture: remote, remote, rent. The child who stands before the woman standing barefoot, sickle forgotten, has fallen through the barrier of an old wooden frame into the picture itself, into the field; into the smell of the field. There is no lark, no birdcall: only the terrible silence of the living room when no one else is there. The grandfather is always there; his eyes keep their vigil. The silence of the field swims up from a time so profoundly lost that it annihilates time. There is the faint weedy smell of thistle: and masses of meadow flowers. In my childhood I recognized violets, lilacs, roses, daisies, dandelions, black-eyed Susans, tiger lilies, pansies (I planted, one summer, a tiny square of pansies, one in each corner, one in the middle), and no more. The lilacs I knew because of the children who brought them to school in springtime: children with German names, Koechling, Behrens, Kuntz.

To annihilate time, to conjure up unfailingly the fragrance in Boaz's field (his field in *The Song of the Lark*), I have the power now to summon what the child peering into the picture could not. 'Tolstoy, come to my aid,' I could not call then: I had never heard of Tolstoy: my child's Russia was the grandfather's portrait, and stories of fleeing across borders at night, and wolves, and the baba yaga in the fairy tales. But now: 'Tolstoy, come to my aid,' I can chant at this hour, with my hair turned silver; and lo, the opening of *Hadji Murad* spills out all the flowers in Boaz's field:

> It was midsummer, the hay harvest was over and they were just beginning to reap the rye. At that season of the year there is a delightful variety of flowers—red, white, and pink scented tufty clover; milk-white ox-eye daisies with their bright yellow centers and pleasant spicy smell; yellow honey-scented rape blossoms; tall campanulas with white and lilac bells, tulip-shaped; creeping vetch; yellow, red, and pink scabious; faintly scented, neatly arranged purple plantains with blossoms slightly tinged with pink; cornflowers, the newly opened blossoms bright blue in the sunshine but growing paler and redder towards evening or when growing old; and delicate almond-scented dodder flowers that withered quickly.

Dodder? Vetch? (Flash of Henry James's Fleda Vetch). Scabious?
Rape and campanula? The names are unaccustomed; my
grandfather in the study-house never sees the flowers. In the
text itself—in the book of Ruth—not a single flower is mentioned. And the harvest is neither hay nor rye; in Boaz's field
outside Bethlehem they are cutting down barley and wheat. The
flowers are there all the same, even if the text doesn't show
them, and we are obliged to take in their scents, the weaker with
the keener, the grassier with the meatier: without the smell of
flowers, we cannot pass through the frame of history into that
long ago, ancientness behind ancientness, when Ruth the
Moabite gleaned. It is as if the little spurts and shoots of
fragrance form a rod, a rail of light, along which we are carried,
drifting, into that time before time 'when the judges ruled'.

Two pictures, divided by an old piano—Ruth in *The Song of
the Lark*, my grandfather in his yarmulke. He looks straight out;
so does she. They sight each other across the breadth of the wall.
I stare at both of them. Eventually I will learn that *The Song of
the Lark* was not painted by Millet, not at all; the painter is Jules
Breton—French like Millet, like Millet devoted to rural scenes.
The Song of the Lark hangs in the Art Institute of Chicago; it is
possible I will die without ever having visited there. Good: I
never want to see the original, out of shock at what a reproduc-
tion now discloses: a mistake, everything is turned the other
way! On our living room wall Ruth faced right. In the Art
Institute of Chicago she faces left. A calendar reversal!—but of
course it feels to me that the original is in sullen error. Breton,
unlike Millet, lived into our century—he died in 1906, the year
my nine-year-old mother came through Castle Garden on her
way to framing *The Song of the Lark* two decades later. About
my grandfather Hirshl there is no 'eventually'; I will not learn
anything new about him. He will not acquire a different maker.
Nothing in his view will be reversed. He will remain a dusty
indoor *melamed* with eyes that drill through bone.

Leaving aside the wall, leaving aside the child who haunts
and is haunted by the grandfather and the woman with the
sickle, what is the connection between this dusty indoor
melamed and the nymph in the meadow, standing barefoot
amid the tall campanula?

Everything, everything. If the woman had not been in the field, my grandfather, three thousand years afterward, would not have been in the study-house. She, the Moabite, is why he, when hope is embittered, murmurs the Psalms of David. The track her naked toes make through spice and sweetness, through dodder, vetch, rape, and scabious, is the very track his forefinger follows across the letter-speckled sacred page.

2. *Mercy*

When my grandfather reads the book of Ruth, it is on Shavuot, the Feast of Weeks, with its twin furrows: the text's straight furrow planted with the alphabet; the harvest's furrow, fuzzy with seedlings. The Feast of Weeks, which comes in May, is a reminder of the late spring crops, but only as an aside. The soul of it is the acceptance of the Torah by the Children of Israel. If there is a garland crowning this festival of May, it is the arms of Israel embracing the Covenant. My grandfather will not dart among field flowers after Ruth and her sickle; the field is fenced round by the rabbis, and the rabbis—those insistent interpretive spirits of Commentary whose arguments and counter-arguments, from generation to generation, comprise the Tradition—seem at first to be vexed with the book of Ruth. If they are not actually or openly vexed, they are suspicious; and if they are not willing to be judged flatly suspicious, then surely they are cautious.

The book of Ruth is, after all, about exogamy, and not simple exogamy—marriage with a stranger, a member of a foreign culture: Ruth's ancestry is hardly neutral in that sense. She is a Moabite. She belongs to an enemy people, callous, pitiless; a people who deal in lethal curses. The children of the wild hunter Esau—the Edomites, who will ultimately stand for the imperial oppressors of Rome—cannot be shut out of the family of Israel. Even the descendants of the enslaving Egyptians are welcome to marry and grow into intimacy. 'You shall not abhor an Edomite, for he is your kinsman. You shall not abhor an Egyptian, for you were a stranger in his land. Children born to them may be admitted into the congregation of the Lord in the third generation' (Deut. 23.8-9). But a Moabite, never: 'none of their descendants, even in the tenth generation, shall ever be admitted into the congregation of the Lord, because they did not meet you with food and water on your journey after you left Egypt, and because they hired Balaam...to curse you' (Deut. 23.4-5). An abyss of memory and hurt in that: to have passed through the furnace of the desert famished, parched, and to be chased after by a wonder-worker on an ass hurling the king's maledictions, officially designed to wipe out the straggling mob of exhausted refugees! One might in time reconcile with Esau, one might in time reconcile with hard-hearted Egypt. All this was not merely conceivable—through acculturation, conversion, family ties and new babies, it could be implemented, it *would* be implemented. But Moabite spite had a lasting sting.

What, then, are the sages to do with Ruth the Moabite as in-law? How account for her presence and resonance in Israel's story? How is it possible for a member of the congregation of the Lord to have violated the edict against marriage with a Moabite? The rabbis, reflecting on the pertinent verses, deduce a rule: *Moabite, not Moabitess*. It was customary for men, they conclude, not for women, to succor travelers in the desert, so only the Moabite males were guilty of a failure of humanity. The women were blameless, hence are exempt from the ban on conversion and marriage.

Even with the discovery of this mitigating loophole (with its odd premise that women are descended only from women, and men from men; or else that all the women, or all the men, in a family line are interchangeable with one another, up and down the ladder of the generations, and that guilt and innocence are collective, sex-linked, and heritable), it is hard for the rabbis to swallow a Moabite bride. They are discomfited by every particle of cause-and-effect that brought about such an eventuality. Why should a family with a pair of marriageable sons find itself in pagan Moab in the first place? The rabbis begin by scolding the text—or, rather, the characters and events of the story as they are straightforwardly set out.

Here is how the book of Ruth begins:

> In the days when the judges ruled, there was a famine in the land; and a man of Bethlehem in Judah, with his wife and two sons, went to reside in the country of Moab. The man's name

was Elimelech, his wife's name was Naomi, and his two sons
were named Mahlon and Chilion—Ephrathites of Bethlehem
in Judah. They came to the country of Moab and remained
there.

Elimelech, Naomi's husband, died; and she was left with her
two sons. They married Moabite women, one named Orpah
and the other Ruth, and they lived there about ten years. Then
those two—Mahlon and Chilion—also died; so the woman
was left without her two sons and without her husband.

Famine; migration; three deaths in a single household; three
widows. Catastrophe after catastrophe, yet the text, plain
and sparse, is only matter-of-fact. There is no anger in it, no-
one is condemned. What happened, happened—though not
unaccoutered by echo and reverberation. Earlier biblical families
and journeys-toward-sustenance cluster and chatter around
Elimelech's decision: 'There was a famine in the land, and
Abram went down to Egypt to sojourn there, for the famine was
severe in the land' (Gen. 12.10). 'So ten of Joseph's brothers
went down to get rations in Egypt... Thus the sons of Israel
were among those who came to procure rations, for the famine
extended to the land of Canaan' (Gen. 42.3, 5). What Abraham
did, what the sons of Jacob did, Elimelech also feels constrained
to do: there is famine, he will go where the food is.

And the rabbis subject him to bitter censure for it. The famine,
they say, is retribution for the times—'the days when the judges
ruled'—and the times are coarse, cynical, lawless. 'In those days
there was no king in Israel; everyone did what he pleased' (Judg.
17.6). Ironic that the leaders should be deemed 'judges', and that
under their aegis the rule of law is loosened, each one pursuing
'what is right in his own eyes', without standard or conscience.
Elimelech, according to the rabbis, is one of these unraveled
and atomized souls: a leader who will not lead. They identify
him as a man of substance, distinguished, well-off, an eminence;
but arrogant and selfish. Even his name suggests self-
aggrandizement: *to me shall kingship come*.[1] Elimelech turns his

1.   Latter-day scholarship avers that Elimelech is a run-of-the-mill
name in pre-Israelite Canaan, 'and is the one name in the Ruth story
that seems incapable of being explained as having a symbolic meaning
pertinent to the narrative' (E.F. Campbell, *Ruth* [AB; Garden City, New

back on the destitute conditions of hungry Bethlehem, picks up his family, and, because he is rich enough to afford the journey, sets out for where the food is. He looks to his own skin and means to get his own grub. The rabbis charge Elimelech with desertion; they accuse him of running away from the importunings of the impoverished, of provoking discouragement and despair; he is miserly, there is no charitableness in him, he is ungenerous. They call him a 'dead stump'—he attends only to his immediate kin and shrugs off the community at large. Worse yet, he is heading for Moab, vile Moab! The very man who might have heartened his generation in a period of upheaval and inspired its moral repair leaves his own country, a land sanctified by Divine Covenant, for a historically repugnant region inhabited by idolators—and only to fill his own belly, and his own wife's, and his own sons'.

Elimelech in Moab will die in his prime. His widow will suffer radical denigration—a drop in status commonly enough observed even among independent women of our era—and, more seriously, a loss of protection. The rabbis will compare Naomi in her widowhood with 'the remnants of the meal offerings'—i.e., with detritus and ash. Elimelech's sons— children of a father whose example is abandonment of community and of conscience—will die too soon. Already grown men after the death of Elimelech, they have themselves earned retribution. Instead of returning with their unhappy mother to their own people in the land dedicated to monotheism, they settle down to stay, and marry Moabite women. 'One transgression leads to another', chide the rabbis, and argue over whether the brides of Mahlon and Chilion were or were not ritually converted before their weddings. In any case, a decade after those weddings, nothing has flowered for these husbands and wives, fertility eludes them, there will be no blossoming branches: the two young husbands are dead—dead stumps— and the two young widows are childless.

This is the rabbis' view. They are symbolists and metaphor-seekers; it goes without saying they are moralists. Punishment is truthful; punishment is the consequence of reality, it instructs in what happens. It is not that the rabbis are severe; they are just the opposite of severe. What they are after is simple mercy: where is the standard of mercy and humanity in a time when careless men and women follow the whim of their own greedy and expedient eyes? It is not merciful to abandon chaos and neediness; chaos and neediness call out for reclamation. It is not merciful to forsake one's devastated countrymen; opportunism is despicable; desertion is despicable; derogation of responsibility is despicable; it is not merciful to think solely of one's own family: if I am only for myself, what am I? And what of the hallowed land, that sacral ground consecrated to the unity of the Creator and the teaching of mercy, while the babble and garble of polymyth pullulate all around? The man who throws away the country of aspiration, especially in a lamentable hour when failure overruns it—the man who promotes egotism, elevates the material, and deprives his children of idealism—this fellow, this Elimelech, vexes the rabbis and afflicts them with shame.

Of course there is not a grain of any of this in the text itself—not a word about Elimelech's character or motives or even his position in Bethlehem. The rabbis' commentary is all extrapolation, embroidery, plausible invention. What is plausible in it is firmly plausible: it stands to reason that only a wealthy family, traveling together *as* a family, would be able to contemplate emigration to another country with which they have no economic or kinship ties. And it follows also that a wealthy householder is likely to be an established figure in his home town. The rabbis' storytelling faculty is not capricious or fantastic: it is rooted in the way the world actually works, then and now.

But the rabbis are even more interested in the way the world *ought* to work. Their parallel text hardly emerges *ex nihilo*. They are not oblivious to what-is: they can, in fact, construct a remarkably particularized social density from a handful of skeletal data. Yet, shrewd sociologists though they are, it is not sociology that stirs them. What stirs them is the aura of judgment—or call it ethical interpretation—that rises out of even the most comprehensively imagined social particularity. The rabbis are driven by a struggle to uncover a moral immanence in every human being. It signifies, such a struggle, hopefulness to the point of pathos, and the texture and pliability of this deeply embedded matrix of optimism is more pressing for the rabbis than any other kind of speculation or cultural improvisation. Callousness and egotism are an affront to their expectations. What are their expectations in the book of Ruth? That an established community figure has an obligation not to demoralize his constituency by walking out on it. And that the Holy Land is to be passionately embraced, clung to, blessed, and defended as the ripening center and historic promise of the covenanted life. Like the Covenant that engendered its sanctifying purpose, Israel cannot be 'marginalized'. One place is not the same as another place. The rabbis are not cultural relativists.

From the rabbis' vantage, it is not that their commentary is 'implicit' in the plain text under their noses; what they see is not implicit so much as it is fully intrinsic. It is there already, like invisible ink gradually made to appear. A system of values produces a story. A system of values? Never mind such Aristotelian language. The rabbis said, and meant, the quality of mercy: human feeling.

3. *Normality*

I have been diligent in opening the first five verses of the book of Ruth to the rabbis' voices, and though I am unwilling to leave their voices behind—they painstakingly accompany the story inch by inch, breath for breath—I mean for the rest of my sojourn in the text (perforce spotty and selective, a point here, a point there) to go on more or less without them. I say 'more or less' because it is impossible, really, to go on without them. They are (to use an unsuitable image) the Muses of exegesis: not the current sort of exegesis that ushers insights out of a tale by scattering a thousand brilliant fragments, but rather the kind that ushers things *toward*: a guide toward principle. The book of Ruth presents two principles. The first is what is normal. The second is what is singular.

Until Elimelech's death, Naomi has been an exemplum of the normal. She has followed her husband and made no decisions or choices of her own. What we nowadays call feminism is of course as old as the oldest society imaginable; there have always been feminists: women (including the unsung) who will allow no element of themselves—gift, capacity, natural authority—to go unexpressed, whatever the weight of the mores. Naomi has not been one of these. Until the death of her husband we know nothing of her but her compliance, and it would be foolish to suppose that in Naomi's world a wife's obedience is not a fundamental social virtue. But once Naomi's husband and sons have been tragically cleared from the stage, Naomi moves from the merely passive virtue of an honorable dependent to risks and contingencies well beyond the reach of comfortable common virtue. Stripped of every social support,[1] isolated in a foreign land, pitifully unprotected, her anomalous position apparently wholly ignored by Moabite practices, responsible for the lives of a pair of foreign daughters-in-law (themselves isolated and unprotected under her roof), Naomi is transformed overnight. Under the crush of mourning and defenselessness, she becomes, without warning or preparation, a woman of valor.

She is only a village woman, after all. The book of Ruth, from beginning to end, is played out in village scenes. The history of valor will not find in Naomi what it found in another village woman: she will not arm herself like a man or ride a horse or lead a military expedition. She will never cross over to another style of being. The new ways of her valor will not annul the old ways of her virtue.

And yet—overnight!—she will set out on a program of autonomy. Her first act is a decision: she will return to Bethlehem, 'for in the country of Moab she had heard that the Lord had taken note of His people and given them food'. After so many years, the famine in Bethlehem is spent—but since Naomi is cognizant of this as the work of the Lord, there is a hint that she would have gone back to Bethlehem in Judah in any event, even if that place were still troubled by hunger. It is no ordinary place for her: the Lord hovers over Judah and

1.   The rabbis' notion of Elimelech as a man of substance is no help to his widow. She has not been provided for; we see her as helpless and impoverished.

its people, and Naomi in returning makes restitution for Elimelech's abandonment. Simply in her determination to go back, she rights an old wrong.

But she does not go back alone. Now, willy-nilly, she is herself the head of a household bound to her by obedience. 'Accompanied by her two daughters-in-law, she left the place where she had been living; and they set out on the road back to the land of Judah.' On the road, Naomi reflects. What she reflects on—only connect! she is herself an exile—is the ache of exile and the consolations of normality.

> Naomi said to her two daughters-in-law, 'Turn back, each of you to her mother's house. May the Lord deal kindly with you, as you have dealt with the dead and with me! May the Lord grant that each of you find security in the house of a husband!' And she kissed them farewell. They broke into weeping and said to her, 'No, we will return with you to your people.'
> But Naomi replied, 'Turn back, my daughters! Why should you go with me? Have I any more sons in my body who might be husbands for you? Turn back, my daughters, for I am too old to be married. Even if I thought there was hope for me, even if I were married tonight and I also bore sons, should you wait for them to grow up? Should you on their account debar yourselves from marriage? Oh no, my daughters!'

In a moment or so we will hear Ruth's incandescent reply spiraling down to us through the ardors of three thousand years; but here let us check the tale, fashion a hiatus, and allow normality to flow in: let young stricken Orpah not be overlooked. She is always overlooked; she is the daughter-in-law who, given the chance, chose not to follow Naomi. She is noone's heroine. Her mark is erased from history; there is no book of Orpah. And yet Orpah *is* history. Or, rather, she is history's great backdrop. She is the majority of humankind living out its usualness on home ground. These young women—both of them—are cherished by Naomi; she cannot speak to them without flooding them in her fellow feeling. She *knows* what it is to be Orpah and Ruth. They have all suffered and sorrowed together, and in ten years of living in one household much of the superficial cultural strangeness has worn off. She pities them because they are childless, and she honors them because they have 'dealt kindly' with their husbands and with their mother-in-law. She calls them—the word as she releases it is accustomed, familiar, close, ripe with dearness—בנתי, 'my daughters', whereas the voice of the narrative is careful to identify them precisely, though neutrally, as כלחיה, 'her daughters-in-law'.

Orpah is a loving young woman of clear goodness; she has kisses and tears for the loss of Naomi. 'They broke into weeping again, and Orpah kissed her mother-in-law farewell.' Her sensibility is ungrudging, and she is not in the least narrow-minded. Her upbringing may well have been liberal. Would a narrow-minded Moabite father have given over one of his daughters to the only foreign family in town? Such a surrender goes against the grain of the ordinary. Exogamy is never ordinary. So Orpah has already been stamped with the 'abnormal'; she is already a little more daring than most, already somewhat offbeat—she is one of only two young Moabite women to marry Hebrews, and Hebrews have never been congenial to Moabites. If the Hebrews can remember how the Moabites treated them long ago, so can the Moabites: traditions of enmity work in both directions. The mean-spirited have a habit of resenting their victims quite as much as the other way around. Orpah has cut through all this bad blood to plain humanity; it would be unfair to consider her inferior to any other kindhearted young woman who ever lived in the world before or since. She is in fact superior; she has thrown off prejudice, and she has had to endure more than most young women of her class, including the less spunky and the less amiable: an early widowhood and no babies. And what else is there for a good girl like Orpah, in her epoch, and often enough in ours, but family happiness?

Her prototype abounds. She has fine impulses, but she is not an iconoclast. She can push against convention to a generous degree, but it is out of the generosity of her temperament, not out of some large metaphysical idea. Who will demand of Orpah—think of the hugeness of the demand!—that she admit monotheism to the concentration and trials of her mind? Offer monotheism to almost anyone—offer it as something to take seriously—and ninety-nine times out of a hundred it will be declined, even by professing 'monotheists'. A Lord of History whose intent is felt, whose Commandments stand with immediacy, whose Covenant summons perpetual self-scrutiny and a continual Turning toward moral renewal, and yet *cannot, may not, be physically imagined*? A Creator neither remote and abstract like the God of the philosophers, nor palpable like the 'normal' divinities, both ancient and contemporary, both East and West? Give us (cries the nature of our race) our gods and goddesses, give us the little fertility icons with their welcoming breasts and elongated beckoning laps, give us the resplendent Virgin with her suffering brow and her arms outstretched in blessing, give us the Man on the Cross through whom to learn pity and love, and sometimes brutal exclusivity! Only give us what our eyes can see and our understanding understand: who can imagine the unimaginable? That may be for the philosophers; *they* can do it; but then they lack the imagination of the Covenant. The philosophers leave the world naked and blind and deaf and mute and relentlessly indifferent, and the village folk—who refuse a lonely cosmos without consolation—fill it and fill it and fill it with stone and wood and birds and mammals and miraculous potions and holy babes and animate carcasses and magically divine women and magically divine men: images, sights, and swallowings comprehensible to the hand, to the eye, to plain experience. For the nature of our race, God is one of the visual arts.

Is Orpah typical of these plain village folk? She is certainly not a philosopher, but neither is she, after ten years with Naomi, an ordinary Moabite. Not that she has altogether absorbed the Hebrew vision—if she had absorbed it, would she have been tempted to relinquish it so readily? She is somewhere in between, perhaps. In this we may suppose her to be one of us: a modern, no longer a full-fledged member of the pagan world, but always with one foot warming in the seductive bath of those colorful, comfortable, often beautiful old lies (they can console, but because they are lies they can also hurt and kill); not yet given over to the Covenant and its determination to train us away from lies, however warm, colorful, beautiful, and consoling.

Naomi, who is no metaphysician herself, who is, rather, heir to a tradition, imposes no monotheistic claim on either one of her daughters-in-law. She is right not to do this. In the first place, she is not a proselytizer or polemicist or preacher or even a teacher. She is none of those things: she is a bereaved woman far from home, and when she looks at her bereaved daughters-in-law, it is home she is thinking of, for herself and for them. Like the rabbis who will arrive two millennia after her, she is not a cultural relativist: God is God, and God is One. But in her own way, the way of empathy—three millennia before the concept of a democratic pluralist polity—she is a kind of pluralist. She does not require that Orpah accept what it is not natural for her, in the light of how she was reared, to accept. She speaks of Orpah's return not merely to her people but to her gods. Naomi is the opposite of coercive or punitive. One cannot dream of Inquisition or *jihad* emerging from her loins. She may not admire the usages of Orpah's people—they do not concern themselves with the widow and the destitute; no-one in Moab comes forward to care for Naomi—but she knows that Orpah has a mother, and may yet have a new husband, and will be secure where she is. It will not occur to Naomi to initiate a metaphysical discussion with Orpah! She sends her as a lost child back to her mother's hearth. (Will there be idols on her mother's hearth? Well, yes. But this sour comment is mine, not Naomi's.)

So Orpah goes home; or, more to the point, she goes nowhere. She stays home. She is never, never, never to be blamed for it. If she is not extraordinary, she is also normal. The extraordinary is what is not normal, and it is no fault of the normal that it does not, or cannot, aspire to the extraordinary. What Orpah gains by staying home with her own people is what she always deserved: family happiness. She is young and fertile; soon she will marry a Moabite husband and have a Moabite child.

What Orpah loses is the last three thousand years of being present in history. Israel continues; Moab does not. Still, for Orpah, historic longevity—the longevity of an Idea to which a people attaches itself—may not be a loss at all. It is only an absence, and absence is not felt as loss. Orpah has her husband, her cradle, her little time. That her gods are false is of no moment to her; she believes they are true. That her social system does not provide for the widow and the destitute is of no moment to her; she is no longer a widow, and as a wife she will not be destitute; as for looking over her shoulder to see how others fare, there is nothing in Moab to require it of her. She once loved her oddly foreign mother-in-law. And why shouldn't openhearted Orpah, in her little time, also love her Moabite mother-in-law, who is as like her as her own mother, and will also call her 'my daughter'? Does it matter to Orpah that her great-great-great-grandchildren have tumbled out of history, and that there is no book of Orpah, and that she slips from the book of Ruth in only its fourteenth verse?

Normality is not visionary. Normality's appetite stops at satisfaction.

4. *Singularity*

No, Naomi makes no metaphysical declaration to Orpah. It falls to Ruth, who has heard the same compassionate discourse as her sister-in-law, who has heard her mother-in-law three times call out 'Daughter, turn back'—it falls to Ruth to throw out exactly such a declaration to Naomi.

Her words have set thirty centuries to trembling: 'Your God shall be my God', uttered in what might be named visionary language. Does it merely 'fall' to Ruth that she speaks possessed by the visionary? What is at work in her? Is it capacity, seizure, or the force of intent and the clarity of will? Set this inquiry aside for now, and—apart from what the story tells us she really did say—ask instead what Ruth might have replied in the more available language of pragmatism, answering Naomi's sensible 'Turn back' exigency for exigency. What 'natural' reasons might such a young woman have for leaving her birthplace? Surely there is nothing advantageous in Ruth's clinging to Naomi. Everything socially rational is on the side of Ruth's remaining in her own country: what is true for Orpah is equally true for Ruth. But even if Ruth happened to think beyond exigency—even if she were exceptional in reaching past common sense toward ideal conduct—she need not have thought in the framework of the largest cosmic questions. Are we to expect of Ruth that she be a prophet? Why should she, any more than any other village woman, think beyond personal relations?

In the language of personal relations, in the language of pragmatism and exigency, here is what Ruth might have replied:

> Mother-in-law, I am used to living in your household, and have become accustomed to the ways of your family. I would no longer feel at home if I resumed the ways of my own people. After all, during the ten years or so I was married to your son, haven't I flourished under your influence? I was so young when I came into your family that it was you who completed my upbringing. It isn't for nothing that you call me daughter. So let me go with you.

Or, higher on the spectrum of ideal conduct (rather, the conduct of idealism), but still within the range of reasonable altruism, she might have said:

> Mother-in-law, you are heavier in years than I and alone in a strange place, whereas I am stalwart and not likely to be alone for long. Surely I will have a second chance, just as you predict, but you—how helpless you are, how unprotected! If I stayed home in Moab, I would be looking after my own interests, as you recommend, but do you think I can all of a sudden stop feeling for you, just like that? No, don't expect me to abandon you—who knows what can happen to a woman of your years all by herself on the road? And what prospects can there be for you, after all this long time away, in Bethlehem? It's true I'll seem a little odd in your country, but I'd much rather endure a little oddness in Bethlehem than lose you forever, not knowing what's to become of you. Let me go and watch over you.

There is no God in any of that. If these are thoughts Ruth did not speak out, they are all implicit in what has been recorded. Limited though they are by pragmatism, exigency, and personal relations, they are already anomalous. They address extraordinary alterations—of self, of worldly expectation. For Ruth to cling to Naomi as a daughter to her own mother is uncommon enough; a universe of folklore confirms that a daughter-in-law is not a daughter. But for Ruth to become the instrument of Naomi's restoration to safekeeping within her own community— and to prosperity and honor as well—is a thing of magnitude. And, in fact, all these praiseworthy circumstances do come to pass: though circumscribed by pragmatism, exigency, and personal relations. And without the visionary. Ideal conduct—or the conduct of idealism—is possible even in the absence of the language of the visionary. Observe:

> They broke into weeping again, and Orpah kissed her mother-in-law farewell. But Ruth clung to her. So she said, 'See, your sister-in-law has returned to her people. Go follow your sister-in-law.' But Ruth replied, 'Do not urge me to leave you, to turn back and not follow you. For wherever you go, I will go; wherever you lodge, I will lodge; your people shall be my people. Where you die, I will die, and there I will be buried. Only death will part me from you.' When Naomi saw how determined she was to go with her, she ceased to argue with her, and the two went on until they reached Bethlehem.

Of course this lovely passage is not the story of the book of Ruth (any more than my unpoetic made-up monologues are), though it might easily have been Ruth's story. In transcribing from the text, I have left out what Ruth passionately put in: God. And still Ruth's speech, even with God left out, and however particularized by the personal, is a stupendous expression of loyalty and love.

But now, in a sort of conflagration of seeing, the cosmic sweep of a single phrase transforms these spare syllables from the touching language of family feeling to the unearthly tongue of the visionary:

> See, your sister-in-law has returned to her people and her gods. Go and follow your sister-in-law.' But Ruth replied, 'Do not urge me to leave you, to turn back and not follow you. For wherever you go, I will go; wherever you lodge, I will lodge; your people shall be my people, and your God my God. Where you die, I will die, and there I will be buried. Thus and more may the Lord do to me if anything but death parts me from you.'

Your God shall be my God: Ruth's story is kindled into the book of Ruth by the presence of God on Ruth's lips, and her act is far, far more than a ringing embrace of Naomi, and far, far more than the simple acculturation it resembles. Ruth leaves Moab because she intends to leave childish ideas behind. She is drawn to Israel because Israel is the inheritor of the One Universal Creator.

Has Ruth 'learned' this insight from Naomi and from Naomi's son? It may be; the likelihood is almost as pressing as evidence: how, without assimilation into the life of an Israelite family, would Ruth ever have penetrated into the great monotheistic cognition? On the other hand, Orpah too encounters that cognition, and slips back into Moab to lose it again. Inculcation is not insight, and what Orpah owns is only that: inculcation without insight. Abraham—the first Hebrew to catch insight— caught it as genius does, autonomously, out of the blue, without any inculcating tradition. Ruth is in possession of both inculcation *and* insight.

And yet, so intense is her insight, one can almost imagine her as a kind of Abraham. Suppose Elimelech had never emigrated to Moab; suppose Ruth had never married a Hebrew. The fire of cognition might still have come upon her as it came upon Abraham—autonomously, out of the blue, without any inculcating tradition. Abraham's cognition turned into a civilization. Might Ruth have transmuted Moab? Ruth as a second Abraham! We see in her that clear power; that power of consummate clarity. But whether Moab might, through Ruth, have entered the history of monotheism, like Israel, is a question stalled by the more modest history of kinship entanglement. In Ruth's story, insight is inexorably accompanied by, fused with, inculcation; how can we sort out one from the other? If Ruth had not been married to one of Naomi's sons, perhaps we would have heard no more of her than we will hear henceforth of Orpah. Or: Moab might have ascended, like Abraham's seed, from the gods to God. Moab cleansed and reborn through Ruth! The story as it is given is perforce inflexible, not amenable to experiment. We cannot have Ruth without Naomi; nor would we welcome the loss of such loving-kindness. All the same, Ruth may not count as a second Abraham because her tale is enfolded in a way Abraham's is not: she has had her saturation in Abraham's seed. The ingredient of inculcation cannot be expunged: there it is.

Nevertheless it seems insufficient—it seems askew—to leave it at that. Ruth marries into Israel, yes; but her mind is vaster than the private or social facts of marriage and inculcation; vaster than the merely familial. Insight, cognition, intuition, religious genius—how to name it? It is not simply because of Ruth's love for Naomi—a love unarguably resplendent—that Naomi's God becomes Ruth's God. To stop at love and loyalty is to have arrived at much, but not all; to stop at love and loyalty is to stop too soon. Ruth claims the God of Israel out of her own ontological understanding. She knows—she knows directly, prophetically—that the Creator of the Universe is One.

5. *Unfolding*

The greater part of Ruth's tale is yet to occur—the greater, that is, in length and episode. The central setting of the book of Ruth is hardly Moab; it is Bethlehem in Judah. But by the time the two destitute widows, the older and the younger, reach Bethlehem, the volcanic heart of the book of Ruth—the majesty of Ruth's declaration—has already happened. All the rest is an unfolding

Let it unfold, then, without us. We have witnessed normality and we have witnessed singularity. We will, if we linger, witness these again in Bethlehem; but let the next events flash by without our lingering. Let Naomi come with Ruth to Bethlehem; let Naomi in her distress name herself Mara, meaning bitter, 'for the Lord has made my lot very bitter'; let Ruth set out to feed them both by gleaning in the field of Elimelech's kinsman, Boaz—fortuitous, God-given, that she should blunder onto Boaz's property! He is an elderly landowner, an affluent farmer who, like Levin in *Anna Karenina*, works side by side with his laborers. He is at once aware that there is a stranger in his field, and is at once solicitous. He is the sort of man who, in the heat of the harvest, greets the reapers with courteous devoutness: 'The Lord be with you!' A benign convention, perhaps, but when he addressed Ruth it is no ordinary invocation: ' I have been told of all that you did for your mother-in-law after the death of her husband, how you left your father and mother and the land of your birth and came to a people you had not known before. May the Lord reward your deeds. May you have a full recompense from the Lord, the God of Israel, under whose wings you have sought refuge!' Like Naomi, he calls Ruth 'daughter', and he speaks an old-fashioned Hebrew; he and Naomi are of the same generation.[1]

But remember that we are hurrying along now; so let Naomi, taking charge behind the scenes, send Ruth to sleep at Boaz's feet on the threshing floor in order to invite his special notice—a contrivance to make known to Boaz that he is eligible for Ruth's salvation within the frame of the levirate code. And let the humane and flexible system of the levirate code work itself out, so that Boaz can marry Ruth, who will become the mother of Obed, who is the father of Jesse, who is the father of King David, author of the Psalms.

The levirate law in Israel—like the rule for gleaners—is designed to redeem the destitute. The reapers may not sweep up every stalk in the meadow; some of the harvest must be left behind for bread for the needy. And if a woman is widowed, the circle of her husband's kin must open their homes to her; in a time when the sole protective provision for a woman is marriage, she must have a new husband from her dead husband's family—the relative closest to the husband, a brother if possible. Otherwise what will become of her? Dust and cinders. She will be like the remnants of the meal offerings.

Boaz in his tenderness (we have hurried past even this, which more than almost anything else merits our hanging back; but there it is on the page, enchanting the centuries—a tenderness sweetly discriminating, morally meticulous, wide-hearted and ripe)—Boaz is touched by Ruth's appeal to become her husband-protector. It is a fatherly tenderness, not an erotic one—though such a scene might, in some other tale, burst with the erotic: a young woman, perfumed, lying at the feet of an old man at night in a barn. The old man is not indifferent to the pulsing of Eros in the young: 'Be blessed of the Lord, daughter! Your latest deed of loyalty is greater than the first, in that you have not turned to younger men.' The remark may carry a pang of wistfulness, but Boaz in undertaking to marry Ruth is not animated by the

1. 'Boaz and Naomi talk like older people. Their speeches contain archaic morphology and syntax. Perhaps the most delightful indication of this is the one instance when an archaic form is put into Ruth's mouth at 2.21—where she is quoting Boaz!' (Campbell, *Ruth*, p. 17).

lubricious. He is no December panting after May. A forlorn young widow, homeless in every sense, has asked for his guardianship, and he responds under the merciful levirate proviso with all the dignity and responsibility of his character, including an ethical scruple: 'While it is true that I am a redeeming kinsman, there is another redeemer closer than I'— someone more closely related to Elimelech than Boaz, and therefore first in line to assume the right, and burden, of kinship protection.

In this closer relative we have a sudden pale reminder of Orpah. Though she has long vanished from the story, normality has not. Who conforms more vividly to the type of Average Man than that practical head of a household we call John Doe? And now John Doe (the exact Hebrew equivalent is Ploni Almoni) briefly enters the narrative and quickly jumps out of it; average-ness leaves no reputation, except for averageness. John Doe, a.k.a. Ploni Almoni, is the closer relative Boaz has in mind, and he appears at a meeting of town elders convened to sort out the levirate succession in Naomi's case. The hearing happens also to include some business about a piece of land that Elimelech owned; if sold, it will bring a little money for Naomi. Naomi may not have known of the existence of this property—or else why would she be reduced to living on Ruth's gleaning? But Boaz is informed of it, and immediately arranges for a transaction aimed at relieving both Naomi and Ruth. The sale of Elimelech's property, though secondary to the issue of marital guardianship for Naomi's young daughter-in-law, is legally attached to it: whoever acquires the land acquires Ruth. The closer relative, Ploni Almoni (curious how the text refuses him a real name of his own, as if it couldn't be bothered, as if it were all at once impatient with averageness), is willing enough to buy the land: John Doe always understands money and property. But he is not at all willing to accept Ruth. The moment he learns he is also being asked to take on the care of a widow—one young enough to bear children, when very likely he already has a family to support—he changes his mind. He worries, he explains, that he will impair his estate. An entirely reasonable, even a dutiful, worry, and who can blame him? If he has missed his chance to become the great-grandfather of the Psalmist, he is probably, like Ploni Almoni everywhere, a philistine scorner of poetry anyhow.

And we are glad to see him go. In this he is no reminder of Orpah; Orpah, a loving young woman, is regretted. But like Orpah he has only the usual order of courage. He avoids risk, the unexpected, the lightning move into imagination. He thinks of what he has, not of what he might do: he recoils from the conduct of idealism. He is perfectly conventional, and wants to stick with what is familiar. Then let him go in peace—he is too ordinary to be the husband of Ruth. We have not heard him make a single inquiry about her. He has not troubled over any gesture of interest or sympathy. Ruth is no more to him than an object of acquisition offered for sale. He declines to buy; he has his own life to get on with, and no intention of altering it, levirate code or no levirate code. 'You do it,' he tells Boaz.

Boaz does it. At every step he has given more than full measure, whether of barley or benevolence. We have watched him load Ruth's sack with extra grain to take back to Naomi. He has instructed the reapers to scatter extra stalks for her to scoop up. He has summoned her to his own table for lunch in the field. He is generous, he is kindly, he is old, and in spite of his years he opens his remaining strength to the imagination of the future: he enters on a new life inconceivable to him on the day a penniless young foreigner wandered over his field behind the harvest workers. *Mercy, pity, peace, and love*: these Blakean words lead, in our pastoral, to a beginning.

The beginning is of course a baby, and when Naomi cradles her grandchild in her bosom, the village women cry, 'A son is born to Naomi!' And they cry, 'Blessed be the Lord, who hath not withheld a redeemer from you today! May his name be perpetuated in Israel! He will renew your life and sustain your old age; for he is born of your daughter-in-law, who loves you and is better to you than seven sons.'

Only eighty-five verses tell Ruth's and Naomi's story. To talk of it takes much longer. Not that the greatest stories are the shortest—not at all. But a short story has a stalk—or shoot—through which its life rushes, and out of which the flowery head erupts. The book of Ruth—wherein goodness grows out of goodness, and the extraordinary is found here, and here, and here—is sown in desertion, bereavement, barrenness, death, loss, displacement, destitution. What can sprout from such ash? Then Ruth sees into the nature of Covenant, and the life of the story streams in. Out of this stalk mercy and redemption unfold; flowers flood Ruth's feet; and my grandfather goes on following her track until the coming of messiah from the shoot of David, in the line of Ruth and Naomi.

BIBLIOGRAPHY

Abel, E. (ed.), *Writing and Sexual Difference* (Chicago: University of Chicago Press, 1982).

Alter, R., *The Art of Biblical Narrative* (New York: Basic Books, 1981).

Ardener, E., 'Belief and the Problem of Woman', in S. Ardener (ed.), *Perceiving Women* (New York: Halstead Press, 1975).

Ardener, S. (ed.), *Perceiving Women* (New York: Halstead Press, 1975).

—*Defining Females* (London: Croom Helm, 1978).

Aries, E., 'Interaction Patterns and Themes of Male, Female, and Mixed Groups', *Small Group Behavior* 7 (1976).

Astour, M.C., *Hellenosemitica* (Leiden: Brill, 1965).

Bal, M., *Femmes imaginaires: l'ancien testament au risque d'une narratologie critique* (Utrecht: Hess; Montreal: HMH; Paris: Nizet, 1986).

—*Murder and Difference: Gender, Genre and Scholarship on Sisera's Death* (Bloomington: University of Indiana Press, 1988).

Barr, J., 'The Vulgate Genesis and St Jerome's Attitude to Women', *Studia Patristica* 18 (1982).

Bass, D., 'Women's Studies and Biblical Studies', *JSOT* 22 (1982).

Berlin, A., *Poetics and Interpretation of Biblical Narrative* (Bible and Literature Series, 9; Sheffield: Almond Press, 1983).

Bickermann, E., *Four Strange Books of the Bible* (New York: Schocken Books, 1967).

Bledstein, A.J., 'The Genesis of Humans: The Garden of Eden Revisited', *Judaism* 26.2 (1977).

Bose, C., 'Dual Spheres', in *Analyzing Gender: A Handbook of Social Science Research* (Minneapolis: University of Minnesota Press, 1988).

Boserup, E., *Women's Role in Economic Development* (London: George Allen & Unwin, 1970).

Bottigheimer, R.B., *Grimms' Bad Girls and Bold Boys: The Moral and Social Vision of the Tales* (New Haven: Yale University Press, 1987).

Brenner, A., 'Esther Through the Looking Glass' (in Hebrew), *Beth Miqra* 86 (1981–83).

—*The Israelite Woman: Social Role and Literary Type in Biblical Narrative* (JSOTSup, 21; Sheffield: JSOT Press, 1985).

—'Female Social Behaviour: Two Descriptive Patterns within the "Birth of the Hero" Paradigm', *VT* 36 (1986); repr. in A. Brenner (ed.), *A Feminist Companion to Genesis* (The Feminist Companion to the Bible, 2; Sheffield: Sheffield Academic Press, 1993).

—*Ruth and Naomi: Literary, Stylistic and Linguistic Studies in the Book of Ruth* (Hebrew; Tel Aviv: Afik/Sifrait Poalim; Hakibbutz Hameuchad, 1988).

Brenner, A., and F. van Dijk-Hemmes, 'On Gendering Biblical Texts' (paper presented to the SBL Annual Meeting, 1992).

—*On Gendering Texts: Female and Male Voices in the Hebrew Bible* (Leiden: Brill, 1993).

Brock, S., *The Luminous Eye: The Spiritual World Vision of St. Ephrem* (Rome: CIIS, 1985).

Burkert, W., *Greek Religion: Archaic and Classical* (trans. J. Raffan; Oxford: Basil Blackwell, 1985).

Cameron, D., *Feminism and Linguistic Theory* (New York: Macmillan, 1985).

Camp, C., *Wisdom and the Feminine in the Book of Proverbs* (Bible and Literature Series, 11; Sheffield: Almond Press, 1985).

Campbell, E.F., *Ruth* (AB; Garden City, NY: Doubleday, 1973; 2nd edn, 1975).

Carmichael, C., '"Treading" in the Book of Ruth', *ZAW* 92 (1980).

Cazelles, H., 'Note sur la composition du rouleau d'Esther', in H. Gross and F. Mussner (eds.), *Lex tua veritas: Festschrift für Hubert Junker* (Trier: Paulinus Verlag, 1961).

Casey, J., *The History of the Family* (Oxford: Basil Blackwell, 1989).

Clines, D.J.A., *The Esther Scroll: The Story of a Story* (JSOTSup, 30; Sheffield: JSOT Press, 1984).

Coats, G.W., *Genesis with an Introduction to Narrative Literature* (FOTL, 1; Grand Rapids: Eerdmans, 1983).

Cross, F.M., Jr, *Canaanite Myth and Hebrew Epic* (Cambridge, MA: Harvard University Press, 1973).

Dällenbach, L., *Le récit spéculaire: essai sur le mise en abyme* (Paris: Seuil, 1977).

Darr, K.P., *Far More Precious than Jewels: Perspectives on Biblical Women* (Gender and the Biblical Tradition; Louisville, KY: Westminster Press/John Knox, 1991).

Delay, J., *La jeunesse d'Audré Gide* (Paris: Payot, 1973).

Dubois, E.C., *et al.*, *Feminist Scholarship: Kindling in the Groves of Academia* (Urbana: University of Illinois Press, 1985).

Edwards, A., *A Child's Bible* (London: Pan Books, 1969).

Eissfeldt, O., *The Old Testament: An Introduction* (trans. P.R. Ackroyd; Oxford: Basil Blackwell, 1965).

Eskenazi, T.C., 'Out from the Shadows: Woman in the Postexilic Period', *JSOT* 54 (1992).

Falk, M., *Love Lyrics from the Bible* (Bible and Literature Series, 4; Sheffield: Almond Press, 1982).

Felman, S., *Le Scandale du corps parlant: Don Juan avec Austin ou la séduction en deux langues* (Paris: Editions du Seuil, 1980).

Fewell, D.N., and D.M. Gunn, *Compromising Redemption: Relating Characters in the Book of Ruth* (Louisville, KY: Westminster Press, 1990).

Flynn, E.A., and P.P. Schweickart (eds.), *Gender and Reading: Essays on Readers, Texts, and Contexts* (Baltimore: Johns Hopkins University Press, 1986).

Fontaine, C.R., 'Proverbs', in *Harper's Bible Dictionary* (San Francisco: Harper & Row, 1988).

Forster, E.M., *Aspects of the Novel* (New York: Harcourt Brace Jovanovich, 1954).

Fox, M., *The Song of Songs and Ancient Egyptian Love Songs* (Madison: University of Wisconsin, 1985).

Friedlander, A.H. (ed. and trans.), *The Five Scrolls* (New York: CCAR Press, 1984).

Fuchs, E., 'The Status and Role of Female Heroines in the Biblical Narrative', *The Mankind Quarterly* 23 (1982).

Gennep, A. van, *The Rites of Passage* (trans. M.B. Vizedon and G.L. Caffee; Chicago: University of Chicago Press, 1960).

Gerleman, G., *Ruth: Das Hohelied* (BKAT, 18; Neukirchen–Vluyn: Neukirchener Verlag, 1981).

Gesenius, W., *Hebrew Grammar* (Oxford: Oxford University Press, 1910).

Ginsberg, L., *Legends of the Jews* (7 vols.; Philadelphia: Jewish Publication Society of America, 1946).

Goitein, S.D., *'Iyyunim ba-miqra* (Hebrew; 'Studies in the Bible'; Tel Aviv: Yavneh, 1957).

—'Women as Creators of Biblical Genres', *Prooftexts* 8.1 (1988).

Golb, I.J., 'Approaches to the Study of Ancient Society', *JAOS* 81 (1967).

Gordis, R., *The Song of Songs and Lamentations* (New York: Ktav, 1974).

—Love, Marriage and Business in the Book of Ruth: A Chapter in Hebrew Customary Law', in H.N. Bream, R.D. Heim and C.A. Moore (eds.), *Light Unto My Path: Old Testament Studies in Honor of Jacob M. Myers* (Philadelphia: Temple University Press, 1974).

Gordon, C., *Forgotten Texts* (New York: Basic Books, 1982).

Gottwald, N.K., *The Tribes of Yahweh: A Sociology of the Religion of Liberated Israel, 1250–1050* (Maryknoll, NY: Orbis Books, 1979).

Gunn, D.M., *The Fate of King Saul* (JSOTSup, 14; Sheffield: JSOT Press, 1980).

Gray, J., *Joshua, Judges and Ruth* (Century Bible; London: Nelson, 1967).

Greenberg, M., *Ezekiel 1–20* (AB; Garden City, NY: Doubleday, 1983).

Gressman, H., *The Tower of Babel* (New York, 1928).

Grimaud, M., 'Sur une métaphore métonymique hugolienne selon Jacques Lacan', *Litterature* 29 (1978).

Gunkel, H., *Genesis* (HKAT; repr.; Göttingen: Vandenhoeck & Ruprecht, 3rd edn, 1964 [1910]).

Gunn, D.M., *The Fate of King Saul* (JSOTSup, 14; Sheffield: JSOT Press, 1980).

Hals, R.M., *The Theology of the Book of Ruth* (Biblical Series, 23; Philadelphia: Fortress Press, 1969).

Hartman, D., *Das Buch Ruth in der Midrasch-Litteratur* (Leipzig: 1901).

Harvey, D., *The Book of Ruth* (IDB, 4; New York: Abingdon Press).

Hubbard, R.L., *The Book of Ruth* (Grand Rapids: Eerdmans, 1991).

Humbert, P., 'Les adjectifs *zâr* et *nokrî* et la "femme étrangère" des Proverbes bibliques', in *Opuscules d'un hébraïsant* (Neuchâtel: Secrétariat de l'Université, 1958).

Jameson, M.H., 'Mythology in Ancient Greece', in S.N. Kramer (ed.), *Mythologies in the Ancient World* (Garden City, NY: Doubleday, 1961).

Jauss, H.R., *Question and Answer: Forms of Dialogic Understanding* (ed. and trans. M. Hays; Minneapolis: University of Minnesota Press, 1989).

Jefferson, A., *'Mise en abyme* and the Prophetic in Narrative', *Style* 17.2 (1983).

Joüon, P., *Grammaire de l'hébreu biblique* (Rome: Pontifical Biblical Institute, 1965).

—*Ruth: commentaire philologique et exégétique* (Rome: Pontifical Biblical Institute, 1953; Subsidia Biblica, 9; Rome: Biblical Institute Press, 2nd edn, 1986).

Kraemer, R.S., 'Women's Authorship of Jewish and Christian Literature in the Greco-Roman Period' (paper presented to a colloquium on Women in Religion and Society, Philadelphia, Annenberg Research Institute, 1991).

Kramarae, C., *Woman and Man Speaking: Frameworks for Analysis* (Rowley, MA: Newbury House, 1981).

Lacan, J., *Ecrits* (Paris: Seuil, 1966).

—*The Language of the Self* (ed. and trans. A. Wilden; York: Delta, 1975).

LaCocque, A., *The Feminine Unconventional: Four Subversive Figures in Israel's Tradition* (Minneapolis: Fortress Press, 1990).

Laffey, A., *An Introduction to the Old Testament: A Feminist Perspective* (Philadelphia: Fortress Press, 1988).

Lambdin, T.O., *Introduction to Biblical Hebrew* (New York: Charles Scribner's Sons, 1971).

Lanser, S.S., 'Feminist Criticism in the Garden: Inferring Genesis 2–3', *Semeia* 39 (1988).

Laslett, P., and R. Wall (eds.), *Household and Family in Past Time* (London: Cambridge University Press, 1972).

Levine, E., *The Aramaic Version of Ruth* (AnBib; Rome: Pontifical Biblical Institute, 1973).

Lord, A.B., *The Singer of Tales* (Cambridge, MA: Harvard University Press, 1960).

MacDonald, E.M., *The Position of Woman as Reflected in Semitic Codes of Law* (Toronto: University of Toronto Press, 1931).

McKane, W., *Proverbs* (OTL; Philadelphia: Westminster Press, 1970).

McVey, K.E., *Ephrem the Syrian: Hymns* (New York: Paulist Press, 1989).

Meek, T.J., *Song of Songs* (IB, V; New York: Abingdon Press, 1956).

Melzer, P., *Ruth* (The Five Scrolls; Jerusalem: Mosad Harav Kuk, 1973).

Meyers, C., 'Gender Imagery in the Song of Songs', *HAR* 10 (1986); repr. in A. Brenner (ed.), *A Feminist Companion to the Song of Songs* (The Feminist Companion to the Bible, 1; Sheffield: Sheffield Academic Press, 1993).

—*Discovering Eve: Ancient Israelite Women in Context* (New York: Oxford University Press, 1988).

—'Everyday Life: Women in the Period of the Hebrew Bible', in C.A. Newsom and S.H. Ringe (eds.), *The Women's Bible Commentary* (Louisville, KY: Westminster Press/John Knox, 1992).

Murphy, R.E., *Wisdom Literature: Job, Proverbs, Ruth, Canticles, Ecclesiastes, Esther* (FOTL, 13; Grand Rapids: Eerdmans, 1981).

Murray, R., *Symbols of Church and Kingdom: A Study in Early Syriac Tradition* (Cambridge: Cambridge University Press, 1975).

Neumann, E., *The Great Mother: An Analysis of an Archetype* (trans. R. Manheim; Princeton, NJ: Princeton University Press, 2nd edn, 1974 [1963]).

Newsom, C., 'Woman and the Discourse of Patriarchal Wisdom: A Study of Proverbs 1–9', in P.L. Day (ed.), *Gender and Difference in Ancient Israel* (Minneapolis: Fortress Press, 1989).

Parry, A. (ed.), *The Making of Homeric Verse: The Collected Papers of Milman Parry* (Oxford: Oxford University Press, 1971).

Perry, M., and M. Sternberg, ''Ha-melek be-mabbat ironi' ('The King in Ironic Perspective'), *Ha-Sifrut* 1 (1968).

Peskowitz, M., '"Set Your Eyes on Family": Thinking about Families in Tannaitic Judaism and Roman Galilean Culture' (paper presented to the SBL Annual Meeting, Kansas City, 1991).

Pope, M.H., *Song of Songs* (AB, 7C; Garden City, NY: Doubleday, 1977).

Propp, V., *Morphology of the Folktale* (ed. L.A. Wagner; Austin, TX, 2nd edn, 1968).

Rad, G. von, *Genesis* (OTL; Philadelphia: Westminster Press, rev. edn, 1972).

Rashkow, I., 'Daughters and Fathers in Genesis...or, What is Wrong with this Picture?' (unpublished paper presented to the SBL Annual Meeting, Kansas City, 1991).

Rendsburg, G.A., *The Redaction of Genesis* (Winona Lake, IN: Eisenbrauns, 1986).

Rich, A., 'Towards a Woman-Centered University', in *On Lies, Secrets, and Silence: Selected Prose, 1966–78* (New York: Norton, 1979).

Richardson, J.E., 'Feminine Imagery of the Holy Spirit in the Hymns of St. Ephrem the Syrian' (PhD dissertation; University of Edinburgh, 1991).

Rosaldo, M.Z., 'The Use and Abuse of Anthropology: Reflections on Feminism and Cross-Cultural Understanding', *SIGNS* 5 (1980).

Rosenberg, A.J., *The Five Megillot* (London: Soncino Press, rev. edn, 1984).

Roth, W.M., 'The Wooing of Rebekah: A Tradition-Critical Study of Genesis 24', *CBQ* 34 (1972).

Rudolph, W., *Das Buch Ruth, Das Hohelied, Das Klagelieder* (KAT; Gütersloh: Gerd Mohn, 1962).

Safrai, S., *The Jewish People in the Days of the Second Temple* (Hebrew; Tel Aviv: Am Oved, 1970).

Sandmel, S., *The Enjoyment of Scripture: The Laws, The Prophets, and the Writings* (New York: Oxford University Press, 1972).

Sarna, N.M., *Genesis* (The JPS Torah Commentary; Philadelphia: Jewish Publication Society, 1989).

Sasson, J.M., 'Ruth', in R. Alter and F. Kermode (eds.), *The Literary Guide to the Bible* (Cambridge, MA: Harvard University Press, 1987).

—*Ruth: A New Translation with a Philological Commentary and a Formalist-Folklorist Interpretation* (Baltimore: Johns Hopkins University Press, 1979; The Biblical Seminar, 10; Sheffield: JSOT Press, 2nd edn, 1989).

Schmidt, S.J., 'Reception and Interpretation of Written Texts as Problems of a Rational Theory of Literary Communication', in *Style and Text: Studies Presented to Nils Erik Enkvist* (Stockholm, 1975).

Schüssler Fiorenza, E., *Bread Not Stone* (Boston: Beacon Press, 1984).

—*In Memory of Her* (New York: Crossroad, 1985).

Scott, R.B.Y., *Proverbs, Ecclesiastes* (AB, 18; Garden City, NY: Doubleday 1965).

Searle, J., *Speech Acts: An Essay in the Philosophy of Language* (London: Cambridge University Press, 1969).

Segal, M.Z., *Introduction to the Bible. III. Ruth* (Hebrew; Jerusalem: Kiryat Sefer, 1955).

Showalter, E. (ed.), *The New Feminist Criticism: Essays on Women, Literature and Theory* (London: Virago, 1986).

Skinner, J., *Genesis* (ICC; Edinburgh: T. & T. Clark, 2nd edn, 1930).

Smith, D.L., *The Religion of the Landless: The Social Context of the Babylonian Exile* (Bloomington, IN: Meyer Stone, 1989).

Smith, L.P., *The Book of Ruth* (*IB*, 2; New York: Abingdon Press, 1954–55).

Speiser, E.A., *Genesis* (AB, 1; Garden City, NY: Doubleday, 1964).

Spender, D., *Man Made Language* (London: Routledge & Kegan Paul, 2nd edn, 1985).

Sproul, B.C., *Primal Myths: Creating the World* (San Francisco: Harper & Row, 1979).

Stager, L.E., 'The Family in Ancient Israel', *BASOR* 260 (1985).

Terrien, S., *Till the Heart Sings: A Biblical Theology of Manhood and Womanhood* (Philadelphia: Fortress Press, 1985).

Trible, P., 'Two Women in a Man's World: A Reading of the Book of Ruth', *Soundings* (1976).

—*God and the Rhetoric of Sexuality* (Philadelphia: Fortress Press, 1978)

Uebersfeld, A., *Le roi et le bouffon* (Paris: José Corti, 1974).

Vawter, B., *On Genesis: A New Reading* (Garden City, NY: Doubleday, 1977).

Wilk, R.R., and R..M. Netting, 'Households: Changing Forms and Functions', in R.M. Netting, R.R. Wilk and E.J. Arnould (eds.), *Households: Comparative and Historic Studies of the Domestic Group* (Berkeley: University of California Press, 1984).

Wilson, R., 'The Family', in *Harper's Bible Dictionary* (San Francisco: Harper & Row, 1985).

Wright, G.E., 'The Provinces of Solomon', *Eretz Israel* 8 (1967).

Zakovitch, Y., *Ruth: A Commentary* (Miqra LeYisrael; Tel Aviv: Am Oved; Jerusalem: Magnes, 1990).

Zlotowitz, M., and N. Scherman, *The Book of Ruth* (Art Scroll Tanach Series; New York: Mesorah Publications, 1976).